MW00527071

A Government that Worked Better and Cost Less?

A Government that Worked Better and Cost Less?

Evaluating Three Decades of
Reform and Change in UK
Central Government

Christopher Hood and Ruth Dixon

OXFORD

UNIVERSITY PRESS

Great Clarendon Street, Oxford, OX2 6DP,
United Kingdom

Oxford University Press is a department of the University of Oxford.
It furthers the University's objective of excellence in research, scholarship,
and education by publishing worldwide. Oxford is a registered trade mark of
Oxford University Press in the UK and in certain other countries

First Edition published in 2015
Impression: 1

Published in the United States of America by Oxford University Press
198 Madison Avenue, New York, NY 10016, United States of America

British Library Cataloguing in Publication Data
Data available

Library of Congress Control Number: 2014954101

ISBN 978-0-19-968702-2

Printed and bound by
CPI Group (UK) Ltd, Croydon, CR0 4YY

Preface and Acknowledgements

This book is meant to fill a gap. It compiles and analyses evidence about what happened to running costs and the perceived consistency and fairness of government administration over a thirty-year period in one of the governmental systems most associated with the development of 'new managerialism' since the 1980s, namely that of the United Kingdom.

In one sense it is surprising that there should be such a gap. After all, millions of words have been written by academics and commentators about the presumed effects of 'New Public Management' (NPM) and cognate developments over recent decades, and a great deal of research funding has been devoted to such issues as well. So why aren't we already drowning in well-established evidence about what happened to cost and performance in the medium to long term?

In the course of writing this book we found out why. It is commonly claimed that we live in an age of transparency and more performance indicators than ever before—a refrain we frequently encountered as we worked on this project. But we also live in an age of highly transient information, where accounting standards and reporting conventions change frequently and often radically. And that means it can be a real challenge to assemble any kind of performance information in a consistent form for more than a few years. 'It's not easy to put trousers on a cat', goes the old saying; and sometimes that was how it felt in our attempts to draw workable time-series out of ever-changing government reports. So in another sense, it is amazing that it has been possible to fill the gap at all, at least to the extent that we have been able to do so.

Readers familiar with Charles Dickens' great novel *Hard Times* will recall the figure of Thomas Gradgrind, the anti-hero of that book (a caricature of what Dickens saw as the blinkered utilitarians of the mid-nineteenth century). Dickens portrays Gradgrind as toiling away in a room full of 'Blue Books' (the term then used in Britain for statistical returns and other official reports) making elaborate calculations to try to prove his theories, and ridicules that approach by likening Gradgrind's room to an astronomical observatory without any windows. In some ways our work for this book was Gradgrind-ish, in that our point of departure was to track down reported numbers about government performance, and follow them through their numerous twists and turns. But we then used those numbers as a basis for conversations and interviews with people working in and around government, so we don't think the 'observatory-without-windows' charge will really stick in our case.

For one of us (Christopher Hood), writing this book was a return to the scene of earlier crimes, of work in the 1970s with Andrew Dunsire on 'bureaumetrics', the quantitative analysis of government agencies. The project was partly motivated by a desire to conduct a 'then and now' analysis of UK central government before and after decades of much-hyped reforms whose professed purpose was to enhance efficiency and make government work better for citizens and customers. And for both of us, the idea for this book grew out of our involvement in a major Economic and Social Research Council-funded research programme (the Public Services Programme) in the 2000s. That programme, which was firmly focused on research on public sector performance rather than descriptions of structures and processes (the traditional focus of much scholarship in public administration), produced a new generation of useful and interesting research. We draw on that initiative in several ways here, both on some specific matters (for instance on the analysis of judicial review and satisfaction with public services) and in methods and approaches (particularly in the use of administrative data for analysis of public service performance). But the programme still left a gap to be filled in providing long-term evidence about how UK government departments performed over a period of decades, particularly on running costs. This book can therefore be seen as a completion, half a decade later, of that aspect of the programme.

We have many debts to acknowledge. This study would not have been possible without the financial support of the Leverhulme Trust, which provided a three-year grant, and the Economic and Social Research Council, which awarded a professorial fellowship to Christopher Hood. Without the time those funds provided, we would never have been able to get to the bottom of understanding the complexities of many of the data-series we looked into for this analysis. And we needed to master those complexities to assess the relevance of administrative numbers to the questions we wanted to answer, to compile consistent series where we could and identify major data breaks where we couldn't.

Nor would this book have been possible without the support and cooperation of many people inside and outside government including the many civil servants and other officials (including local government people) who gave generously of their time and expertise to provide us with datasets and answer our questions in a series of interviews which culminated in a focus group comprising current and former civil servants with a wealth of experience from different backgrounds to discuss and interpret our findings in the summer of 2013. We also gratefully acknowledge our debt to All Souls College for allowing us to use the college's facilities for conducting that focus group.

We are grateful for research assistance from Susan Divald, Karina Gould, Imogen Peck, Rikki Dean, and Emma Anderson, who also helped with preparing the manuscript. We are also indebted to Gillian Hood for compiling the index.

Other individuals helped us by giving valuable advice as we started to delve into areas where we needed expert help. One, Brian Hogwood, even let us use his valuable dataset on 'quangos' from the 1970s to the 1990s, and offered advice for which we are very grateful. As we came to write up the analysis, many others (sometimes the same people) helped us to clarify our arguments, sharpen up our text and rethink our analysis by reading all or part of the manuscript of this book in various stages of draft. In particular we would like to thank Gwyn Bevan, Thomas Elston, Dennis Grube, David Heald, Martin Lodge, Alasdair Roberts, Martin Stanley, and Tony Travers for their valuable advice, criticism, and contributions. While deficiencies inevitably remain, they would have been far worse without the perceptive criticisms and comments of all these people.

In the age of the 'blogosphere', short versions of some elements of the analysis have appeared in various blogs. Parts of this book have also been presented at various conferences and seminars over the years and part of the analysis of running costs and tax collection costs in Chapters 4 and 5 is developed from a paper originally published in the journal *Public Administration* in 2013.

Christopher Hood and Ruth Dixon
Oxford, October 2014

Contents

List of Figures and Tables

Figures

Tables

1

Yesterday's Tomorrows Revisited—the Route to Better and Cheaper Public Services

He was the future once.[1]

1.1 Thirty Years of Public Management Makeovers—Evidence-Based or Evidence-Free?

This book shows that over a thirty-year period of successive reforms, one of the most commented-on government systems in the world (the UK) exhibited a striking increase in running or administration costs in real terms, while levels of complaint and legal challenge also soared. So why should that matter?

It matters because those three decades have witnessed repeated reform efforts, not just in the UK but around the world, to cut the costs of government and make it work better for citizens or users. Back in 1980, in the early days of Margaret Thatcher's government in Britain, one of her most powerful lieutenants of that time (Lord Heseltine) famously declared that, 'the management ethos must run right through our national life—private and public companies, civil service, nationalized industries, local government, the National Health service'.[2] Indeed, during the 1980s the Thatcher government introduced successive 'managerialist' reform initiatives of a kind that were destined to become familiar in the UK and in many other countries in later decades—attempts to bring greater business efficiency to government by corporatization, performance indicators, new financial frameworks,

---

[1] How David Cameron (then newly elected leader of the UK Conservative Party) referred to then British Prime Minister Tony Blair in their first official parliamentary confrontation (in Prime Minister's Questions, Hansard, 7 December 2005: Column 861).

[2] Quoted in Christopher Pollitt, *Managerialism and the Public Services: The Anglo-American Experience* (Oxford: Blackwell, 1990), p. vi.

outsourcing, performance-related pay, and more emphasis on effective management.[3] Of course these changes had their antecedents, both in the twentieth century and earlier. Indeed, in some respects such initiatives harked back to the utilitarian philosopher Jeremy Bentham's early nineteenth-century ideas about how to cut the costs of government and make it more responsive to users, which were partly summed up in Bentham's famous slogan, 'aptitude maximized, expense minimized'.[4]

In the early 1990s Bentham's slogan was memorably (though probably unconsciously) reworked into the title of a well-known report by Al Gore, then vice-president under the Bill Clinton presidency in the United States: *Creating a Government that Works Better and Costs Less*.[5] Similar documents—albeit seldom with quite such rhetorical zing—became commonplace in many other countries. Indeed, in recent decades the preoccupation with 'reinventing government'[6] has reached the point where governments almost everywhere have had to develop reform plans to improve and 'modernize' their administration and public services. For some, the drive has been to satisfy demands from international donors or lenders or as part of a set of adjustments to meet accession conditions for the European Union or other international bodies. For others, the drive was to display an image of competence, modernity, and managerial 'grip' to their voters and to give themselves 'bragging rights' in the international community. (And those bragging rights themselves may have translated into marketing opportunities for consultants, who often included the former politicians or public servants who introduced the reforms.)

Those recipes for modernization varied. For instance, anti-corruption measures tended to figure more prominently in the plans of developing and transitional countries than in those of the developed countries. But there were some common and recurring themes. One was the idea that the way to make government work better and cost less was to *manage* it differently, on the grounds that poor management in one form or another was the main obstacle to greater efficacy.[7] What was seen as the key to better management varied according to the ideology and worldview of would-be modernizers,

---

[3] See for example George W. Jones, 'A Revolution in Whitehall? Changes in British Central Government since 1979', *West European Politics* 12, no. 3 (1989): 238–61; Peter Kemp, 'Next Steps for the British Civil Service', *Governance* 3, no. 2 (1990): 186–96; Joe Painter, 'Compulsory Competitive Tendering in Local Government: The First Round', *Public Administration* 69, no. 2 (1991): 191–210.

[4] Jeremy Bentham, *Constitutional Code* (Oxford: Clarendon, [1830] 1983), p. 297: 'Indicated in these few words are the leading principles of this Constitution on the subject of remuneration.'

[5] Al Gore, *From Red Tape to Results: Creating a Government That Works Better and Costs Less*, Report of the National Performance Review (Washington: US Government Printing Office, 1993).

[6] The title of one of the few bestsellers ever written in the field of public management: David Osborne and Ted Gaebler, *Reinventing Government: How the Entrepreneurial Spirit is Transforming the Public Sector* (Reading, MA: Addison-Wesley, 1992).

[7] On the 'management factor', see for instance Erik-Hans Klijn, *It's The Management, Stupid! On the Importance of Management in Complex Policy Issues* (The Hague: Lemma, 2008).

and often comprised a rather eclectic set of ideas and practices. But recurring ideas included drawing on what were seen as successful recipes from business, bringing in new kinds of people to do the managing, and structural makeovers of various kinds. Such reforms, it was claimed, would make government more focused or responsive or 'joined-up', including changes in politician–bureaucrat relationships to improve 'accountability' (which often served as a code word for making civil servants take more of the blame for government failures, particularly in the UK and similar Westminster-model bureaucracies). A second recurring theme was a strong belief in the capacity for new types of information technology (IT), if boldly and intelligently applied, to transform costly, outdated, and user-unfriendly bureaucratic processes. A third was a stress on improved presentation and packaging of initiatives and ideas, drawing on modern marketing, new media, and other forms of persuasive expertise based on psychological insights.

Such ideas and the reform efforts associated with them have not lacked for critics and commentators—quite the reverse. A huge international academic industry—interacting and overlapping with the world of consultants, non-governmental organizations, and governments' own reform bureaucracies—has grown up to chronicle, compare, explain, and criticize such developments, particularly the so-called New Public Management movement that rose to prominence in the 1980s.[8] Things have got to the point where the literature is almost impossible to survey (a search of Google Scholar alone for 'New Public Management' yields over 84,000 hits, and a Google search for the same phrase gives a hundred times more),[9] and from the sheer volume of writing about such matters, you could be excused for thinking that the last word must surely have been said on this well-worn subject.

But there are at least two reasons for suggesting it has not. One is that the world has changed, as it is apt to do, in a way that shows up gaps and mismatches in the received interpretations and studies. The great financial crash of 2008 and the continuing repercussions of the fiscal stress and crisis that resulted from it across much of the world have put the spotlight sharply on cost containment in many governments, notably but not only in those eurozone countries that have dramatically hit the debt wall in recent years and have not yet been able to inflate or devalue their debts away.[10] It is one thing for governments to 'talk the talk' about efficiency and cost containment at a

---

[8] One of us must take at least part of the blame for introducing this term: see Christopher Hood, 'Public Administration and Public Policy: Intellectual Challenges for the 1990s', *Australian Journal of Public Administration* 50 (1989): pp. 346–58; and by the same author, 'A Public Management for All Seasons', *Public Administration* 69, no. 2 (1991): pp. 3–19.

[9] Searches made in June 2014.

[10] See for example Christopher Hood, David Heald, and Rozana Himaz (eds), *When the Party's Over: The Politics of Fiscal Squeeze in Perspective*, Proceedings of the British Academy 197 (Oxford: Oxford University Press, 2014).

time when public revenues are buoyant and it is easy to leverage public borrowing. In those comfortable conditions governments can readily invest more in shiny new public service facilities, and the efficiency agenda is consequently likely to be about 'spending to save' and getting 'more for more', as it was for much of the 2000s.[11] But it is quite another thing for governments to find themselves so strapped for cash that they have to aim for cost containment in absolute terms and/or on a scale that make 'good times' efficiency strategies (such as 'protecting the front line' of public services by cutting down on the back-office facilities and other 'management magic') insufficient, unfeasible, unaffordable, or all of the above. So the long-term track record of management, IT, and other changes which claim to be able to deliver 'more for less' merits a closer—and much harder—look than it has received up to now.

Second, and relatedly, much more has been written about the promises and the processes than about the documented results of those reform efforts of the recent past, and the tendency both for governments and the public-management commentariat is to focus on the latest reform ideas, on the rhetoric and ideology of the reformers, and on what is happening right now rather than a careful examination of what happened to previous reform efforts. That tendency to focus on the present and the future is understandable enough, given the obvious financial and political incentives to do so, but it means that past experience tends to get little systematic examination, and we tend to lack clear evidence about the outcomes of previous government makeovers. Did governments really end up 'working better and costing less' over the past thirty years or so, as all those once-important reformers who 'were the future once', so confidently expected and intended?

That bottom-line question has not been very clearly answered by the vast international public management research industry, and as far as cost is concerned it has barely been answered at all. Evaluation of results has mostly been based on the analysis of rhetoric and ideology rather than careful digging into the more prosaic issues of cost. While there is certainly an interest in matters of administrative quality, it tends to get reduced to perception indices and 'expert surveys' rather than careful before-and-after analysis of administrative data, and hence tends to be limited in validity and replicability over time. Forty years ago a senior British civil servant (Desmond Keeling) drily remarked of the reform ideas of the 1960s: 'It was a decade in which management in the public service developed greatly . . . in assertions of realized or potential benefits, but less frequently in their measurement or proof.'[12] Exactly

---

[11] Christopher Hood, 'Reflections on Public Service Reform in a Cold Fiscal Climate', in *Public Services: A New Reform Agenda*, edited by Simon Griffiths, Henry Kippen, and Gerry Stoker (London: Bloomsbury, 2013), Chapter 13, pp. 215–29.

[12] Desmond Keeling, *Management in Government* (London: George Allen and Unwin, 1972), p. 11.

the same comment could be made about most of the later decades as well, despite institutional developments accompanying frequent pious assertions about the importance of evaluation and desirability or necessity of policy to be 'evidence-based'.[13]

There are several good—well, understandable—reasons for that continuing absence of 'measurement or proof'. One is that cross-national datasets of the kind that can be found for tracing items like national income or demography over time are still in their infancy for issues of government operating cost and even for measures of administrative quality, consistency, or fairness that go beyond broad-brush (and often not very meaningful) survey questions about trust or satisfaction with government. So there is still no real alternative to tackling the analysis country by country and, as we shall show later, that tends to be highly labour-intensive in the effort required to standardize the relevant numbers over time. And such difficulties in turn limit the scope for 'quick wins' and 'low-hanging fruit' in this kind of analysis. That may be why so little progress has been made even after three decades in answering some of the basic bottom-line questions about what have been the results of so many managerial reforms in government and whether they really ended up improving government's aptitude and reducing its expense.

Another thing that has worked against such evaluation is that the quality of debate about public management and government reform tends to be surprisingly ideological in practice. At first sight you might expect aspirations to make government and public services 'work better and cost less' to be wholly unexceptionable—after all, who could possibly want the opposite? Policies for making government more effective or efficient should surely be of the type that political scientists call 'valence' issues—that is, the sort of issue over which leaders, candidates, and parties compete for votes on the basis of their perceived competence in delivering generally agreed goals— rather than 'positional' issues where politicians compete for votes over goals that are contested (such as pro-choice or pro-life, teaching of creationism or evolution in schools, higher taxes or lower spending).[14] Indeed, Tony Blair (the subject of our epigraph: he helped to rebrand the British Labour party as 'New Labour' in the 1990s and is the only British Labour leader to date who has led the party to three successive general election victories) presented the public-service delivery problem as precisely that sort of valence issue in a

[13] See for example David Taylor and Susan Balloch (eds), *The Politics of Evaluation: Participation and Policy Implementation* (Bristol: Policy Press, 2005), pp. 3–5.

[14] See for example, Donald Stokes, 'Spatial Models of Party Competition', *American Political Science Review* 57, no. 2 (1963): pp. 368–77; David Butler and Donald Stokes, *Political Change in Britain* (London: Macmillan, 1969); Jane Green, 'When Voters and Parties Agree: Valence Issues and Party Competition', *Political Studies* 55 (2007): pp. 629–55.

famous and beguiling slogan 'what matters is what works [to give effect to our values]'.[15] Many other politicians and reform leaders have more or less explicitly advanced a similar claim that the public-management problem can be depoliticized and turned into a matter of common sense or well-understood paths to effective 'modernization'—itself a term whose meaning is often misleadingly presented as self-evident and unexceptionable.

But in practice public service reform tends to be surprisingly hotly contested, for several reasons. One is that such changes so often turn on the visceral issues that divide powerful cultural worldviews—for example about the virtue or otherwise of markets and competition in social life, about the supposed collective wisdom of groups and bottom-up participation, about the proper authority to be given to experts or bosses. Because humans tend to have very strong and contradictory priors (beliefs or assumptions) on such matters, arguments about organization that link to favoured worldviews often tend to be advanced in an evidence-free fashion and are relatively impervious to contrary evidence.[16] Related to that, visceral issues of identity may cut across debates that at first sight might be expected to focus on humdrum questions about what is the most practical and cost-effective way to collect the garbage or run the schools, as they typically do in societies strongly divided by race, ethnicity, religion, or language. And yet another reason for the ideological character of such policies—their apparent imperviousness to evidence—is what Thomas Ferguson calls the 'investment theory of politics'.[17] The theory posits that the choice of policies, in public management as in any other domain, can be driven as much by what influential backers and funders of parties and politicians want as by the wants of the median voter (voters who are situated in the middle of preference orderings or income distributions), the focus of so many standard models of party competition in political science since the 1960s.[18]

But explanation of a state of affairs is not the same as justification. And the fact that debates about public management reform have often been relatively evidence-free, evidence-light, or at least based on highly selective evidence, even on the very valence issues that reform advocates have typically stressed, makes it all the more important to pin down what can be said about when

---

[15] Tony Blair, *The Third Way: New Politics for the New Century* (London: Fabian Society, 1998), p. 4; see also Tony Blair, 'New Politics for the New Century', *The Independent*, 21 September 1998.

[16] Christopher Hood, *The Art of the State* (Oxford: Clarendon, 1998).

[17] Thomas Ferguson, *Golden Rule: The Investment Theory of Party Competition and the Logic of Money-Driven Political Systems* (Chicago: University of Chicago Press, 1994); David Craig and Richard Brooks, *Plundering the Public Sector: How New Labour are Letting Consultants Run off with £70 Billion of Our Money* (London: Constable, 2006).

[18] Donald Black, 'On the Rationale of Group Decision-making', *Journal of Political Economy* 56 (1948): pp. 23–34; Anthony Downs, 'An Economic Theory of Political Action in a Democracy', *Journal of Political Economy* 65 (1957): pp. 135–50.

and whether the last three decades of government reforms have really produced a system that 'works better and costs less'. And that is what this book aims to do, for the critical case of the United Kingdom.

1.2 Potential Discontinuities in the Operation of Government over Three Decades: Managerialism, Digitization, Spin-Doctoring

Chapter 2 lays out what happened to some of the major features of UK central government over the three decades or so we are exploring here—for example in features such as the size of the cabinet, the number of government departments and 'quangos', the size and shape of the civil service, and the overall pattern of public spending. The aim of that broad-brush description is to put the changes of the last few decades into context. But, as we have already suggested, some bold claims have been made about changes over that period that are said to have had a big impact on what executive government cost and how it worked. Three common claims of that sort relate to the effects of managerial makeovers, to the effects of the digital revolution in government, and to the rise of spin-doctoring and related techniques of communication and information architecture.

1.2.1 *Better Government Through Management Makeovers*

The idea that government could be improved through better management is probably as old as government itself, and there are plenty of historical recipes for better public management. Over forty years ago Andrew Dunsire and Richard Chapman[19] remarked that there had always been two strains of thinking about the civil service in Britain, the Macaulayite strain and the Benthamite strain. The Macaulayite strain, deriving from those nineteenth-century writers and politicians who admired the Chinese Confucian tradition of government by a meritocracy of scholar-administrators, stressed the role of civil servants as policy advisers, intellectuals, philosophers, and guardians of constitutional convention. The Benthamite strain, deriving from Jeremy Bentham's distillation of a set of supposedly rational principles of public management some two hundred years ago, as mentioned at the outset, put more stress on the importance of management and service-delivery expertise to maximize 'aptitude' and minimize 'expense'.[20]

---

[19] Richard Chapman and Andrew Dunsire (eds), *Style in Administration* (London: Allen and Unwin, 1971), p. 17.
[20] Leslie J. Hume, *Bentham on Bureaucracy* (Cambridge: Cambridge University Press, 1981).

During the two world wars of the twentieth century, the Benthamite or 'management' view was necessarily accorded a key role in UK central government, with many people brought in from business firms to organize production and service supply functions, from the production of munitions to the supply and distribution of basic goods and services like milk and timber. But after each of those wars, the civil service tended to revert to a more 'Macaulayite' position as the wartime command economy was turned back into a market or mixed economy. After the First World War there were criticisms of management ineptitude in UK central government in the 1920s from a business perspective, for example by Sir Stephen (Stephanos) Demetriadi (a businessman and civil servant who had been Director of Naval and Military Pensions during the First World War),[21] and numerous articles on the subject of management and efficiency in the then newly established journal *Public Administration*.[22] But there was no real equivalent to the stress laid on the potential for management in federal government in the United States by the famous Brownlow Committee of 1937, which presented management as a vital ingredient to the achievement of 'social justice, security, order, liberty, prosperity, in material benefit and in higher values of life'.[23] Perhaps the leading UK textbook on British central government in the 1950s, Mackenzie and Grove's *Central Administration in Britain*,[24] had much of value to say about the recurrent rhetoric of reform and restructuring and of some of the folkways of Whitehall, but little or nothing about issues of operating costs or performance in service delivery.

However, a renewed stress on management in UK government started to emerge in the 1960s and 1970s. Desmond Keeling detected early manifestations in a 1957 Treasury circular by Sir Norman Brook (then head of the British civil service) which urged the higher ranks of the civil service (the 'administrative class', as that group was then called) to pay more attention to 'management matters', and to the stress on improving management of the public services which came from a major committee on the control of Public Expenditure (the Plowden Committee), which was appointed in 1959 and reported in 1961. But, as Keeling shows, 'management' at that time came to be conceived narrowly as the conduct of personnel and pay matters in the

[21] Sir Stephen Demetriadi, *A Reform for the Civil Service* (London: Cassell, 1921).
[22] See Christopher Hood, 'British Public Administration: Dodo, Phoenix or Chameleon?', in *The British Study of Politics in the Twentieth Century*, edited by Jack Hayward, Brian Barry, and Archie Brown (Oxford: Oxford University Press for the British Academy, 1999), pp. 309–10.
[23] Brownlow Committee on Administrative Management, *Report of the Committee, with Studies of Administrative Management in the Federal Government* (Washington, DC: Government Printing Office, 1937).
[24] William J.M. Mackenzie and Jack W. Grove, *Central Administration in Britain* (London: Longmans, 1957).

public service rather than the broader sense intended by Sir Norman Brook and the Plowden Committee.[25]

That broader view of management as the key to better government started to develop in local government in the 1960s and 1970s,[26] but only emerged in full-blown form at central government level in the 1980s, reaching a point that led Christopher Pollitt to characterize it as a dominant ideology of the public services in the UK and the USA at that time.[27] This era culminated with a senior civil servant (Sir Peter Kemp) directing a programme of 'agencification' in the civil service in the late 1980s and early 1990s, who refused even to use the word 'administration' rather than 'management' for any part of the conduct of executive government. Such individuals clearly had very high expectations of what a new managerial approach to make a big difference to how government operated. Three decades later, what can we say about the observable results?

1.2.2 *Salvation Through Information Technology*

Fifteen years or so ago, Helen Margetts observed,

> Information technology has been heralded as a new fairy godmother for government. Politicians in the 1990s compete to associate themselves with the magical effects of her wand, which they claim will wave in the new age of government and an end to the ills of administration . . . Politicians' speeches [in the USA and UK at this time] were peppered with the words 'new,' 'modern,' and dazzling images of the twenty-first century.[28]

Margetts pointed out that such soaring rhetoric, implying that the IT revolution would transform bureaucracy in politically desired directions (making government more flexible, more intelligent, more accountable, and providing new standards of customer service), picked up on portentous claims from management gurus and futurologists in an earlier era, such as Daniel Bell and Alvin Toffler, about the power of new technologies to radically reshape society and organizations.[29]

The US 1993 National Performance Review, mentioned earlier, is a clear example of what Margetts was referring to. US Vice-President Al Gore's

---

[25] Desmond Keeling, *Management in Government* (London: George Allen and Unwin, 1972), pp. 18–20.

[26] See for example Jeffrey Stanyer, *Understanding Local Government* (Glasgow: Fontana/Collins, 1976), pp. 234–63.

[27] Christopher Pollitt, *Managerialism and the Public Services: The Anglo-American Experience* (Oxford: Blackwell, 1990), p. vi.

[28] Helen Z. Margetts, *Information Technology in Government: Britain and America* (London: Routledge, 1999), pp. xiii–xiv.

[29] Margetts, *Information Technology*, pp. xiv–xv.

preface to that document declared with utter confidence, 'As everyone knows, the computer revolution allows us to do things faster and more cheaply than we ever have before . . . ' and referred to an impressive number of billions of dollars' worth of projected savings arising from new IT in the federal government.[30] Later in the review document it was said that 'opportunities abound for cutting operating costs by using telecommunications technologies', but also claimed that far more than just cost-cutting could be achieved. The report envisaged far better service to users and citizens through digital technologies than through old-fashioned paper-based bureaucracy, with all its accompanying frustrations: 'With computers and telecommunications . . . we can design a customer-driven electronic government that operates in ways that, 10 years ago, the most visionary planner could not have imagined.'[31]

Nor was it just such purple passages from politicians that conveyed expectations and beliefs about the power of IT developments to cut costs and improve customer service in government. For example, in the mid-1980s, the UK department then responsible for collecting direct taxes (the Inland Revenue, which merged with the Customs and Excise Department twenty years later) introduced a long-awaited new computer system for the PAYE (Pay as You Earn) withholding system,[32] which it described as 'a massive project that will bring large savings in our administrative costs' and added that it would enable a move from a manual system that 'both our staff and "customers" have increasingly come to regard as antiquated, to one more in keeping with modern business methods . . . '[33] Fifteen years or so later, a controversial new mega-contract for outsourcing the department's entire IT operations to the data-processing firm EDS (Electronic Data Systems) was announced, with the claim that 'Information technology unit cost reductions of 15–20 per cent are anticipated over the [ten year] life span of the contract',[34] which in money terms was expected to lead to savings of hundreds of millions of pounds.[35] Again, decades later, what can be said about the outcome of such developments, from which so much was claimed and expected?

---

[30] Gore, *From Red Tape to Results*, p. iv.

[31] Gore, pp. 114 and 112, respectively.

[32] That system, originally introduced during the Second World War, involves employers deducting income tax according to a code issued by the tax department, before paying employees' wages or salaries, and then paying the money to government, usually with a small delay that enables employers to earn a 'turn' on the money in return for their costs.

[33] *Report of the Commissioners of Her Majesty's Inland Revenue for the year ended 31st December 1983* (Cmnd 9305, 1984), p. 1.

[34] *Report of the Commissioners of Her Majesty's Inland Revenue for the year ending 31st March 1997* (Cm 3771, 1998), p. 28.

[35] *Report of the Commissioners of Her Majesty's Inland Revenue for the year ending 31st March 1999* (Cm 4477, 1999), p. 31.

1.2.3 *On Message: Controlling the Story*

At the 1993 launch of the ' . . . *Works Better and Costs Less*' report mentioned above, it is reported that, after making his opening speech, Vice-President Al Gore turned the meeting over to a motivational consultant (John Daly) who stressed that optimism and effective communication were key to the success of the programme, declared that 'it doesn't matter how good you really are but *how you communicate how good you are*' [our emphasis], proceeded to discuss customer strategies used by the Disney company, and indeed concluded in that spirit by leading the assembled company in the 'off to work we go' song from *Snow White and Seven Dwarfs*.[36] And that introduces another element of change affecting government over the last thirty years or so, namely claims about how much can be achieved by new presentational techniques, improved 'framing' and tighter control of corporate 'messages'.

The word 'spin doctor' is said to have been coined in the 1970s by the Canadian-American novelist Saul Bellow,[37] although of course the phenomenon of 'message control' goes back long before that. For example, propaganda (both of the overt variety and the 'black' or disavowable kind) was a major activity of UK central government in both of the twentieth-century world wars. Indeed, the UK is said to have had a rather larger information and propaganda ministry during the Second World War than did Nazi Germany,[38] but again it was reined back after that war to a more modest and relatively neutral role.

However, powerful claims came to be made from the late 1950s about the new power of advertising, based on improved understanding of human psychology and linked with increased ability of pollsters to gauge public moods and sensitivities.[39] That percolated into party politics, with the rise of private polling and associated message control, as parties developed methods of fine-grained polling to target and craft policies for key swing voters,[40] and started to shape the conduct of executive government as well, as presentation, media control, and branding received more emphasis and their practitioners acquired more authority. By the 1990s, 'spin' became a central theme

[36] Ronald C. Moe, 'The "Reinventing Government" Exercise: Misinterpreting the Problem, Misjudging the Consequences', *Public Administration Review* 54, no. 2 (1994): p. 111.

[37] Frank Esser, 'Spin Doctor' in *The International Encyclopedia of Communication*, edited by Wolfgang Donsbach (London: Wiley Blackwell, 2008), pp. 4783–7, says '[Saul Bellow] spoke in his 1977 Jefferson Lecture about political actors "capturing the presidency itself with the aid of spin doctors"'.

[38] Sir Bernard Ingham, *The Wages of Spin* (London: John Murray, 2003), p. 40.

[39] See for example Vance O. Packard and Mark C. Miller, *The Hidden Persuaders* (New York: Pocket Books, 1957) and James A.C. Brown, *Techniques of Persuasion: From Propaganda to Brainwashing* (Harmondsworth: Penguin Books, 1963).

[40] See for example Stephen Mills, *The New Machine Men: Polls and Persuasion in Australian Politics* (Ringwood, VIC: Penguin, 1986).

of political commentary in both the USA and the UK,[41] with the idea that new and more powerful methods were being applied to present government leaders and policies in a favourable light, countering 'negativity bias' in the media by a variety of techniques, such as taking advantage of diversions or depriving the most critical journalists of attractive stories.

For example, one of us encountered minatory wall posters in one major UK department in the early 2000s warning its civil servants that 'there are 152 political journalists noting your every word'.[42] A year or two after that, in the mid-2000s, the UK's Department of Health went further in its efforts at message control, commissioning consultants to construct a database of print and broadcast journalists writing about the department, coding every story about the department by every journalist according to the degree of positivity or otherwise it showed towards the department's operations and policies.[43] In the later 2000s major claims were made about the ability of governments and corporations to shape the behaviour of citizens and customers by using insights drawn from marketing and psychology, for example by the way default options were set, such that big changes in behaviour by citizens (such as tax compliance) could be engineered by low-cost changes in information system architecture.[44] If such developments were as transformational as some have claimed, we might expect these changes to have had a noticeable impact on government's ability to deliver effective policy at lower cost over several decades.

1.3 The 'Works Better and Costs Less' Test: Nine Possible Outcomes

These three changes in government—in the stress laid on a new generation of managerialism, on the development of modern IT and the stress on modern techniques of controlling the story, framing the debate, and shaping citizens' choices—developed simultaneously over recent decades, and are therefore not easy to separate. For example, IT system development has been closely interrelated with approaches to management systems and with broader

---

[41] See for example, Howard Kurtz, *Spin Cycle: Inside the Clinton Propaganda Machine* (New York: Free Press, 1998).

[42] See Christopher Hood and Martin Lodge, *The Politics of Public Service Bargains: Reward, Competency, Loyalty—and Blame* (Oxford: Oxford University Press, 2006), p. viii.

[43] *National Media Coverage of Public Health Issues and the NHS*, December 2004–November 2006. <http://webarchive.nationalarchives.gov.uk/+/www.dh.gov.uk/en/FreedomOfInformation/Freedomofinformationpublicationschemefeedback/Classesofinformation/Communications research/DH_4130120>.

[44] Richard H. Thaler and Cass R. Sunstein, *Nudge: Improving Decisions about Health, Wealth, and Happiness* (New Haven: Yale University Press, 2008); Cass R. Sunstein, *Simpler: The Future of Government* (New York: Simon & Schuster, 2013).

presentational strategies. But if there is any truth in the claims put forward about the quantum impact that might be expected from such changes on the cost and performance of government, we might expect to find clear step changes in what government cost to run and how it worked over the past few decades.

If the aspirations of the modernizers, managers, and other reformers was indeed to produce a government that worked better and cost less, the range of possible results after a generation of reform are laid out in Table 1.1, which presents the nine possible permutations of better, worse, and no change outcomes on the two dimensions of cost and performance.

Those who expect the three developments discussed above to have introduced quantum change or major discontinuities in the factors that shape the relationship between cost and outcomes in government might expect to find the outcomes at the outer ends of the northwest–southeast diagonal of Table 1.1. Optimists within this 'discontinuity' school might expect to find the overall result shown in cell 1 of Table 1.1—the 'dream' outcome in which government did indeed work better and cost less, 'doing better with less' as a result of smarter management, better technology, or methods of marketing or presentation that elicited readier compliance or promoted a more favourable image of government. But 'discontinuity pessimists' would expect to find precisely the opposite, as shown in cell 9—the 'nightmare' outcome in which government ends up with higher costs and lower levels of performance, 'doing worse with more' as a result of dysfunctional management, failing technology, and self-defeating spinmanship.

Those who take neither a utopian nor a dystopian view of the management and technological developments we discussed earlier, and who believe that in government, as in many other things in life, you tend to get what you pay for, would expect to find the results on the other, northeast to southwest,

Table 1.1. How Government Works and What It Costs: Nine Possible Outcomes

Cost level →		
1 Worked better, cost less *Did better with less* *('Dream' outcome)*	2 Worked better, cost the same *Did better with the same*	3 Worked better, cost more *Did better with more*
4 Worked the same, cost less *Did the same with less*	5 Worked the same, cost the same *No change*	6 Worked the same, cost more *Did the same with more*
7 Worked worse, cost less *Did worse with less*	8 Worked worse, cost the same *Did worse with the same*	9 Worked worse, cost more *Did worse with more* *('Nightmare' outcome)*

Quality level

diagonal of Table 1.1. If you want Scandinavian levels of public service performance, this view would go, you must expect to pay the Scandinavian price for it in your tax bill. If you follow this sort of approach, said by some to be associated with less individualist cultures,[45] you would expect to find either the positive result shown in cell 3, where improved performance goes along with rising costs—doing better with more—or the result shown in cell 7, where lower costs are paid for in lower levels of performance and government ends up doing 'worse with less'.

But again, there are some who might believe that what happens in society and policy, outside the machinery of government and the deliberate actions of those who manage that machinery, is likely to have the biggest impact on the relationship between what government costs and how well it does its job. From this viewpoint—that changing social context can be more important than whizzy management or other internal factors in determining government cost and performance—there would be no compelling reason to expect the relationship between cost and performance to be confined to the four corners of Table 1.1, and good reasons to expect that many kinds of change would produce the relationship between cost and quality that is described by the diamond between the mid-points of each side of the square. For example, if society changes in such a way that government and public services must operate in a larger number of languages than before (as has happened with successive enlargements of the European Union, or in cities receiving immigrants from multiple language groups), then the extra need for translation and interpretation could be expected to increase government's administration costs without any necessary changes in the general level of public performance. Contrariwise, if politicians decide to move from a complex tax code, with many levels, categories exemptions, and abatements, to a flat-tax regime, as has happened in some Eastern European countries, the surveillance and inspection costs of the tax authorities could be expected to fall without any necessary change in the performance of tax administration.

Finally, fatalists and sceptics who do not subscribe to the 'get what you pay for' view of government; do not see management, technology, or marketing and presentation as either good or bad magic; and might not expect contextual changes to relate to what happens inside government in any coherent way either, will not be surprised if the observed result is that represented by cell 5 in Table 1.1. From this perspective, in spite (or maybe because) of all the hot air and purple prose accompanying a generation of reform initiatives,

---

[45] See for example, Ashok K. Lalwani and Sharon Shavitt, 'You Get What You Pay For? Self-Construal Influences Price-Quality Judgments', *Journal of Consumer Research* 40, no. 2 (2013): pp. 255–67.

government might well be expected to end up costing much the same and performing at much the same level, for better or worse.

1.4 New Public Management Poster Child—the UK Case

Any study of what government cost and of changes in the perceived fairness and consistency of administration has to balance breadth against depth, weighing the advantage of the big comparative sweep as against that of a narrower but deeper trench. There are pros and cons of both approaches. But this book mostly goes for the 'deep trench' approach and concentrates on the UK, one of the 'poster children' of the New Public Management.

In fact, it could almost be argued that the UK was not just a 'poster child' but the 'vanguard state,' of the New Public Management movement, given that (as was mentioned at the outset) the more business-oriented approach associated with the Thatcher government's famous drive to cut 'bloated bureaucracy' in the 1980s preceded several other parallel moves elsewhere in the world (for instance by US President Ronald Reagan, Canadian Premier Brian Mulroney, and the New Zealand Labour government led by David Lange and Roger Douglas in the 1980s). UK reformers often boasted about their influence on reform drives elsewhere in the world, many reformers in other countries in turn acknowledged a debt to the UK's influence on their efforts, and the UK has often been said to have been one of the world's most prolific producers of government reform plans and efficiency makeovers over the past three decades.[46] But what exactly has been the result of all those much-publicized efficiency drives and that portentous reform rhetoric?

The UK's new managerialism movement presented itself as a hard-headed, business-minded, cost-conscious, and data-driven approach to government makeover. So it deserves a correspondingly hard-headed, business-minded, cost-conscious, and data-driven assessment of its results, confronting received claims or interpretations with systematic quantitative evidence from the past three decades. That is what this book tries to provide. As will be seen in later chapters, the analysis is not based on a quick survey or a *jeu d'esprit*, but rather has been developed out of three years of detective work involving careful combing through decades of documentary data, backed up with material drawn from interviews with a range of current and retired players and observers in the government-reform process about issues of cost and quality in government and public services.[47]

---

[46] See for example, Christopher Pollitt, 'The Evolving Narratives of Public Management Reform: 40 Years of Reform White Papers in the UK', *Public Management Review* 15, no. 6 (2013): pp. 899–922.

[47] The roles of individual interviewees are shown in anonymized form in Appendix 1 at the end of this book.

1.5 Plan of the Rest of the Book

Of course some of the expectations that we sketched out in Section 1.3 are easier to test than others. But this book looks carefully for evidence of how the costs of running government changed over a period of three decades in the UK, what happened to indicators of perceived fairness and consistency in government administration, and what seems to have been the relationship between the two (to test 'get what you pay for' relative to 'discontinuity' views).

Before we get to that, we have two scene-setting chapters. Chapter 2 follows on from this one by sketching out some of the broad changes that took place in UK central government over the thirty years we are putting under the spotlight here. We explore what changed and what remained relatively constant under four broad headings, namely, the basic legislative, electoral, and constitutional features of the UK as a state; the place of the bureaucracy in the political system; the place of government in the economy and wider society; and the technology of government. Under most of those headings, there were continuities as well as changes, and it is necessary to identify both to get a balanced picture of the background to efforts to cut cost and improve administrative quality.

Chapter 3 then turns to the data that documents government performance over time, showing that, despite government's protestations about the desirability of evidence-based policy and management, the continued destruction of consistent data-series over time often makes it impossible or at least very laborious for anyone to possess evidence about whether government is doing better or worse over a period of more than a few years. We examine why that should be so, what sort of factors seem to be behind this evidence-destroying data 'churn', and what its consequences are.

Now, as we also argue in Chapter 3, the study of data breaks and data volatility is valuable in itself for the light it can throw on changing priorities, preoccupations, and ways of working over a generation. One of us was once told (perhaps with some exaggeration) by a senior Australian public servant that the whole history of the public service could be told by exploring changing arrangements for pay and reward over time. And in similar vein it can be argued that tracking changes in the way performance numbers are recorded is a key to understanding changes in values, culture, and practice in the bureaucracy over time. Chapter 3 goes into some of those issues, looking at the causes of data changes and the relative incidence of different kinds of change. But as well as being a window into such bureaucratic changes, data changes also present a challenge for the sort of long-term analysis of government performance that this book aims to provide. How can we reach any firm conclusions about such performance if the evidence keeps changing?

We deal with that challenge in two main ways, as will be shown in later chapters. One is to 'call back yesterday', that is, to adjust runs of performance numbers after a data break into the previous format wherever we can. That sort of adjustment is possible when there is an overlap in reporting the relevant data at the change-over point, but not in those cases (far from infrequent) where there is no such overlap. The other is to practise 'redundancy' in data analysis, placing heavy reliance on a form of what was been called 'consilience' in the collection and assessment of evidence. Consilience means putting evidence together from more than one source, no one of which is perfect on its own, but which, if combined, provide more powerful evidence than any one element would do on its own if those various sources point in the same direction.[48] The term itself dates from the nineteenth century,[49] the method has been and continues to be applied in many branches of science, and in the following chapters we use this method wherever we can to add to the robustness of our conclusions about changes in performance.

Accordingly, putting together the available fragments of data in the same sort of way as an archaeologist or forensic scientist might reassemble broken pottery shards or put together scraps of other evidence, we start by examining what happened to indicators of administration cost in central government (ostensibly the central target of many of the management reformers, as we have seen). Chapters 4 and 5 look respectively at what happened to reported running costs in UK civil departments as a whole and in the tax-collecting departments (arguably a set of organizations where one might expect the promise of more focused management allied with changes in technology to have a particularly strong impact). We show that in both cases administration costs—so far as they can be reliably tracked—rose substantially in real terms over the period. There certainly were times when those costs fell relative to total spending or total tax revenue collected, if that is how 'costs less' should properly be construed—but this past performance provides only very limited inspiration for current and recent plans to cut administration costs drastically in absolute terms.

Chapter 6 turns from what government cost to administrative performance in the sense of indicators of perceived unfairness or inconsistency or sloppy administration on the part of citizens or users. Of course, 'performance', like 'modernization', is a term that different people interpret in different ways, dependent on their outlook or worldview. Some people believe government

---

[48] Christopher Hood and Ruth Dixon, 'The Political Payoff from Performance Target Systems: No-Brainer or No-Gainer?', *Journal of Public Administration Research and Theory* 20, Suppl. 2 (2010): pp. i281–98.

[49] William Whewell, *The Philosophy of the Inductive Sciences: Founded upon their History* (Whitefish, MT: Kissinger, [1847] 2007).

should be extensively engaged in social engineering and management in everything from diet, exercise, and obesity to thought and language policing, while others take a much more minimal view of the proper role of the state. But irrespective of whether you take a maximalist or minimalist view of government as a manager of society and the economy, whatever government does do can be expected to be conducted fairly and consistently, carefully applying rules to put cases into categories reliably and treat like cases alike—and indeed some of the critics of 'new managerialism' argued that it is precisely those rather traditional administrative virtues that tend to suffer under the pressure of cost control and greater managerial freedom. Accordingly, we put the emphasis here on the changing incidence of formal complaints and legal challenges to government decisions, which have the advantage both of being a relatively technology-free way of assessing administrative performance over a period in which technology changed so markedly and also of getting precisely at those issues of perceived consistency and fairness of government operations. Our analysis suggests a mixed picture, but one that is hard to reconcile with the 'working better' aspirations and expectations of those reformers of two decades or more ago.

In Chapter 7, we widen our focus to explore how far the cost and performance of the UK central government machine can be compared with those of other countries, with local government (often said to embody very different approaches and cultures), with those delivery ('executive') agencies placed at arms-length from central departments to allow greater scope for focused management, and with the Scottish group of departments and agencies headquartered in Edinburgh (or other Scottish cities), which arguably share few of the characteristics of central government at UK level. So far as such comparisons are possible, we find little evidence of a marked difference in performance between UK central government and these comparators, which raises puzzling questions about what exactly was the dividend reaped by extra focus on management in executive agencies from the early 1990s or by the emphasis on developing large-scale new tax IT systems at central government level as against the more pluralist and variable approach taken in local government.

We then (in Chapter 8) turn from cost and perceptions of administrative fairness or consistency to the way the process of government worked over the period—a feature stressed by numerous commentators, especially those critical of change. We focus in particular on the process of drafting and managing legislation, the keeping of accounts and records, and the degree of turnover in institutions and people (politicians and bureaucrats of various types). Again, the picture that this analysis suggests is nuanced, but is more consistent with government working worse or about the same, rather than working better over this period.

18

Finally, Chapter 9 then returns to the broader issue of what overall conclusions can be drawn from this analysis of cost and performance in UK central government over three decades. It goes back to the nine possible outcomes that we laid out in Table 1.1 above and shows that the outcomes that most plausibly fit our analysis fit within a range between government costing about the same (but not less) and working about as well (but not better), to a darker picture of government costing substantially more and working decidedly worse. That suggests that the battle for better management in government has by no means been won, in this particular case at least, and the book concludes by exploring the implications of our findings for widely held ideas about public management, the puzzling or intriguing questions they present for further analysis, and their policy implications for a period in which pressures to make government 'work better and cost less' are unlikely to go away.

2

The General Background

What Changed and What Didn't in the UK Central Governance Landscape

Bien perdu, bien connu (French proverb)[1]

2.1 Introduction: Identifying Change and Continuity in the Landscape

This chapter sketches out some of the general background against which efforts to cut running costs of UK central government and to make it work better took place between 1980 (the first full year of Margaret Thatcher's government) and the early 2010s. As already explained, this book aims to examine the effects of three decades of reform on running costs and perceived consistency and fairness of administration, rather than to identify the causes of those reforms, so the purpose of this chapter is simply to set the reforms into context. To do that, we give a brief account of what happened over that period under four broad headings, namely

(1) the legislative, electoral, and constitutional features of the UK as a state;

(2) the place of the bureaucracy in the political system;

(3) the place of government in the economy and wider society; and

(4) the technology of government.

Under the first heading (the main legislative, electoral, and constitutional features of the state, the conventional starting point of comparative-politics scholars), one well-known characterization of what has traditionally made the UK's version of democracy distinctive comes from the distinguished

---

[1] Meaning the true value of something is clearly perceived (only) when it is lost.

comparative political scientist Arend Lijphart, who in successive writings since the 1970s has identified the UK as the world's leading example of what he called majoritarian democracy. By that is meant a democratic system combining a concentrated executive dominating the legislature with a highly unitary state comprising very few 'veto points' (that is, points in the decision-making structure where players can block a change from the status quo).[2] Some have argued that such features may help to explain the UK's prominent international profile as an apparent 'poster child' of New Public Management and similar reforms, since it created the opportunity to drive reform efforts from a single centre of power.[3] So what changed and what didn't about this feature of UK government over the period?

Under the second heading (the place of the bureaucracy in the political system) it is often said that the UK is distinctive (though not necessarily unique) in the type of 'bargain' that its civil service has operated under since the nineteenth century. That is, senior civil servants, relatively insulated from party affiliations, obtained a degree of permanence and influence in the policy process in exchange for anonymity and loyalty to the elected government of the day.[4] Again, it can be argued that such a system might possibly be more conducive to 'managerial' reforms than one in which the civil service is more closely intermeshed with party politics, so we need to consider what happened to this part of the background over our thirty-year period.

The third heading (the place of government in the economy and wider society) takes us into the province of political economy and political sociology scholars. Over at least part of the period considered here, notably under the Thatcher government, there was much heady rhetoric about 'rolling back' or at least substantially restructuring the state[5] and there were also frequent assertions of long-term changes in social attitudes towards government, notably in sharply declining trust and confidence in government, politics, and indeed other institutions too.[6] And here too it can be claimed that

---

[2] See for example Arend Lijphart, *Patterns of Democracy* (New Haven: Yale University Press, 1999).

[3] See Christopher Hood, 'Exploring Variations in Public Management Reform of the 1980s', Chapter 13 in *Civil Service Systems in Comparative Perspective*, edited by Hans Bekke, James Perry, and Theo Toonen (Bloomington: Indiana University Press, 1996), pp. 268–87.

[4] See Lesley Lipson, *The Politics of Equality* (Chicago: Chicago University Press, 1948), p. 479; Bernard Schaffer, *The Administrative Factor* (London: Frank Cass, 1973), p. 252; Christopher Hood and Martin Lodge, *The Politics of Public Service Bargains: Reward, Competency, Loyalty—and Blame* (Oxford: Oxford University Press, 2006).

[5] See for example Andrew Gamble, *The Free Economy and the Strong State: The Politics of Thatcherism* (Basingstoke: Macmillan, 1988).

[6] For example, Joseph Nye, Philip Zelikow, and David King, *Why People Don't Trust Government* (Cambridge, MA: Harvard University Press, 1997) and from a different point of view, Lord Richard Wilson (former UK cabinet secretary), 'Trust in Public Life', *British Academy Review* 12 (2009): pp. 1–4.

an emphasis on 'managerial' reforms of the state might fit with a post-Cold War era in which mainstream political parties all came to compete on the basis of some version of 'managed capitalism' rather than by pitting 'free enterprise' against full-blown socialism. In those conditions, politicians and parties more shallowly rooted in society than in earlier times and less ideologically distinct needed to find new ways to persuade sceptical voters of their ability to manage public services effectively. So what signs can we see of a changing role of that state and of changed citizen attitudes towards government and politics?

Under the final heading (the technology of government), much has been said about the changes associated with the 'digital age', the effect of such changes on what government can do (for example in surveillance), and the new pressures those changes put governments under.[7] Those who think social change (and the pay-offs associated with different systems of state management) is dependent on long-term economic cycles linked to particular leading technologies (so-called Kondratieff cycles)[8] might well see the reforms of the thirty years considered here as belonging to the age of developing digital technology. What is more debatable is what kind of management systems fit best with such technology, and some scholars have claimed that the effective use of digital technology in government demands special and different kinds of management.[9] So we need to review what changed in digital technology over the period.

We do not claim that those four headings are jointly exhaustive, or even mutually exclusive. But together they can help us to take stock of both the fixed points and the things that changed in the background during the thirty years of reform we are concerned with here. As the proverb given as the epigraph to this chapter implies (and there are variants of it in other languages), change and loss tends to draw attention and comment, while continuity is taken for granted and invisible. So we can only put our thirty-year period in perspective by trying to identify parts of the government landscape that were more-or-less stable, as well as those parts which changed. When we look at the four elements mentioned above, we find some things changed more than others, and so the extent to which the era is to be classed as revolutionary or otherwise depends what weight is placed on each element.

---

[7] See Christopher Hood and Helen Margetts, *The Tools of Government in the Digital Age* (Basingstoke: Palgrave Macmillan, 2007).

[8] See for example Herbert Kitschelt, 'Industrial Governance Structures, Innovation Strategies, and the Case of Japan: Sectoral or Cross-National Comparative Analysis?', *International Organization* 45, no. 4 (1991): pp. 453–93, especially pp. 472–5.

[9] See Patrick Dunleavy, Helen Margetts, Simon Bastow, and Jane Tinkler, *Digital Era Governance: IT Corporations, the State and E-Government* (Oxford: Oxford University Press, 2006).

2.2 The Legislative, Electoral, and Constitutional Features of the UK as a State

Some of the main political, legislative, and constitutional features noted by Lijphart as characteristic of the UK's majoritarian democracy remained clearly in evidence throughout the period, such as dominance of the executive over the legislature, a weakly bicameral legislature with a non-elected upper house, an atomistic rather than corporatized interest-group structure, and a first-past-the-post electoral system for the lower house that mostly produced a majoritarian style of government at UK level led by one or other of the two main parties. Over our three decades, there was one minority government in Westminster (John Major's Conservative government between December 1996 and May 1997, when it had lost its original parliamentary majority as a result of numerous resignations and by-election defeats) and one coalition government (David Cameron's Conservative–Liberal Democrat coalition formed after the 2010 general election produced a hung Parliament), but otherwise the UK central government was single-party majoritarian.

Some other related basic features of domestic political architecture stayed fairly constant. One was the basic political geography and policy competencies of UK central government at the topmost level, concerning matters such as defence, intelligence, foreign affairs, finance, taxation, immigration, and welfare benefits. Of course, the political geography of the UK state was contested during the period by republicans in Northern Ireland and by nationalists in Scotland (and to a lesser extent in Wales), but these functions continued to be exercised on a UK basis throughout the three decades considered here. Similarly, some of the legislation enacted by government originated from the European Union, but that legislation nevertheless had to be transposed into British law, applied and enforced through the government machine.[10]

Additional more-or-less constant features included the size of the UK Cabinet (formed of about twenty ministers) and the overall number of major government departments, albeit with many of their portfolios successively reorganized as political needs changed.[11] Similarly, the size of the Westminster Parliament remained constant with about 650 elected members of the lower house and about 1000 non-elected members of the upper house (although this stability masks an important change in the composition of the House of Lords in 1999 when most of the hereditary peers were replaced by

---

[10] See Jørgen Christensen, 'EU legislation and National Regulation: Uncertain Steps Towards a European Public Policy', *Public Administration* 88, no. 1 (2010): pp. 3–17, for a wider discussion of national impacts of EU legislation.

[11] Anne White and Patrick Dunleavy, *Making and Breaking Whitehall Departments: A Guide to Machinery of Government Changes* (London: Institute for Government and LSE Public Policy Group, 2010).

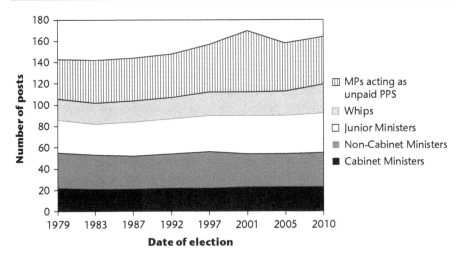

Figure 2.1. Number of Ministers 1979–2010 (number after each general election)

Source: House of Commons Library, *Limitations on the Number of Ministers and the Size of the Payroll Vote* (SN/PC/03378, 2010).

appointed life peers). As Figure 2.1 shows, the number of salaried politician office-holders at the upper levels was very stable, while the number of Junior Ministers and 'whips' (the term used for the official and paid parliamentary managers of both the government and opposition parties) increased by some 15 per cent.

Beyond central government, a further relatively stable feature was a local government system (albeit much reorganized, and with its competences changed in numerous important ways) that had extensive service delivery responsibilities but which raised only a small proportion of the associated revenue as local taxes (themselves radically changed during the period, as we discuss in Chapter 5). Throughout the period local government was therefore heavily dependent on central government funding for its operations and all the various and changing strings that accompanied such funding.

Against these more-or-less stable features of the legislative, electoral, and constitutional make-up of the UK went several changes that markedly weakened several of the majoritarian elements that Lijphart took as distinctive to the UK's model of democracy. Perhaps the change that struck most directly at the 'unitary' feature noted by Lijphart was the devolution of legislative and oversight powers for many domestic public services and policy responsibilities to elected governments or assemblies in Scotland and Wales in 1999. That move, twenty years after earlier proposals for devolution had failed (resulting in the general election of 1979), put electoral representation on top of a pre-existing pattern of extensive administrative devolution, particularly in Scotland, and indeed it was accompanied by the development of a Lijphart-style 'consociational' regime in Northern Ireland under a de facto condominium with the Republic of Ireland since 1998. Even though it arguably made more changes to the parliamentary than the administrative landscape, devolution was a major constitutional change, which together with the assignment of more co-legislative powers in the European Parliament after the Lisbon Treaty of 2009 marked a development of a new 'intergovernmental relations'—a phrase which still might have seemed alien to many within the UK at the start of our period.

Another striking change that went along with devolution was a marked growth in the number of full-time politicians. At the Westminster level, while the number of senior paid political offices at the topmost level stayed fairly stable, as Figure 2.1 shows, the number of MPs acting as unpaid Parliamentary Private Secretaries (and thus not covered by statutory limits on the number of paid officeholders allowed to sit in the Parliament) increased by about 15 per cent. And while the number of Westminster MPs remained constant at about 650 since 1983, Scottish and Welsh devolution added 189 salaried politicians (including about thirty-six extra ministers) into the political system, and the post-1998 Northern Ireland government increased the number of elected politicians from seventy-eight to 108. Together, those changes meant that numbers of full-time salaried politicians in the United Kingdom increased by about 30 per cent between 1979 and 2010, over a period when the total number of civil servants fell by about a third.

Along with that increase in the size of the 'salariat' of full-time elected politicians competing to make the various administrative machines serve their agendas came an increase in the public resources commanded by those politicians. Although Westminster MPs' basic salaries remained at about 2.5 to three times UK average earnings, their allowances for office expenses and support staff increased rapidly, rising from about half of an MP's official salary in 1980 to more than twice that salary by 2009.[12] These changes were paralleled by developments at local government level where substantially increased allowances allowed greater professionalization of municipal politics as well. Whether that increase in numbers and resources of the salaried political class produced a commensurate rise in the quality of government in the UK is of course a matter of opinion, but it certainly changed the level of political surveillance, pressure, and intervention to which the executive machinery of government and public services was subject over the period considered by this book.

---

[12] Calculated from data in *Member's Pay, Pensions and Allowances* (House of Commons Information Office, Factsheet M05, 2011).

Along with this notable shift towards a larger 'salariat' of politicians in general went changes affecting the balance of powers, duties, and responsibilities of central relative to local government. Writing in the mid-1960s about the relationship between central government and local authorities in England and Wales, John Griffith observed that 'the period since 1945 has shown a progressive growth in the power of the central government',[13] pointing to transfer of functions away from local authorities (such as the former municipal hospitals and local government utilities including gas and electricity) and increasing central government attempts to subject local government spending to the dictates of national economic and financial policy. Over the thirty years considered here, that process went further. Several key functions were removed from local government control, such as (taking English examples) for key regeneration projects in the 1980s, for further education colleges in the early 1990s, and for secondary and some primary schools in the 2000s, with the creation of state-funded schools ('Academies') intended to be independent of direct control by local education authorities.

In addition, while the general feature of a local government system with extensive service delivery responsibilities but largely funded from central government did not change (as noted earlier), there were certainly attempts to tighten overall financial control by central over local government from the 1980s. Those efforts included exercise of rate-capping powers (restricting increases in the levels of property tax that locally elected councils could levy to fund their services),[14] and the imposition of a radical new form of local taxation (the Community Charge or 'Poll Tax') in Scotland in 1989 and in England and Wales in 1990, only to be scrapped after massive levels of protest and replaced with a modified form of the earlier property tax. And further controls were imposed on how local authorities could provide services, notably in the form of centrally imposed compulsory competitive tendering requirements after 1980 for what had previously been direct labour organizations in local government. While political parties in opposition at Westminster typically championed 'localism', in government such parties tended to impose new central controls over local authorities, often in the name of avoiding 'postcode lotteries' in variations of service provision. That occurred for instance in the *soi-disant* 'Localism Act' of 2011 (which despite its title gave central government over a hundred new powers to control local authorities in England).

---

[13] John Griffith, *Central Departments and Local Authorities* (London: Allen and Unwin, 1966), p. 19.
[14] However, despite a succession of new frameworks for controlling local government spending, we show in Chapter 7 that such spending increased at a similar rate to central government spending, more than doubling in real terms since 1980.

2.3 The Place of the Bureaucracy in the Political System

Some of the basic characteristics of the top civil service comprised a relatively unchanging feature of UK central government over this period, despite repeated and heated discussion of what many saw as moves towards 'politicization' and 'managerialism'. The top of the civil service continued to be broadly divided between less than 100 overtly political civil servants ('special advisers'), appointed during the tenure of the ministers they served, and about 4000 overtly non-party-political appointees on indefinite or fixed-term contracts. And those top departmental civil servants and the political civil service broadly continued to operate in what Charles Sisson[15] nearly forty years ago identified as a 'courtier' style, meaning a mode of operation characterized by skill in moving within the inner circles of political power and competing for the ear and favour of ministers rather than by certificated technical expertise or hands-on management at the front line.

Those top departmental civil servants broadly operated under a form of what one of us in earlier work with Martin Lodge has called an 'agency bargain' with ministers, in which officials appointed on indefinite contracts were expected to give loyal support and assistance to each minister they served with rather than making autonomous judgements in the style of a judge.[16] Moreover, in contrast to states such as Germany in which each department pursues its own management system within a general constitutional and legal framework (the *Ressortsprinzip*, in German parlance), overall civil service policy continued to be broadly controlled from the centre, although the details and nomenclature of the relevant units kept changing.

In addition to the government departments and civil servants populating them, another continuing feature of the bureaucratic structure was a large group of 'quangos'—a term often used loosely to denote special-purpose appointed bodies of various types delivering advice, services, watchdog, and complaint-handling functions at some official distance from the core of central government, typically headed by individuals serving under a different kind of 'public service bargain'. Over our thirty-year period, as Figure 2.2a shows, reported numbers of non-departmental public bodies (NDPBs)—the official term for many centrally appointed bodies that were not directly part of departments—fell sharply as a result of amalgamations and other reorganizations, with the biggest fall in the number of bodies classed as advisory and roughly a halving of those classed as executive. But much of that apparent fall

---

[15] Charles Sisson, 'The Civil Service After Fulton', in *British Government in an Era of Reform*, edited by William Stankiewicz (London: Collier Macmillan, 1976), p. 262.

[16] Christopher Hood and Martin Lodge, *The Politics of Public Service Bargains* (Oxford: Oxford University Press, 2006), pp. 42–59.

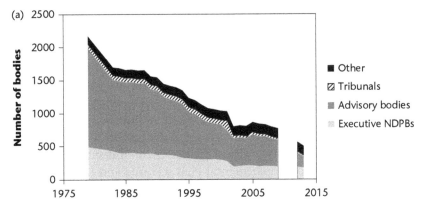

Figure 2.2a. Number of Non-Departmental Public Bodies 1979–2013

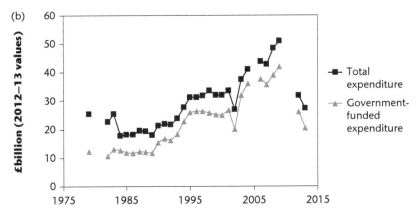

Figure 2.2b. Spending of Executive Non-Departmental Public Bodies in Real Terms (£ billion 2012–13 values) 1979–2013

Source: Annual editions of *Public Bodies* (Cabinet Office, London: HMSO). Unless otherwise noted, all dates in figures and tables in this book refer to *financial year ending* or *calendar year* depending on the data source. Real terms costs were calculated by dividing the nominal costs by the 2012–13 GDP deflator series provided by HM Treasury.

can probably be put down to 'numbers games' by successive governments keen to show the voters and the media that they were 'tough on quangos', and despite the apparent fall in numbers of bodies, as Figure 2.2b shows, reported spending by executive NDPBs in constant prices roughly quadrupled from 1980 to 2010.[17]

[17] That rise was curtailed after 2011 by a programme which led to the closure, merger, or reabsorption into parent departments of numerous organizations and functions over the following two years. The cost savings of this reorganization were more modest than the £15 billion that Figure 2.2b suggests, since many former functions of NDPBs were transferred to other parts of government. The Cabinet Office intended a £2.6 billion saving in administrative spending by 2014–15, and the National Audit Office estimated that £0.7 billion of savings had been realized by 2012–13 (see National Audit Office, *Reorganising Central Government Bodies* [HC 1703, 2010–12], and *Progress on Public Bodies Reform* [HC 1048, 2013–14]).

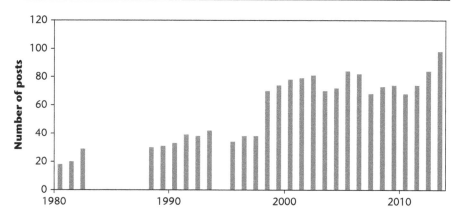

Figure 2.3 Numbers of Special Advisers (Political Civil Servants) 1980–2013

Sources: House of Commons Treasury and Civil Service Select Committee, *Civil servants and ministers: duties and responsibilities* (HC 92-II, 1985–86), Annex 2, pp. xlii–liii; Hansard Written Answer (10 June 1993) vol. 226 c314W; House of Commons Library, *Special Advisers* (SN/PC/03813, 2013).

Along with these relatively enduring features went several notable changes. We referred at the outset to the notion of public service bargains—that is, the deals or ground rules public servants were subject to. Writing in the 1970s, Bernard Schaffer argued that the predominant bargain that had applied to civil servants in Whitehall since the later nineteenth century was one in which they gave up the right to make independent comments on government policy or to refuse to implement policies with which they disagreed, in exchange for indefinite employment and an element of anonymity.[18]

But almost as soon as Schaffer's elegant analysis had been published, a process of complexification or multiplication of 'civil service bargains' began to develop. Arguably the first step in that process of complexification was the formal creation of a political civil service (known as 'special advisers') in the mid-1970s, involving a different kind of bargain (with tenure linked to that of the tenure in office of the minister for whom such individuals worked). As can be seen from Figure 2.3, the numbers of those political civil servants roughly quadrupled over the thirty years covered by this book, and as Figures 2.4a and 2.4b show, the senior ranks of the civil service also grew markedly with an increasing proportion of women in those senior grades. The civil service as a whole showed a fall in numbers over the same period, losing staff mainly from non-managerial grades.

A decade after the creation of a new formal bargain in the form of special advisers in the 1980s, a new breed of semi-independent regulators (many

[18] Bernard Schaffer, *The Administrative Factor* (London: Frank Cass, 1973), p. 252.

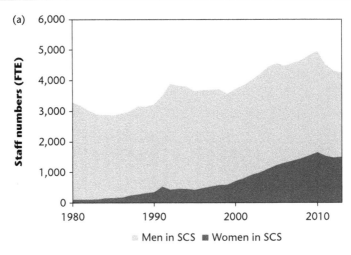

Figure 2.4a. Number of Civil Servants in Upper Management Grades 1980–2013—Senior Civil Service (SCS, Grades 1–5 until 1996)

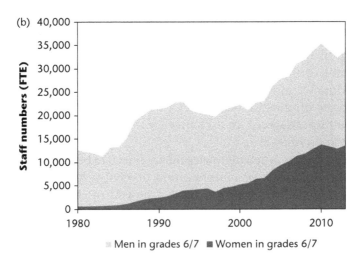

Figure 2.4b. Number of Civil Servants in Upper Management Grades 1980–2013—Civil Service Grades 6–7

Source: Civil Service Statistics, annual editions. Full-time equivalents (FTE).

of them coming from the academic world or from outside the civil service) was established for the formerly privatized utilities (and later for other public services as well), and the 'bargain' in that case involved limited tenure but semi-independent powers to apply regulatory policies.

Following that development there was a marked growth in arms-length regulation, audit, assurance, and other compliance activity in public services.

Although public management reformers often used slogans such as 'from red tape to results' (as we noted in Chapter 1) or from 'rules-based' to 'results-based' management, one of the frequent characteristics of traditional management practices in the UK's public services was a remarkable indefiniteness of the rules of the game, for example over issues such as entitlement to pensions or conflict of interest rules. Fifteen years or so ago, a UK civil servant who had worked in the US federal civil service in Washington described the contrasting British style in a Cabinet Office seminar as 'a constant search for consensus over rules that no one ever quite specifies'.[19] But one of the developments over the period covered by this book was a proliferation of independent or semi-independent regulators to generate and apply more rules and standards in public services, for example in setting and seeking to enforce ethical codes, quality systems, and 'best practice' of one kind or another.

The creation of the Audit Commission in the early 1980s to oversee local government spending in England and Wales was a key step in the process, and the Commission came to have its counterparts in other services, with special-purpose, semi-independent bodies developing and applying more explicit standards and rules. A case in point is the beefing up of the Civil Service Commissioners in the mid-1990s. This body, originally created by Treasury minute in the 1850s to oversee a Chinese-style examination system for selecting civil servants on merit, had hitherto been headed by a mid-career civil servant who in principle could climb higher up the promotion ladder (and thus was hardly independent from the service being overseen). From the early 1990s the Commission was put onto a statutory basis, turned into a body headed by outsiders, and with more explicit and extended responsibilities for audit, enforcement, and oversight of appointments.[20]

That process of developing more explicit arms-length oversight by inspectors and regulators in place of a once cosier and more indefinite process of controlling UK public services might be argued to have been part of a wider move from 'club government' towards a modern regulatory state in the UK, as claimed by Michael Moran.[21] Indeed it partly resembles what David Levi-Faur and Jacint Jordana found as a widespread pattern of an increase in formally independent regulatory units overseeing public utilities across many countries in the 1990s and 2000s,[22] though some scholars such as

[19] Quoted in Christopher Hood, Oliver James, George Jones, Colin Scott, and Tony Travers, *Regulation inside Government: Waste Watchers, Quality Police and Sleaze-Busters* (Oxford: Oxford University Press, 1999), p. 73.

[20] See Richard Jarvis, *The UK Experience of Public Administration Reform* (London: Commonwealth Secretariat, 2002).

[21] Michael Moran, *The British Regulatory State: Hyper-Modernism and Hyper-Innovation* (Oxford: Oxford University Press, 2003).

[22] See David Levi-Faur, 'The Global Diffusion of Regulatory Capitalism', *The Annals of the American Academy of Political and Social Science* 598 (2005): pp. 12–32.

Cristopher Ballinas Valdés have questioned whether the underlying pattern quite matched the formal frameworks.[23]

While one form of 'complexification' of the public service bargain took the form of a new breed of arms-length regulators, during the 1990s another new class of senior civil servants was created to act as managers of executive or service-delivery agencies, again with limited tenure combined with formal responsibility for policy delivery.

This new bargain went along with a move to 'managerialization' (delegating more executive and discretionary power to named executives) and 'corporatization' (breaking up large departments and organizations into manageable chunks). Both changes were much commented on, particularly in the 1990s, when some 140 executive agencies[24] were rapidly spun out from central departments and subjected to a form of arms-length control through an elaborate process of performance indicators and framework agreements concluded with their chief executives, albeit with no statutory basis for those arrangements. Figure 2.5 shows the changing number of such agencies. By 1998 over three-quarters of civil servants worked in executive agencies (or on 'Next Steps lines' in organizations that were not formally agencies)—though this proportion subsequently fell as a result both of reabsorption of functions within central departments and of further changes of structure, notably by privatization or by restructuring agencies into more independent bodies.[25]

A further major development involving yet another new public service bargain came in 1998 with an Act reconstituting the central bank (the Bank of England) as an independent public body with autonomy in setting monetary policy (albeit with a reserve power of direction by Treasury with the support of Parliament). This move changed the status of one of the key players in economic and financial policy, produced new 'bargains' applying to the Governor of the Bank and the members of the committee to which the powers of managing monetary policy were devolved, and thus created another set of public servants who were more like 'judges' than 'agents'.

Finally, in the 2000s there was much discussion of what was seen as a new breed of quasi-political civil servants, particularly in senior communications,

---

[23] Cristopher Ballinas Valdés, *Political Struggles and the Forging of Autonomous Government Agencies* (Basingstoke: Palgrave Macmillan, 2011).

[24] These agencies were also known as Next Steps Agencies after the report from the Cabinet Office's Efficiency Unit that led to their formation (Kate Jenkins, Karen Caines, Andrew Jackson, *Improving Management in Government: The Next Steps* [London: HMSO, 1988]—also known as the Ibbs Report after Sir Robin Ibbs, who led the Efficiency Unit at that time).

[25] Formally these agencies were part of their parent department and staffed by civil servants. Other types of public bodies, notably 'non-departmental public bodies' could be more independent of central departments and were typically not staffed by civil servants. See Oliver James, *The Executive Agency Revolution in Whitehall: Public Interest versus Bureau-Shaping Perspectives* (Basingstoke: Palgrave Macmillan, 2003); Colin Talbot and Christopher Pollitt, *Unbundled Government* (London: Routledge, 2003).

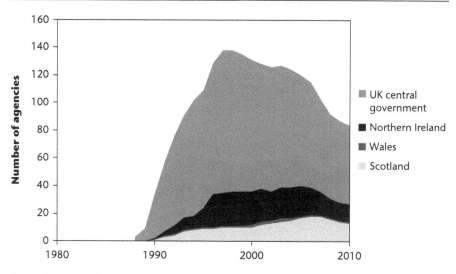

Figure 2.5. Number of Executive Agencies 1988–2010

Source: Thomas Elston, 'Developments in UK executive agencies: Re-examining the "disaggrega-tion-reaggregation" thesis', *Public Policy and Administration* 28, no. 1 (2013): pp. 66–89.

public relations, or policy advisory roles, who were not formally appointed as special advisers but nevertheless seen as political appointments, and indeed by the 2010s moves were afoot to give ministers the power to appoint departmental heads and other senior civil servants. If Bernard Schaffer could have been brought back to life in the early 2010s he would therefore have found the public service bargain he had described thirty years before as the central feature of the constitutional position of the civil service to be surrounded by a host of rather different bargains and, at least in the eyes of many, to be hanging by a thread.

2.4 The Place of Government in the Economy and Wider Society

Despite the rhetoric of 'rolling back the state', the UK's profile as a major European member state with a mixed economy and a broadly 'European' welfare state profile did not change out of recognition. As Figure 2.6a shows, total managed expenditure (TME, an official term introduced in the 1990s for total public spending[26]) as a percentage of GDP ranged between the

---

[26] The term was introduced in 1998, replacing the earlier public spending aggregate 'General Government Expenditure' which had a slightly different definition. The Office for National Statistics calculated a series equivalent to TME dating back to the mid-1940s. See Rowena Crawford, Carl Emmerson, and Gemma Tetlow, *A Survey of Public Spending in the UK* (London: Institute for Fiscal Studies, 2009).

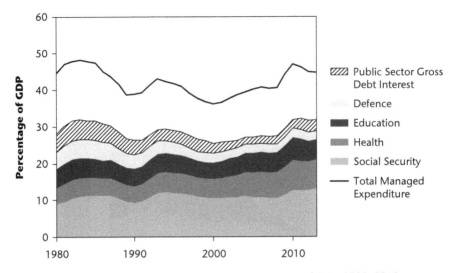

Figure 2.6a. Total Managed Expenditure as a Percentage of GDP 1980–2013

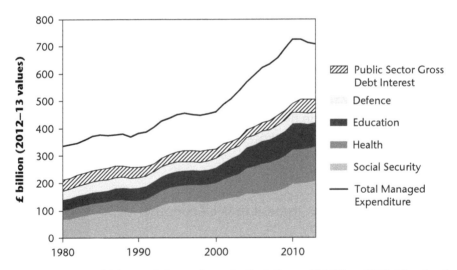

Figure 2.6b. Total Managed Expenditure in Real Terms (£ billion 2012–13 values) 1980–2013

Source: Institute for Fiscal Studies, *Fiscal Facts* (2014).

middle 30s and upper 40s, with a broadly downward trend over the period of Conservative rule (1979–1997) followed by a broadly upward trend over the subsequent period of Labour rule (1997–2010). The corollary of that, as Figure 2.6b shows, is that public spending in constant price terms roughly doubled, with education, health, and welfare spending responsible for much of that increase. So in terms of overall public spending relative to GDP, the UK state was neither dramatically 'rolled back' nor 'rolled forward' over the period as a whole, though there was some ebb and flow, and substantial changes in the composition of that spending.

Similarly, it is not clear that there was a seismic shift in public attitudes towards government and public services, even though, as already noted, there are numerous claims that trust and confidence in government plummeted over recent decades, both in the UK and elsewhere. Not many relevant survey questions were asked consistently over the whole of our period or even for much of it; but what was available, taken together, did not point to dramatic change. Figure 2.7 presents four runs of survey data drawn from sources which had indicators that dated back to the late 1970s or early 1980s. The survey responses shown in Figure 2.7 are not the only ones that were available, but they are the most consistent long-term indicators of public attitudes to government, politicians, and bureaucracy that we could find.

What Figure 2.7 demonstrates (and the same conclusion can be drawn from other survey datasets not included in that figure) is that, far from all available survey data pointing in the same direction, we can find some reputable and consistently conducted surveys showing a marked fall in trust, confidence, or satisfaction in government, some that indicate a marked rise, and some that indicate no discernible change. An example of the first (marked fall in trust and confidence) is the pattern of responses to questions about how far British government was trusted to 'put the interests of the nation above party' (whatever respondents made of that gnomic phrase). An example of the second (marked rise in trust and confidence) is the pattern of responses to questions about how far 'civil servants'—however respondents interpreted that term—were trusted to tell the truth. An example of the third (no discernible change) is the pattern of responses to questions about how far politicians were trusted to tell the truth, or satisfaction with government. Satisfaction with how the government was running the country peaked after every change of government, most notably after the election of Tony Blair's New Labour government in 1997, but declined thereafter, showing no overall trend over the whole period. Overall, those responses show much less change than might have been expected, given claims that trust in politics was plumbing ever-lower depths as a result of scandals over abuse of parliamentary expense allowances and public disillusionment with political spin (politicians were consistently among the least trusted professions since the Ipsos-MORI surveys began in 1983). Altogether, unless we selectively put all the emphasis on a minority of the measures and ignore the others, it is hard to discern a clear long-term pattern here.

However, along with some relatively stable elements went some marked changes in the role of government in the economy and society, which are

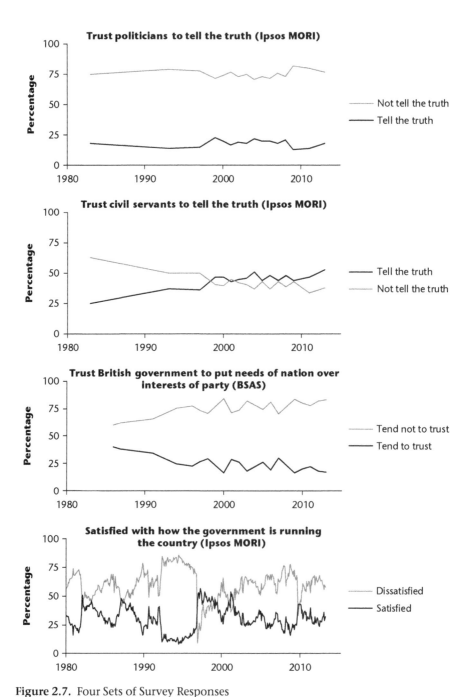

Figure 2.7. Four Sets of Survey Responses

Sources: Ipsos MORI, *Trust in Professions* and *Political Monitor: Satisfaction Ratings* and British Social Attitudes Survey (BSAS), indicator 'GOVTRUST'.

masked by the aggregate spending to GDP ratio noted earlier. Over the period covered by this book, a sizeable proportion of employment and GDP that had once been the province of a set of nationalized public corporations—covering not just utilities but also other parts of the manufacturing economy such as automobile, steel, coal, and oil production—were turned into company-law entities and sold to private buyers, subject to a measure of continuing regulation by new arms-length bodies in the case of utilities.

Moreover, over these thirty years there was a decisive move towards a more developed 'contract state' in the form of greater private sector provision in public services. A generation ago, the UK could be described as a 'public bureaucracy state' in that it relied on direct employment to provide many kinds of public services. Over the thirty years considered here there was a steady move away from that model, beginning with the privatization of public corporations and public utilities (with some notable exceptions, such as the BBC) and the outsourcing of work previously done by thousands of so-called industrial (blue-collar) civil servants, such as maintenance and cleaning. That was followed by the outsourcing of white-collar professional service support such as IT services (once developed exclusively in-house by civil service experts, interacting with a handful of companies all sponsored by government in one way or another), and even some uniformed functions, for instance custodial services such as prisons, job placement, and management of offenders.

The development of private financing initiatives across much of the public sector from the 1990s was a key shift in this direction, since it moved to a position in which public service facilities—including the buildings of government departments, such as the Treasury itself—were provided and managed by private firms on long-term contracts, replacing an older model in which government had managed the development and management of such facilities itself. By the 2010s the shift had gone from the older 'public bureaucracy state' model towards a variant of the US-type mixed economy of public administration in some domains (such as prisons and health care) and a pattern of private oligopolies if not monopolies in a range of service domains, such as IT and security.

Further, somewhere between the 'place of the bureaucracy in the political system' and 'the place of government in the economy and wider society', we can note the development of a professional and international reform industry for government and public services, devoted to advocating, planning, and reacting to government and public service makeovers. New players came to join what had once been a smaller epistemic industry in which public management knowledge had been concentrated in small groups of civil servants, academics, politicians, and journalists, and in which reform had developed episodically through key 'blue-ribbon' committees or Royal Commissions over the previous three decades.

Part of that process consisted of a development of the public-service consulting, auditing, outsourcing, and professional services industry within the UK, as big corporate players such as McKinsey and PricewaterhouseCoopers became major players in government reform plans. But part of it came from the establishment of a range of not-for-profit policy think-tanks—such as the Institute of Public Policy Research (founded in 1988), Demos (founded in 1993), and the Institute for Government (founded in 2008)—to add to the relatively small number that had existed at the start of this period, such as the Institute for Fiscal Affairs (founded in the early 1970s) and the Policy Studies Institute, founded in 1978. And, as already mentioned, a professional reform industry developed at an international level as well, as organizations such as the OECD, World Bank, the European Commission, and independent bodies such as Transparency International started to concern themselves with issues of governance and bureaucracy in the developed countries. That development produced a significant expansion of capacity to articulate and develop ideas for reorganization and reform outside the public service and the universities.

2.5 The Technology of Government

One of the dramatic changes over the period considered here, already mentioned in Chapter 1, consisted of a presentational and informational revolution. Many kinds of administrative work were changed in ways that made the styles and systems of the late 1970s almost unrecognizable by the 2010s. The technological changes associated with the digital age transformed office work previously centred on fixed-line telephony linked to paper-based communication, storage, and handling of data. Anyone walking along a typical corridor in Whitehall (or town hall, for that matter) in 1980 would have seen no desktop, laptop, or tablet computers, and some important parts of government (like No. 10 Downing Street) had no computers at all at the start of Margaret Thatcher's government.

Back then, there were only a few terminals and keyboards in specialized offices linked to a handful of inflexible mainframe computers operated by a small corps of separate IT staff (and still activated in many cases by paper tape or punched cards rather than keyboards: even the computer mouse was only available for one or two computers in 1980). Those computers were only used for tasks involving repetitive or complex calculations, such as payroll, tax, and weather or economic forecasting. Outside that limited domain, the clacking of manual or electric typewriters accompanied by the ringing of landline telephones (mobile phone technology was in its early infancy in 1980) was the normal soundtrack of government offices. We have an inventory dating from 1977 which lists all the 321 computers costing over £10,000 (in 1977 money) owned by UK central government at that time.[27] Many of those machines were already museum pieces, and some were models that had been a commercial flop and had therefore ended up in government use to help support the still fledgling computer industry.

Out of those 321 computers in 1977, the most expensive, and by far the most powerful, was a 1970 IBM 360/195 that was at that time the top of IBM's range, with a speed—then deeply impressive—of some 30 MIPS (million instructions per second). Its proud owner was the Ministry of Defence, and it was used by the Meteorological Office for weather forecasting and research. But the subsequent pace of change was such that by the late 1980s a run-of-the-mill desktop 386 PC had roughly comparable computing power.

Whereas most government work had been a 'computer-free zone' in the heyday of that once-fêted IBM 360/195, almost everyone who worked in government over the succeeding thirty years saw their work transformed by digital-age developments that eventually led to virtually all office work becoming screen-based, to paper files and records giving way to (often much less durable and secure) digital ones, and to communication and information collection through the internet and associated developments (search engines, social media, intranet). By the 2010s computers of one kind or another were pervasive in government and public services, but most of them were being used for communications (largely replacing mail and intersecting with phone communication), for writing, recording, reporting, and research (replacing typewriters and traditional libraries and filing systems), and for processing decisions not involving massive calculations of the payroll or tax variety.

Even though the qualitative change is striking, it is effectively impossible quantitatively to compare the computing power available to government today compared to what it was thirty years ago. Even three decades ago, there was no standard metric for comparing computing power across different departments. The same applies even more so to comparison over time, and the difficulty arises because of the changing functionality of the technology. Not all technologies are like that. For example, we could compare a 1915 car with a 2015 car using metrics that would be reasonably meaningful at both times—such as power, top speed, acceleration, stopping distance, reliability, fuel consumption—even though the social context of motoring was completely transformed over that time (for instance with the advent of mass motoring, road rage, and ever-more-dense regulation). But unlike the car example, where use has not changed out of recognition over a century, we cannot do the same for IT in government even over thirty years.

---

[27] Obtained by one of us from the then Civil Service Department in 1977. See Christopher Hood and Andrew Dunsire, *Bureaumetrics: The Quantitative Comparison of British Central Government Agencies* (Farnborough: Gower, 1981), pp. 100–2.

One marked change enabled by these developments (and far from unique to government bureaucracy) was that most 'office work' no longer took place in individual offices. For most of the civil service below the highest levels, there was a shift to open plan working in 'Dilbert'-type cubicles and even in some cases to hot-desking and the like. One of us remembered interviewing middle-level civil servants in their own (often cramped) offices in Whitehall in the 1970s, but almost all of our civil service interviews for this project took place in meeting rooms booked for the purpose, often in buildings whose occupancy by departments was fluid and rapidly changing. As we have already noted and will explore further in later chapters, IT changes produced much debate and expectation about their potential for cutting costs and transforming the way government worked.

But even for IT developments, the extent and even existence of change depends on what we choose to look at. We can see more change from some angles than from others. If we could count aggregate MIPS (million instructions per second) available to UK central government through its IT over the thirty years as a measure of absolute computing power, it would show growth of massive, almost unimaginable, orders of magnitude. But if we had a measure for government's *relative* computing power as against other players in society (such as drivers using satnavs with speed camera alerts), it is far from clear whether such relativities radically changed. And the *cost* of UK government's IT spending did not fall in real terms, despite an enormous general drop in the cost of computing power over the three decades. That one-time flagship Meteorological Office computer we mentioned earlier cost £3.75 million when it was bought in 1970 (approximately £45 million in 2013 prices), as against the reported cost of some £33 million for a powerful computer acquired by the same department in 2008 and a projected £97 million for a model to be installed in 2015.[28] In other cases, reported costs doubled or tripled. For example, four decades ago the two central government tax departments, which we discuss in Chapter 5, were operating computers that had cost about £5 million to buy between 1972 and 1977 (about £35 million in 2013 prices). In the mid-1990s they were spending about £100 million per year on the capital costs of information technology (about £150 million in 2013 prices). By the early 2010s the equivalent department was spending about £250 million annually on its IT contract with the multinational IT service corporation Capgemini.[29]

---

[28] Source for the 2008 purchase: <http://www.computerweekly.com/news/2240103049/Photo-story-Met-Office-agrees-33m-deal-for-IBM-supercomputer> and for the 2015 purchase: <http://www.metoffice.gov.uk/news/releases/archive/2014/new-hpc>.

[29] *Report of the Commissioners of Her Majesty's Inland Revenue for the year ending 31st March 1995* (Cm 3014, 1995), p. 70; *Report of the Commissioners of Her Majesty's Customs and Excise for the year*

Along with those technological changes in office work went new ways of attempting to 'control the story' in interactions with the media, and this change fits somewhere in the interface between 'the place of the bureaucracy in the political system' and 'the technology of government'. At the start of our period, government and public services worked in a media environment consisting of a handful of national or regional newspapers, each producing a single daily edition, along with a few radio and TV programmes operating on slightly less leisurely news cycles. The now ubiquitous term 'spin doctor'—said to have been invented in the 1970s, as noted in Chapter 1—had not yet appeared in the press.[30] At that time, as we will show in Chapter 8, government had an army of specialized information officers mainly concerned with getting relatively non-political messages across to the public about issues such as road safety or public health, but it had a much more haphazard approach to keeping its various organizations politically 'on message' more broadly, and there were no presumptions that official information should be available to the general public (quite the reverse).

That world was also totally transformed over the period considered here. A new media environment developed in which news appeared continually, and in which the few national or regional media sources of earlier days had been replaced by an online environment of social media such as Twitter that enabled virtually anyone, anywhere, to become a 'broadcaster'. At the same time, a new legislative and regulatory approach developed to determine who could hold (or withhold) information about whom (or what) in the form of Freedom of Information and Data Protection Laws.

Both of those developments formed the background for greater emphasis on high-powered 'spin machines' within ministers' immediate entourages to keep control of political stories, while outsourcing much of the less politically charged information work to the private sector, and we shall put some of that transformation into numbers in Chapter 8. This difference shows up clearly in the contrast between the bureaucratic and governmental world portrayed by the BBC TV series *Yes Minister* of the early 1980s (a smash-hit sitcom about the subtle machinations of Whitehall mandarins trying to outwit their ministers) and the far less genteel, more frenetic world portrayed by the BBC some twenty-five years later in the series *The Thick of It*, first broadcast in 2005, in which everything in the inner workings of the upper levels of government is driven by a twenty-four-hour struggle involving aggressively warring spin

---

ended 31 March 1995 (Cm 2980, 1995), p. 68; *HM Revenue & Customs Annual Report and Accounts 2011–12* (HC 38, 2012–13), p. 93.

[30] Frank Esser, 'Spin Doctor', in *The International Encyclopedia of Communication Vol. X*, edited by Wolfgang Donsbach (London: Blackwell, 2008), pp. 4783–7.

doctors, politicians, and senior civil servants trying to shut down negative stories and control the news agenda.

2.6 Conclusion

As explained at the outset, this book focuses mainly on the observable results of three decades of reform in terms of running costs and perceived fairness and consistency in UK central government, rather than what the causes of those reforms might have been (partly because so much less has been said on

Table 2.1. A Summary of What Changed and What Didn't from the Early 1980s to the Early 2010s

Relatively stable	Markedly changed
Main legislative, electoral, and constitutional features of the state	
Weakly bicameral legislature, first-past-the-post elections to lower house, generally majoritarian government. Numbers of Westminster MPs and peers remained constant (though composition of upper house changed).	New forms of 'intergovernmental relations', notably through devolution to elected parliaments in Scotland and Wales in 1999 and a new 'consociational' regime in Northern Ireland after 1998. More co-legislative powers with European Parliament.
UK-wide system for tax collection, social security, currency, defence, immigration, and foreign affairs.	About 30 per cent growth in the number of full-time elected politicians.
Local government with extensive service delivery responsibilities but limited tax collection powers.	Autonomy of local authorities progressively reduced.
The place of the bureaucracy in the political system	
Senior ranks of civil service comprised a small number of political civil servants and about 4000 overtly non-party-political appointees on permanent contracts.	Numbers of 'special advisers' (political civil servants) quadrupled, and the senior civil service also grew, while the overall size of the civil service fell by about a third, weakening traditional civil service bargain.
Beyond government departments, several hundred quangos headed by government appointees provided advice, delivered services, and conducted watchdog and complaint-handling functions.	New kinds of 'public service bargains' with arms-length semi-independent regulators for utilities and public services.
	Central bank gained autonomy to set monetary policy.
The place of government in the economy and wider society	
Mixed economy, major EU member state with 'European'-type welfare state. Public spending 35–45 per cent of GDP.	Public utilities and other key industries privatized.
Public attitudes to government and public services constant.	Private provision of public services increased.
	Development of a professional 'reform industry'.
The technology of government	
Government's computing power relative to other players in society changed less than its absolute computing power.	Government office work was transformed by information technology.
	New methods of information management and control.

the former than on the latter, as we argued in Chapter 1). But as a scene-setting exercise this chapter has attempted to sketch out some of the background against which attempts to make UK central government 'work better and cost less' took place over the thirty years we examine in this book. Table 2.1 summarizes the earlier discussion, highlighting what changed and what didn't for each of the four elements discussed in Sections 2.2 to 2.5.

The picture conveyed here is necessarily sketchy, selective, and indeed subjective as well. No doubt other observers would pick aspects of the social or governmental system not mentioned here, and might also differ in their assessment of what to categorize as big or small change for each of the four aspects of government and society considered here. The analysis is also necessarily time-bound, in that features that can be counted as relatively stable about the UK central state over the three decades considered by this book will not necessarily continue into the future, including such basic issues as the future of the UK as a state, whether all or part of it would continue to be a member state of the European Union on the same terms as previously and the (perhaps less fundamental) issue of whether most of the upper civil service would continue to be mostly appointed on indefinite contracts by a notionally meritocratic procedure, or by something approximating to a party-spoils system. The future of all of those elements is uncertain.

But that is for the future, and the aim of this chapter was to focus on the past by indicating the sort of backdrop against which efforts to cut cost and improve the quality of public services took place during this thirty-year period, and the sort of instruments and institutions that were in play. And after considering what happened to performance data over the same period in the next chapter, we turn in later chapters to assess what was achieved against the background of this mixture of unchanging and more changing features in UK central government.

3

Performance Data Breaks

Breaking the Mould and Burying the Evidence

> *[The First Emperor] discarded the ways of the former kings and burned*
> *the books of the hundred schools of philosophy . . .* [1]

3.1 The Paradox of Evidence-Hunger Combined with Evidence-Destruction in Government and Public Services

It is often claimed that a distinctive feature of government and public services over the past thirty years has been the development of 'management by numbers', that is, of performance management through the use of quantitative indicators such as school league tables or measures of customer satisfaction.[2] And an emphasis on performance numbers is often related to aspirations for public policy and management to be more analytic and evidence-based in its pursuit of performance improvement than in earlier less enlightened times. A recurring trope of public service reform is the argument that policies to improve public management and service delivery ought to be based on proper evidence of 'what works', and that 'proper evidence' is often taken to mean well-developed performance numbers. Such numbers, it is held, can provide policymakers and managers (in some versions the public more generally) with dials and dashboards[3] to help them better understand how to

---

[1] Ssu-Ma Ch'ien, *Records of the Grand Historian of China* (*Shih Chi 48*, about 91 BCE) translated by Burton Watson (New York: Columbia University Press, 1971), p. 32. The first Ch'in emperor who unified China in 221 BCE is often said to have had most of the historical books in his kingdom burned so that history would begin with him.

[2] Christopher Hood, 'Public Service Management by Numbers: Why Does it Vary? Where has it Come From? What are the Gaps and the Puzzles?', *Public Money and Management* 27, no. 2 (2007): pp. 95–102.

[3] Or 'dials and tin-openers', following a well-known distinction by Neil Carter, who distinguishes between using performance numbers as directly actionable 'summative' measures of performance and using them to open up qualitative investigations about organizational performance

improve policy interventions and drive up performance, rather than ad hoc 'stories' or unsystematic qualitative assertions about how to improve services.

Now sceptics might argue there is actually nothing very new about public management by numbers, that such a focus commonly goes with developed bureaucracies, and can often be traced back a surprisingly long way.[4] Historical cases in point include the elaborate performance target system developed in the former Soviet Union in the 1930s,[5] the system of rewarding school teachers according to their students' exam results in England and Wales in the late nineteenth century,[6] the elaborate statistics about mortality rates and treatment of military casualties in the American Civil War of the 1860s (at least on the Union side) that fed into the efforts of the Medical Corps and the Sanitary Commission,[7] even the efforts of eighteenth-century German forestry bureaucrats to count the growth of the trees for what they termed 'scientific management' of state forests (with disastrous results, according to a well-known book by James Scott).[8]

But even if we lay aside such academic scruples about the novelty of this phenomenon, and accept at face value the common assumption that public management by numbers is something distinctively associated with present-day preoccupations for an evidence-based and performance-enhancing approach to public policy and management, another puzzle arises. How can that assumed concern for evidence be reconciled with the observation that governments often tend to systematically *destroy* the quantitative evidence for the efficacy or otherwise of their policy measures, by changing administrative record-keeping in ways that make it impossible to make before-and-after comparisons, on which cumulative evidence about 'what works' could be built?

before taking any action. See Neil Carter, 'Learning to Measure Performance—The Use of Indicators in Organizations', *Public Administration* 69, no. 1 (1991): pp. 85–101.

[4] After all, a century or so ago Max Weber argued that the 'increased intellectualization and rationalization' that he associated with social modernity meant 'the knowledge or belief . . . that one can, in principle, master all things by calculation'. Max Weber, 'Science as a Vocation', in *From Max Weber: Essays in Sociology*, edited and translated by Hans H. Gerth and C. Wright Mills (London: Routledge and Kegan Paul, 1948), p. 139.

[5] See for example Maurice Dobb, *Socialist Planning: Some Problems* (London: Lawrence and Wishart, 1970); Alec Nove, *The Soviet Economy: An Introduction* (New York: Praeger, 1961).

[6] See Richard Aldrich, 'Educational Standards in Historical Perspective', in *Educational Standards, Proceedings of the British Academy 102*, edited by Harvey Goldstein and Anthony Heath (Oxford: Oxford University Press for the British Academy, 2000), pp. 39–67.

[7] See Bernard Rostker, *Providing for the Casualties of War: The American Experience Through World War II* (Santa Monica, CA: Rand Corporation, 2013), pp. 75–111.

[8] James C. Scott, *Seeing Like a State: How Certain Schemes to Improve the Human Condition Have Failed* (New Haven: Yale University Press, 1998), pp. 14–21. According to Scott's account, productivity plunged after mixed forests were replaced with regular plantations of single species cleared of undergrowth for ease of measurement and management. Because productivity was excellent for the first crop from such forests (a period of some eighty years), this model of 'scientific forestry' spread across the world before the problems became apparent.

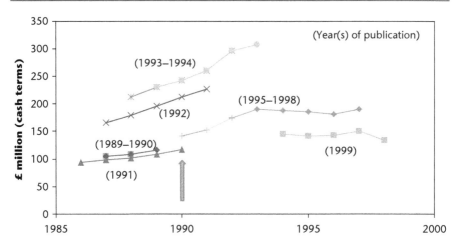

Figure 3.1. Reported Gross Running Costs of 'The Scottish Office' (£ million Cash Terms) 1986–1998

Source: Data from successive editions of *The Government's Expenditure Plans (Departments of the Secretary of State for Scotland)*. Dates of publication shown alongside each data series.

Figure 3.1 shows a particularly glaring example of the type of data break that we mean. As we were finalizing the manuscript of this book, arguments were raging about what would be the costs of running Scotland's government in the event of a 'yes' vote in the 2014 independence referendum (which, as it turned out, produced a majority for 'no').Widely varying numbers were propounded by different players at a key point in the referendum campaign. But as Figure 3.1 shows, it is hard enough to figure out what Scottish government cost to run in the past, let alone what it might cost in the future. The figure shows that the apparent running costs of the central administration of Scotland prior to devolution in 1999 (the Scottish Office, as it was then called) varied enormously depending on which year's report was consulted (by over a factor of two for 1989–90 [arrowed]). Readers who worked hard enough comparing the texts of the different reports available could eventually discover that the differences arose mainly from which aspects of prisons and arms-length agencies were included or excluded in each successive report, and how staff costs were calculated. And Figure 3.1 is far from an isolated case. Many of the performance data-series we encountered showed a similar pattern, if not always so extreme as this example.

To compare and explore such discontinuities, we developed an 'index of volatility' for performance indicators which showed that changes in data-series in four domains of management information for UK central government over three decades came to be so frequent that they stacked the odds heavily against assessment of long-term government performance in terms of what it cost or how well it worked, either from inside or outside the government machine. Perhaps unintentionally, the process of reform itself contrived to make it as difficult as possible for the impact of reforms to be demonstrated.

Of course, we are not the first to have made the point that performance indicators often prove so ephemeral as to prevent anything but the most short-term evaluations of how much better or worse government and public services perform over time. Christopher Pollitt, one of the leading international analysts of managerialism and performance evaluation, has commented on the tendency of performance indicator regimes to be complex and unstable, with the consequence that only a few experts at most can understand them and that synchronic comparison (comparison of units at a single point in time) is heavily privileged over diachronic comparison, that is, comparison over time.[9] In 2007, Bill Martin, a leading Cambridge Business School academic, wrote to the *Financial Times* observing that errors in some key official UK economic indicators were so extensive, endemic, and changing that 'every quarterly release is a voyage into an undiscovered country',[10] and that same telling phrase could be applied to many other runs of government numbers that we came across in writing this book.[11] For example, Colin Talbot showed that only just over a third of the key performance indicators applying to UK central government departments and executive (service delivery) agencies in 1995 were comparable with those of only two years earlier,[12] and in the mid-2000s Oliver James showed that many of the then 'public service agreements' (performance targets that were linked to budgetary settlements at that time) were changed on a two-year cycle.[13] Indeed, writing about Australian Commonwealth government performance indicators in the early 2000s, Tyrone Carlin and Nigel Finch noted that some indicators had such a short lifetime that those indicators were changed before any actual outcomes were reported, thus completely undercutting the performance accountability the measures ostensibly underpinned.[14]

[9] Christopher Pollitt, 'Performance Blight and the Tyranny of Light', Chapter 5 in *Accountable Government: Problems and Promises*, edited by Melvin J. Dubnick and H. George Frederickson (Armonk, New York: M.E. Sharpe, 2011), pp. 86–7.

[10] Bill Martin, 'The Puzzle behind Britain's Lamentable Statistics', *Financial Times*, 23 February 2007.

[11] Including, disconcertingly, the GDP deflator series, which in 2012 was changed by ONS resulting in a lower apparent rate of inflation during the 1980s than when earlier editions of the series were used. This retrospective change made a substantial difference to some key economic indicators, as discussed by Samuel Williamson at <http://www.measuringworth.com/datasets/ukgdp/RewriteUK.php>.

[12] Colin Talbot, *Ministers and Agencies: Control, Performance and Accountability* (London: CIPFA, 1996).

[13] Oliver James, 'The UK Core Executive's Use of Public Service Agreements as a Tool of Governance', *Public Administration* 82, no. 2 (1994): pp. 397–419.

[14] Tyrone M. Carlin and Nigel Finch, 'Performance in Flux—An Investigation of New Public Financial Management Reform in Action'. In 34th Annual Meeting of the Western Decision Sciences Institute (2005).

Now what might be called the 'standard social science response' to such observations of data discontinuity consists mainly of complaining about it, as an egregious inconvenience to scholars and evaluators, and in some cases to putting considerable time and effort into repairing or reconstructing 'broken' data-series into a consistent form such that more-or-less meaningful comparisons can be made over time.[15]

We certainly do not want to dismiss that 'standard social science' response of complaining about lack of data continuity, though we recognize that the design of performance data necessarily involves several trade-offs. One of those trade-offs is between maintaining full consistency over time (necessary for managers, those to whom they are accountable, and evaluators of various kinds to have any means of assessing whether performance is improving, deteriorating, or staying the same) and on the other hand maintaining relevance for present-day concerns and conditions (necessary for performance statistics to reflect current values, technology, and methods of work).[16] Go too far towards over-time consistency, and you risk loss of relevance, as would happen for example if we went on collecting data about consumption of candles or coal in government offices long after these items had lost their importance.[17] Go too far towards relevance for the present—for example starting afresh a new set of data every year—and you risk being unable to compare one year's performance with another. Such trade-offs are inexorable; it is how such trade-off is set, and how it may have changed over the thirty-year period considered by this book, that interests us here.

In this chapter, therefore, we focus on trying to explain when, why, and how performance data discontinuities come about. How can we explain how the UK, one of the countries best known internationally for its enthusiasm both for public management reform in general and for the development of performance indicators in particular, has apparently been so prone to such evidence-destroying behaviour? How can we explain what lies behind those data discontinuities?

[15] For example, Bill Martin painstakingly reconstructed historic sector UK national accounts and Stuart Soroka and colleagues reconstructed UK public spending data into a consistent form. See Bill Martin, 'Resurrecting the UK Historic Sector National Accounts', *The Review of Income and Wealth* 55, no. 3 (2009): pp. 737–51; and Stuart N. Soroka, Christopher Wlezien, and Iain McLean, 'Public Expenditure in the UK: How Measures Matter', *Journal of the Royal Statistical Society: Series A (Statistics in Society)* 169, no. 2 (2009): pp. 255–71.

[16] A point made clearly by William Gormley Jr., and David Weimer, *Organizational Report Cards* (Cambridge, MA: Harvard University Press, 1999).

[17] We found very little evidence of pressure to retain indicator series. Only one of our interviewees volunteered the observation that developing a new data series represents a monetary opportunity cost. And we found just one example of an external pressure, when the Customs and Excise department discontinued publication of their costs of collection in 1988–89, the Public Accounts Committee asked the department 'to reconsider' that decision, and the metric was reinstated the following year (*Report of the Commissioners of Her Majesty's Customs and Excise for the year ended 31 March 1990* [Cm 1223, 1990], pp. 10–11).

In an attempt to explore that issue, this chapter begins by describing and measuring the incidence of volatility (or evidence-destroying change) in four key sets of UK central government performance numbers that we will encounter again in the chapters that follow. We then turn to ways of accounting for those observations, exploring the plausibility of four possible explanations for such evidence-destroying behaviour.

3.2 An 'Index of Volatility'

As we have already indicated, our aim here is to move from the frequent observations of lack of consistency of many public service performance indicators to develop an index of indicator volatility over time. And as a first step towards classifying and comparing data breaks and discontinuities in performance indicators, Table 3.1 offers the basis of a simple three-step 'index of volatility'.

The aim of the index is to measure and track the impacts of discontinuities in performance data, turning such discontinuities themselves into an indicator of bureaucratic and other politics. By 'volatility', we mean the type of discontinuity that arises when the methodology, classification, presentation, or scope of any given indicator of interest change in ways that make before-and-after comparison difficult or impossible. Such changes in data collection or classification should not of course be confused with actual changes in the phenomena that indicators track, for example if the staff size of a public bureaucracy suddenly grows or falls in a dramatic way, as opposed to appearing to grow or fall as a result of different ways of counting

Table 3.1. A Simple Three-Step Classification of Indicator Volatility

Consequence for the indicator time series	Examples
Impact of discontinuity: *Small*	
Comparison of the indicator over time requires some effort, but does not require corrections to be made	Format of tables or report style changes markedly
Medium	
The published indicator is inconsistent with previous reports but a consistent dataset can be calculated with substantial labour	Basis of classification changes in reported numbers, but with an overlap period of reporting in the old and new way, such that a conversion formula can be estimated
Large	
Comparison before and after the discontinuity is impossible or subject to major uncertainties. The indicator may disappear altogether or be calculated on a materially different basis	Radically different reporting categories introduced with no overlap period

staff.[18] Of course, it is quite possible for both types of change (apparent and real) to occur simultaneously, which makes detecting true changes even more difficult.

The three steps here begin at the lowest level with changes in reporting that require some effort to match 'before' and 'after' numbers to form a consistent series, but the effort needed is not unduly time-consuming and does not require assumptions to be made to estimate equivalence or that the reporting organization provides additional information. Changes of that type often arise when series of annual reports change their format, reporting system, or level of aggregation (of staff costs, for example). To match the old system of reporting with the new requires some labour and intelligence (to find the relevant numbers in new and different places and ensure that they are compatible with previous figures), but not more than that. We classify that sort of change at the lowest level of volatility.

Beyond that comes the sort of change in reporting that requires more intellectual and other effort, perhaps requiring some plausible assumptions and successful contact with the providing organizations, to reconstruct a consistent series. To take a real example, suppose that an organization changed the reporting basis of administration costs to include superannuation, casual staff costs, and the like. That would appear in the accounts as a sudden increase in costs, but given sufficient time and effort (albeit more than any casual reader might be expected to have), it may be possible either to convert the earlier numbers into the later basis, or the later into the earlier, providing that the organization reported overlapping years calculated on the different assumptions. That is exactly what we had to do to provide a consistent series for departmental running costs over time, which we discuss in Chapter 4.[19] That sort of before-and-after conversion requires active input in arriving at plausible assumptions since it needs to be based on a thorough understanding of the changes involved,[20] possibly involving a degree of cooperation from the organization concerned, and the patience to wade through complicated footnotes and gnomic bureaucratic prose. But it is nevertheless possible, and that is why we classify that sort of change at the medium level of volatility.

At the highest level of discontinuity comes the sort of change at which even with ample supplies of time, energy, and intellectual acuity, a before-and-after

---

[18] Sudden actual changes in spending have been used, for example, to identify policy shifts (see e.g. Bryan Jones, Frank Baumgartner and James True, 'Policy Punctuations: US Budget Authority, 1947–1995', *The Journal of Politics* 60, no.1 [1998]: pp. 1–33).

[19] Appendix 3 at the end of this book shows how it was done, using the 'overlap' period to rework the numbers on the previous basis to make a consistent series.

[20] Such understanding is needed to avoid conflating actual spending changes with reclassification changes if they occurred within a data-series, and to ensure the numbers being compared do not differ in any other systematic way.

data-series cannot be constructed. Suppose that the organization in question stops reporting any numbers at all relating to its total staff, delegates personnel management to lower levels without any detailed reporting to the central level, and instead starts to provide only information about its 'top team', without specifying who is included in that category. At that point, only the highest level of outside diktat or persuasion (to make those delegated units provide the numbers in the old way) could secure a consistent data-series, and no amount of time or energy from outside could reconstruct the numbers on the basis of available documents. So here we reach the limits of 'before' and 'after' conversion, and hence arrive at the highest level of discontinuity.

Of course this three-level distinction according to the consequentiality of data discontinuities is crude, and as with all such categorizations, there are bound to be cases that straddle the boundaries. For example, somewhere between 'medium' and 'large' discontinuities comes the sort of case where the organization possesses but does not publish the information, such that with sufficient 'clout', goodwill, threats, or actual invocation, of freedom-of-information procedures,[21] the data can be produced. That applied to the reconstruction of national accounts by Martin and public expenditure series by Soroka and colleagues that we referred to earlier. So we do not claim this index of volatility is a perfect measure, or incapable of further development. What we do claim is that it represents a step beyond complaining about discontinuities towards more systematic analysis, and that there are several important things that can be learnt by developing such an index to represent volatility systematically across several decades of performance indication. For example, it can tell us whether performance indicator volatility is some sort of constant in human life, like death and taxes, or whether such volatility changes over time. It can help us to pinpoint those domains or types of indicators that show higher or lower levels of volatility. And it can help us to pinpoint what might be accounting for higher or lower levels of volatility.

3.3 Observing Indicator Volatility over Time: Four Cases

Figure 3.2 applies the categorization of indicator validity developed in Table 3.1 to four key indicators that appear in the next three chapters, all taken from administrative datasets or annual reports of government

---

[21] In fact none of the data for this book was obtained through Freedom of Information requests (apart from Bill Files classed as 'closed' under the thirty-year rule which were released by the Parliamentary Legislation Office formally under FOI). All other data that were not publicly available were supplied voluntarily by the organizations and departments concerned. But in several cases our requests for information went unanswered or we were simply told that the data series in question was unavailable or discontinued.

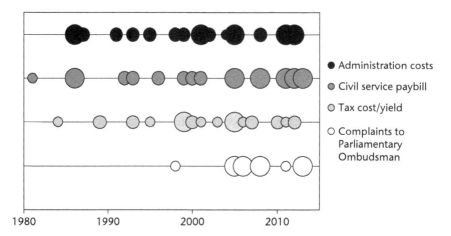

Figure 3.2. 'Large', 'Medium', and 'Small' Discontinuities (as Defined in Table 3.1) in Four Indicators 1980–2013

See Appendix 2 for sources and coding decisions.

departments or agencies. As mentioned earlier, the indicators classified for discontinuities were the reported numbers for the 'running' or 'administration' costs of UK central government departments, for the paybill or hiring costs of the civil service, for the cost of collecting the main central government taxes, and for complaints received by the Parliamentary Ombudsman (Parliamentary Commissioner for Administration) concerning possible 'maladministration' by central government departments and agencies. Appendix 2 at the end of the book describes the data breaks in each of these four series in more detail.

The coding exercise involved three steps. First, we identified data discontinuities in the four series, a discontinuity defined as when a data-series showed a substantial numerical difference from the previous edition of its source, or was reported in a very different way. Second, we classified them into the three categories shown in Table 3.1, and third, we chose an appropriate weighting for each type of discontinuity. Figure 3.2 represents those scores graphically, and Figure 3.3 shows the sum of the discontinuity scores for each five-year period since 1980. As with any classification of this type, definitions can slip and particular coding decisions can be challenged, so we do not pretend this analysis represents the final word on the subject, only that Figures 3.2 and 3.3 represent a first step towards constructing a comparative and historical index of volatility in performance indicators.

As Figure 3.2 shows, there were discontinuities in all of the cost data-series in almost every five-year period. There was no period of complete stasis, but the overall index of volatility shows a general increase over time. The

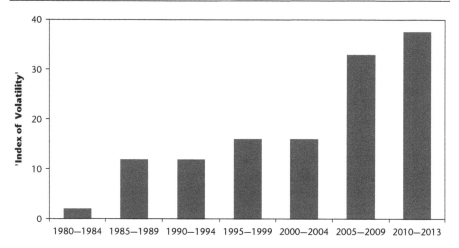

Figure 3.3. Index of Volatility for Five-Year Intervals Since 1980 (Final Period Scaled *Pro Rata*)

Weighting: 'small' discontinuities counted as 1, 'medium' discontinuities as 2, and 'large' discontinuities as 4. The final period covers four years, namely 2010 to 2013 inclusive, scaled up by 25 per cent to estimate the five-year total.

Blair–Brown Labour government's third term (2005–10) stands out both in terms of the total number of discontinuities and of discontinuities that were coded as 'large' according to our index of volatility. The Cameron–Clegg Conservative–Liberal Democrat coalition government formed in 2010 also scored high on the volatility index up to the time of writing. What this suggests is that data discontinuities may be like death or taxes in the sense that no period in the thirty years considered here was entirely discontinuity-free, but there were clear signs of an upward movement in the incidence and consequentiality of data breaks from our four-series analysis over this time.

As shown in more detail in Appendix 2, one of the largest discontinuities in the administration and staff costs series (the top two lines in Figure 3.2) came with the introduction of a new running costs regime and an accompanying break in reporting of civil service wage costs in the mid-1980s. That data break reflects a key reform, discussed in Chapter 4, which was intended to reveal the true costs of 'running government' and making each department responsible for the costs of services such as accommodation and IT that had previously been provided by specialist common service departments or agencies. But it was hard even for the civil servants themselves (let alone ministers, Parliament, public interest bodies, or academics) to figure out at a glance from the published numbers whether those costs were increasing, decreasing, or staying about the same because of the frequency with which the categories of expenditure defined as running or administration costs changed from one year to another.

Another major discontinuity in the top series shown in Figure 3.2 involved the reclassification of a large but unspecified number of front-line civil servants out of 'administration' into 'programme' costs following a major efficiency review in the mid-2000s.[22] That date also marked the end of systematic public reporting of the pay costs of the civil service.[23] More recent changes included further reclassifications of staff in the 2010s, and the inclusion of arms-length bodies (hitherto excluded) within the administration budget in 2011.

The indicator shown in the third line of Figure 3.2 is the reported cost-to-yield of tax collection, the traditional performance measure applied to central government tax collection (though not, as we show in Chapter 5, to the collection of local taxes). In contrast to numbers reported for the whole of central government, which inevitably reflect all the shifting-of-deckchairs that happens among departments and agencies, this specimen indicator relates to the costs of a single—and basic—government activity. One of the major discontinuities in this indicator came in 1999 when one of the tax departments (after a long bureaucratic turf battle) was credited with formal responsibility for collecting the main social security tax (National Insurance contributions) and at the same time, started to be responsible for paying Tax Credits. Another came in 2005 with the merger of the two main central government tax departments into a single body (HMRC), at which time a key table showing the individual components that went into the overall cost-to-yield calculation disappeared from sight.

As far as complaints to the Parliamentary Ombudsman were concerned (the fourth line in Figure 3.2), the main break was in 2005 when the number of complaints received via MPs—a number that had been reported consistently for over two decades, and a criterion that remained a formal requirement up to the time of writing—disappeared from the reports, and was not replaced by a consistent series. We obtained the total number of complaints submitted via MPs from a personal communication with the Ombudsman's Office, but we could not obtain data on complaints by department or outcome in a form that allowed comparison of those numbers before and after 2003–04. Two editions of a statistical summary were produced in 2010–11 and 2011–12, but that summary too was later discontinued.[24] So a lot of bureaucratic effort seemed to be going into producing annual figures that were incommensurable

---

[22] Peter Gershon, *Releasing Resources to the Front Line: An Independent Review of Public Sector Efficiency* (London: HMSO, 2004).

[23] The only published source available of civil service paybill costs on a consistent basis for the 2000s was a National Audit Office report *Managing Staff Costs in Central Government* (HC 818, 2010–12), drawing on Cabinet Office estimates. Thereafter, our only source of matching numbers was through direct contact with the Cabinet Office statisticians, which naturally depended on being able to identify the relevant unit and to secure its cooperation in the face of all the other demands on its time (a process which took over a year in our case, and is not for the faint-hearted).

[24] Parliamentary and Health Service Ombudsman. *Responsive and Accountable?* (HC 1551, 2010–12 and HC 800, 2012–13). A less detailed (and undated) spreadsheet appeared on the PHSO website in 2013.

with previous ones, and that presented us with one of those 'zero versus infinity' classification problems, since either we had to count almost every year as a 'large' change on our index of volatility or as not representing anything that could meaningfully be called a series at all.

Some of these data breaks coincided with major restructuring or reorganization of the government machine, as in the case of the merger of the tax departments mentioned above. But that was not always the case: for example, the much-trumpeted proliferation of executive agencies for service delivery at arms' length from core departments in the early 1990s did not change the way that administrative spending was classified and reported at that time although it may well have been part of a process that led to extensive classification changes later. Similarly, as we will see in Chapter 7, devolution of control of much of domestic administration to the newly (re)formed Scottish Parliament in 1999 (and parallel developments in Wales and Northern Ireland) caused 'medium' data breaks as a result of reclassification of the administrative units, but did not alter the way paybill or running costs were defined. So what explains the pattern depicted in Figure 3.2? We turn to that question in Sections 3.4 and 3.5.

3.4 Explaining Performance Data-Breaking: Democracy, Modernity, Conspiracy, Bureaucracy?

Table 3.2 summarizes four possible ways of accounting for data discontinuities of the kind discussed in Section 3.3, namely 'democratic responsiveness', 'sociotechnical responsiveness', 'track-covering activity', and 'organizational dynamics'. These four possible explanations, all of which figure in Christopher Pollitt's account of the causes of performance indicator churn,[25] can be roughly arrayed on two dimensions, namely the extent to which they manifest themselves in high-level strategic decisions or in more mundane processes or responses, and the extent to which they are more-or-less officially 'mentionable'.

Table 3.2. Four Possible Explanations of Evidence-Destroying Behaviour

Level of action	Official 'Mentionability'	
	More mentionable	Less mentionable
High-level, strategic	Democratic responsiveness	Track-covering activity
Lower-level, operational	Sociotechnical responsiveness	Organizational dynamics

[25] Christopher Pollitt, 'Performance Blight and the Tyranny of Light', in *Accountable Governance: Problems and Promises*, edited by Melvin J. Dubnick and H. George Frederickson (New York: M.E. Sharpe, 2010), p. 87.

By 'democratic responsiveness' we mean those decisions about changes in performance indicators coming from shifts in values, agendas, and ideologies that clearly link to democratic processes, such as changing governments after elections or ministers in between elections. Changes in performance indicators that stem from such electoral shifts could be regarded as a variant of the democratic doctrine (albeit honoured more in the breach than in the observance) that no Parliament can bind its successor. And to the objection that such changes might get in the way of evidence-based policy, the democratic rejoinder would be that election results are themselves the most important kind of 'evidence' about the views of the electorate. For example, if a right-wing government concerned mainly with keeping costs of bureaucracy down is voted out in an election and replaced by a left-wing government concerned mainly with the social or ethnic representativeness of the public service, we can expect indicators of cost to be downplayed or even scrapped relative to indicators of representativeness. In the UK one of the campaign pledges made by the Conservative Party in the 2005 general election was to immediately abolish all central government performance targets and the bureaucracy then responsible for managing them (the Prime Minister's Delivery Unit) if it won government. As it happened, the incumbent Labour government was re-elected in 2005 and the Conservatives were defeated, but if the election had gone the other way the resulting performance data discontinuity would have been a clear case of democratic responsiveness in this sense.

By 'sociotechnical responsiveness' we mean performance numbers changing as a neutral and pragmatic response to changes in technology and society, with the implication that it is those technological and social changes that undermine efforts to pin down evidence of failure or success rather than egregious interference with data continuity. For example, in the early days of government computing in the UK, central records were kept of every computer in every department, including its purchase costs and other technical details, but now computing is an everyday part of almost every government worker's life, such central records would be almost impossible to collect today, and would serve no obvious purpose. Similarly, as ways of working changed in such a way that more part-time and flexible contracts replaced an older pattern in which the overwhelming majority worked a standard forty-hour week, the original way of counting 'full-time equivalent' (in which part-time staff were simply counted as 0.5 full-time persons) came to be superseded by a more accurate count of hours to represent civil service numbers in the mid-1990s.[26]

---

[26] *Civil Service Statistics 1997* (London: HMSO, 1998), p. 2, para 2.2.

Turning to less 'mentionable' sources of data discontinuity, we mean by 'track-covering activity' a process of evidence-destruction through data breaks as a product of willed and deliberate efforts to obscure failure or success by tampering with the numbers. For example, if reported performance numbers turn out to be highly embarrassing for politicians or senior managers, we can expect strong pressure from those quarters to change the basis of counting to produce more favourable outcomes or even to drop 'bad news' indicators altogether. Emmanuel Todd, the radical French historian who in the late 1970s predicted the future collapse of the Soviet Union, noticed that the USSR stopped publishing infant mortality figures after 1974, and concluded that the statistical break must presage bad news.[27] The Thatcher Conservative government of the 1980s was frequently accused of changing the way unemployment figures were counted so as to put its economic policies in a more favourable light—for example, changing what counted as 'unemployment' from simply being registered as seeking work (the original basis of the count) to claiming unemployment *benefits*, then reducing eligibility for such benefits (which had the effect of cutting the numbers further), and starting to count training and work programmes for the first time as 'employment', such that people on such programmes also disappeared from the unemployment count.[28]

By the rather anodyne term 'organizational dynamics', we mean that the source of evidence-destruction comes as much from processes going on within and between agencies and bureaucracies (and the personalities and politics in play at that level) as from the declared agendas and changing preoccupations of elected politicians claiming to represent the will of the electorate. By that we mean changes such as the rate of turnover of those in policy or strategic roles, their capacity and disposition to control the story by reworking numbers, changes in the pecking order of different kinds of players, bureaucratic turf battles, or battles over gaming of numbers. Such processes are partly what lies behind 'Goodhart's Law' of indicative numbers, a famous proposition that (based on Charles Goodhart's observation of changing definitions of 'money supply' by the Bank of England in the 1970s) states that any statistics used for administrative purposes will over time tend to become progressively denuded of meaning as a result of opportunistic gaming and strategic reinterpretation.[29]

---

[27] Emmanuel Todd, *La Chute Finale: Essai sur la décomposition de la sphère Soviétique* (Paris: Robert Lafont, 1976).

[28] See for example Michael Jacobs, 'Margaret Thatcher's Economic Jackpot: Miracle or Myth?', *Economic and Political Weekly* 23, no. 3 (1988): p. 1520. Another example of the 'conspiracy' view, this time from the United States, is John Williams' website 'Shadow Government Statistics: Analysis Behind and Beyond Government Economic Reporting' (<http://www.shadowstats.com/>).

[29] Charles Goodhart, *Monetary Theory and Practice* (Basingstoke: Macmillan, 1984).

But such gaming may also interact with other changing features of organizations. For example, one well-known account of organizational decision-making over time, the so-called 'garbage can model' developed by three leading organizational theorists (Cohen, March, and Olsen) in the 1970s, argued that in some kinds of organization (typified, they thought, by universities), factors such as indefinite technology and an ever-changing cast of decision-makers could lead to a high degree of time-inconsistency in organizational decisions, and such a pattern might well account for discontinuities in the collection and use of performance data.[30] For example, if the relevant culture values short-term entrepreneurial 'creative destruction' activity over continuity and organizational memory, we cannot expect stability and over-time consistency in performance numbers. The same goes if there is no check against data discontinuities being caused simply by carelessness and ignorance (i.e. unawareness of the long-term difficulties being created) at an everyday level.

Indeed, the story behind the major discontinuities in UK historic sector income and expenditure accounts highlighted (and partially corrected) by Bill Martin, to which we referred earlier, seems to have been a product of changes of precisely that type. Far from being the result of some high-level cover-up or 'democratic' choice, it seems to have resulted from a fatal mix of IT system changes rendering older data corrupt or inaccessible, a decline in the status of professional statisticians relative to managers with less grasp of the analytic importance of historic data, and partially exogenous developments, notably in the form of a new statutory accounting framework (the European System of Accounts [ESA95]) introduced in the UK in 1998. In fact, such organizational dynamics reflect a combination of just the three changes we highlighted in Chapter 1—namely more emphasis on managerial control (in this case, more pressure to change performance numbers so that they fit the current preoccupations of managers), the effects of the digital age (in this case, more ability to change and finesse those numbers with lower cost and effort than in the pre-digital age), and more emphasis on spin-doctoring (in the sense of more ability to 'control the story' by ensuring that the performance regimes and the way numbers are reported avoid reputational damage).

A striking example of performance data changes that occurred when we were drafting this book, incorporating all of those three processes, was a 2014 claim by HM Revenue and Customs that the government had raised a record £23.9bn in additional tax as a result of its enforcement efforts in 2013–14, accompanied by another claim that HMRC expected to secure some £100bn

---

[30] Michael Cohen, James March, and Johan Olsen, 'A Garbage-Can Model of Organizational Choice', *Administrative Science Quarterly* 17, no. 1 (1972): pp. 1–23.

from its compliance activities between 2010 and 2015, over double what had been reported (£52bn) as having been secured in the previous five-year period. These numbers indicating apparently increased organizational efficiency appeared at an opportune time, when instances of tax avoidance by large corporations had been in the news and the enforcement efforts of the tax bureaucracy had been criticized. But in fact the basis of the numbers had been changed substantially over those two time periods, with the earlier figures representing only the extra cash taken in as a result of enforcement activity, but the later ones including in addition the organization's estimate (which it had every incentive to exaggerate) of the extra future tax it hoped or believed would be paid as a result of its enforcement efforts.[31]

Of course it is not hard to find examples of each of these types of evidence-destroying behaviour, and these explanations certainly overlap at the margin. It is also possible to envisage more than one behaviour applying within an organization at the same time, leading to 'hybrid' explanations. The challenge, however, is to estimate what the relative power of each of these explanations is for the discontinuities shown in Figure 3.2, and we explore that in Section 3.5.

3.5 The Observed Pattern

Table 3.3 presents an approximate scorecard of how some of the data breaks in the four series we summarized in Table 3.1 seemed to fit into the four categories discussed earlier (and summarized in Table 3.2).

Four main conclusions can be drawn from this admittedly limited analysis. One is that most of the data breaks considered here were hybrids in the sense that they seemed to arise from more than one of the four possible sources of discontinuity that we identified earlier, and indeed it may be that changes are more likely to occur when several of the factors we identified as possible causes of performance indicator churn are working together.

A second is that—perhaps contrary to stereotype—almost none of those discontinuities seemed to be unambiguously attributable to 'track covering activity' (only one possibility is shown in Table 3.3, and even that was debatable). Of course the strongest version of this 'cover-up' explanation is hard to demonstrate, since it requires clear evidence of high-level involvement in

---

[31] These claims were made in the HMRC Bulletin *Fast Facts: Record Revenues for the UK* (May 2014) which was amended in July 2014 to remove the five-year comparison first reported by *Private Eye* ('HMRC: Think of a Number . . . ', *Private Eye*, no. 1368, 13–26 June 2014, p. 29). HMRC was criticized by the National Audit Office for having 'inadvertently overstated the degree of improvement' (*Report on HM Revenue & Customs 2013–14 Accounts* [London: NAO, July 2014], p. R29).

Table 3.3. Accounting for Discontinuities in the Four Cases: Ten Examples

Changes to indicator series	More mentionable		Less Mentionable	
	Democratic responsiveness	Socio-technical responsiveness	Track-covering activity	Organizational dynamics
1980s: Introduction of 'running costs'	✓			✓
1990s and 2000s: Defence running costs reporting discontinued/reinstated				✓
Late 1990s: Devolution to Scotland and Wales	✓			
Early 2000s: Parliamentary Ombudsman complaints reporting altered		✓		✓
Early 2000s: Resource accounting introduced		✓		✓
Early 2000s: Merger of tax and benefit systems	✓			?
Mid-2000s: Gershon reclassifications	✓		?	✓
Mid-2000s: Reporting of tax cost-to-yield ceased				✓
Early 2010s: Costs of arms-length bodies included	✓			?
All decades: Minor changes of running costs reporting practice				✓

dropping or 'fiddling' statistical series. Equally, the weaker version (put to us by more than one disgruntled academic colleague), that governments and bureaucracies may often find it highly convenient for consistent evidence about their performance over time to be as difficult as possible to retrieve, is almost impossible to falsify. But even in candid conversations on an anonymous basis, across a range of civil service interviewees, we picked up few if any indications that such factors figured large for the data breaks in the four series shown in Figure 3.2, as against rather less dramatic considerations. The sort of deliberate evidence-destroying activity said to have been practised by the first Ch'in emperor, as noted in the epigraph, does not seem to have been behind many of these discontinuities.

A third is that relatively few were plausibly attributable to 'democratic responsiveness' or 'sociotechnical responsiveness', but those elements certainly seemed to play into some of these data breaks. For example, it is plausible to attribute some of the data break in reporting of complaints to the Parliamentary Ombudsman in the early 2000s (the fourth series in Figure 3.2) to sociotechnical changes, in the sense that the Ombudsman's reports on the count of letters and telephone calls had clearly become obsolete as a valid indicator of communication levels as a result of the advent of email and websites from the 1990s.

Similarly, 'democratic responsiveness' as we defined it above seems to have been at least partially behind some of these data breaks. For example, as we will see in Chapter 4, at least part of the impetus for the introduction of 'running costs' as a concept seems to have come from high-level political frustration in the early days of the Thatcher government about the fact that it was very hard to identify the total costs of running government departments at that time, and that those numbers were not brought together at a point where any single individual or group could be made responsible for managing the total. And some two decades after that, the idea of changing the count of administration costs to distinguish back-office from front-line staff (a pattern of evolution in which the 2004 Gershon report represented a decisive step) was something that at least had strong 'politician appeal' at the top level, because it played into beguiling rhetoric about protecting or strengthening the (good) front-line rather than the (bad) back-office bureaucrats, even if that distinction is highly problematic to draw in practice. But it is hard to explain most of the data breaks shown in Figure 3.2 as clear instances of democratic responsiveness, and indeed in both of the examples mentioned earlier, internal organizational dynamics seem also to have been behind those changes, in the form of the Treasury's need for new expenditure-control levers over spending departments in the first example, and of attempts to stop departments responding to budget pressures by passing all the pain down to the front line in the second one.

Fourth, the overwhelming majority of data breaks considered here seemed to be attributable, at least in part, to some form or other of 'organizational dynamics'—that is, evidence-destruction coming mainly from internal processes and politics within and between agencies and bureaucracies rather than simple cover-ups, adaptations to technological or social change, or responses to democratic pressures. For example, many of the early running-cost discontinuities seem to be explicable as attempts to block loopholes or rectify what were seen as anomalies. More than one interviewee from the Treasury told us more or less explicitly that performance indicators that link to resource allocation have an inherently limited shelf-life, because they tend to become 'gamed out' as strategizing bureaucrats learn to manipulate them to their advantage, thus leading to shifts in what gets counted and how to limit gaming processes. Several of our interviewees from spending departments and agencies also alluded to ways that cost figures could be finessed to take advantage of gaps or weaknesses in the official distinction between running and programme costs at any point in time.

Several of the other observed discontinuities seem to be explicable in terms of bureaucratic politics with a small 'p'—not linked to big-picture electoral politics but reflecting turf battles, changed managerial strategies, or other bureaucratic wars. The disappearance of the Ministry of Defence from the running costs count for over a decade seems most plausibly explained by this sort of dynamic, and the same can be said for the inclusion of National Insurance as part of the Inland Revenue's cost-to-yield ratio in 1999, after a long period in which the Inland Revenue had complained[32] about the adverse effect on its cost-to-yield figures that arose from that department's lack of 'ownership' of the collection cost figures for this tax (the additional collection costs of which, on top of income tax, were relatively low). Other discontinuities seem to reflect new managerial brooms and the visions and preoccupations of people at the top. The change in the way the Parliamentary Ombudsman recorded complaints in the early 2000s seems to have been a combination of a semi-political move reflecting a long-standing frustration on the part of the Ombudsman's office with the 'MP filter' (the rule that complaints had to go through MPs)[33] and a changed managerial view of how to conceive of and handle complaints, introduced by a new leader.

3.6 Conclusion: Data Breaks as Problems, Mirrors, or Tin-Openers

As we explained at the outset, breaks and discontinuities in performance data about government and public services can be seen as both a problem and a puzzle. They are a problem in that they make it hard for anyone—managers, ministers, governments, Parliaments, think-tanks, scholars, and others—to say whether government is doing better or worse over time. If your blood pressure is checked with different and hard-to-compare metrics every time you go to the doctor, how can you—or anyone—know whether your health is improving or deteriorating? Such churn seems all too likely to lead what the organization theorist Haridimos Tsoukas in a well-known article has called 'the tyranny of light'—namely that attempts to develop indicators can be self-defeating in their ostensible purpose to make organizational performance more transparent to the public at large, because they produce such a strong divide between those with the relevant expertise to understand the indicators and the public at large that citizens become less rather than more trustful

---

[32] See for example *Reports of the Commissioners of Her Majesty's Inland Revenue* (Cmnd 8514, 1982, p. 11, and Cmnd 9305, 1984, p. 34). Political decisions at that time to merge the tax and welfare systems may well have provided the window of opportunity for this change of bureaucratic ownership.

[33] See Parliamentary and Health Service Ombudsman, *Annual Report 2010* (HC 274, 2010–12), p. 8, where the Ombudsman called for the abolition of the MP filter.

of the numbers.[34] Indeed, in the case of the cost numbers discussed earlier, even the experts were floundering to keep track of the volume of year-to-year changes.

That is why what we called the 'standard social science' response to performance data breaks and discontinuities is to deprecate them, treat them as a problem, and laboriously try to rework data-series into a consistent form by various workarounds. We had to do plenty of that in the analyses that follow in the next five chapters.

Of course there are limits to the pursuit of consistency in performance measures in any organization. As we mentioned earlier, consistency has to be traded off against other important values such as economy (for example if the price of consistency is to keep records in old as well as new forms), current relevance, even democratic responsiveness. The idea that consistent measurement over time is always a key to performance improvement can be challenged as well; some would argue that designing performance-improving *incentives* (for example by rivalry and competition or other methods) often gets in the way of centralized data collection. After all, the elaborate statistical series relating to production volumes in the days of the USSR were not retained by post-Soviet Russia as it shifted from central planning to a form of capitalism. And having your blood pressure checked in a consistent form over time might well turn out to be less important for health outcomes than effective incentives for healthy living. At least one of the practitioners we spoke to thought it might not seriously matter if governments destroy historical data-series, given what he saw as the more powerfully performance-enhancing effects of modern ways of collecting and retrieving evidence. Examples include crowd-sourcing, web-crawling, or the laboratory experiments which form the favoured source of evidence of today's behavioural economics in its search for evidence about ways to 'nudge' effectively.

Such objections to all-out pursuit of consistency cannot be dismissed. But the alternative sources of evidence, powerful as they may be for other purposes, cannot really answer the historical question this book addresses, namely how far were aspirations for a government that cost less and worked better realized over a generation? And while cost is no doubt a factor in data collection and reporting, it is remarkably rare that management-by-numbers systems are carefully costed in government or public services, modern digital age information systems ought to be capable of being able to report data in different ways with very little extra cost, and indeed governments are

---

[34] See Haridimos Tsoukas, 'The Tyranny of Light: The Temptations and Paradoxes of the Information Society', *Futures* 29, no. 9 (1997): pp.827–43. Pollitt's 'Performance Blight and the Tyranny of Light' notes the relevance of Tsoukas' analysis to the understanding of performance indicator systems.

perfectly capable of reporting data on multiple bases when it is politically convenient to do so, as the UK did after nationalizing Northern Rock and other banks in the aftermath of the 2008 financial crash, when it carefully kept accounts in two ways.

But the main point of this chapter is to show that data breaks and discontinuities can be an opportunity as well as a problem. They can themselves be categorized and compared, and used as a way of observing change in and around government bureaucracy. As we noted earlier, Neil Carter has made a well-known distinction between the use of performance numbers as 'dials' and as 'tin-openers', and data breaks can themselves be used as analytic tin-openers in that sense. It has often been observed that the budget serves as a mirror of political life (because it 'reflects the ability of certain parties to defend their interests better than the other parties'),[35] and data breaks and discontinuities can also serve as mirror of bureaucratic and other kinds of politics. From our examination of the discontinuity record of the four indicators considered here, relatively few of the data breaks could be plausibly accounted for as simple responses to electoral changes or sociotechnical changes, or even very clearly as attempts to bury evidence of poor performance. The majority of the cases related more to the inner lives of bureaucracies and their internal dynamics of gaming, strategizing, 'creative destruction', staff turnover, and attempts at rationalization.

That seems to be the closest we can get from this analysis to solving the puzzle we started with, namely how we can account for the apparent contradiction between strongly professed hunger for quantitative 'evidence' in public management policy and the systematic destruction of the bases on which such evidence can be drawn. And that answer has both practical and theoretical implications. On the theoretical side, it shows some of the complications in the way that the much-discussed process of 'path dependence' plays out in bureaucratic and institutional development. On the practical side, the implication is that only very short-term evidence-based performance management is likely to be possible—and if the data on our volatility index is anything to go by, there are indications that the time-frame actually got shorter over the period considered here.

---

[35] Erik Lindhahl, 'Just Taxation: A Positive Solution', in *Classics in the Theory of Public Finance*, edited by Richard A. Musgrave and Alan T. Peacock (London/New York: Macmillan, 1958), pp. 174–5.

4

Did Government Cost Less?

Running Costs and Paybill

. . . saving candle-ends and cheese-parings . . . [1]

4.1 Universally Acknowledged Truths? NPM as Cost-Cutting in Government

As we pointed out in Chapter 1, New Public Management (NPM), particularly in its early stages in the 1980s, is often said to have concentrated on cost-cutting. Indeed, one of the few assumptions that many of NPM's advocates and detractors have in common is the view that the NPM movement was strongly motivated by a drive to improve 'efficiency' (in some, often undefined, sense) in the public sector. This claim has approached the status of 'a truth universally acknowledged'. For example, Tom Christensen and Per Laegreid, two of the leading and most prolific international scholars concerned with describing and assessing the development of NPM, describe it as 'a global reform movement . . . inspired by . . . economic theories and normative values whose main focus is on increasing efficiency'.[2] For Christensen and Laegreid, 'The main ideas of NPM were focused on economy and efficiency, and the organizational changes made were efficiency-focused'.[3]

In fact, as we also pointed out in Chapter 1, one (perhaps 'the') standard line of criticism of NPM is that the movement—particularly in the UK—took the pursuit of cost-cutting in government to the point where it risked

---

[1] Words from a famous speech given by William Gladstone in Edinburgh, printed in *Political Speeches in Scotland, November and December 1879* (Edinburgh: Andrew Elliot, 1880), p. 148.

[2] Tom Christensen and Per Laegreid (eds), *New Public Management: The Transformation of Ideas and Practice* (Aldershot: Ashgate, 2001), p. 1.

[3] Christensen and Laegreid (eds), *New Public Management*, p. 15. Exactly the same words are used to describe NPM's essential qualities in Tom Christensen and Per Laegreid (eds), *Transcending New Public Management* (Aldershot: Ashgate, 2007), p. 4.

undermining other important values in public administration. And one of the key values that NPM was said to threaten was the 'rule of law' aspect of bureaucracy as an instrument for upholding correct processes and fitting cases carefully into categories, as emphasized by classic writers such as Jeremy Bentham and Max Weber. But some critics saw the movement as a potential threat to other perhaps more subtle values such as political control, resilience, and coordination across the various departments and units of government. Reflecting this view, for example, Torben Beck Jørgensen and Lotte Andersen declared that 'In the UK, the home of NPM, the counter-reaction was prompt and strongly focused on values. The dangers of one-sided values and of efficiency crowding out other—classical—values were pointed out . . . '[4] Gerard Maas and Frits Nispen made similar observations about aspirations to cut costs in government in the late 1990s,[5] and in the early 2000s, Ezra Suleiman went so far as to claim that NPM's attacks on traditional bureaucracy in the name of efficiency risked undermining democracy itself by weakening one of its key constitutional underpinnings.[6]

In Chapter 6 we will come back to assessing claims that quality, especially in those Weberian 'rule-of-law' aspects of public administration at central government level in the UK, suffered as a result of managerial and other changes during the NPM period. But the job of this chapter is to carefully explore that 'universally acknowledged'—yet surprisingly little-examined—claim about the cost-cutting side of NPM.

In exploring what happened to costs, we need to note that some influential observers have argued that the cost-cutting focus changed over time in the UK, rather than remaining constant over the whole NPM period. In particular, Christopher Pollitt has argued that there was a difference between the earlier and later eras of managerial reform.[7] Pollitt saw the early version as a 'neo-Taylorist' approach to public services management under the Thatcher Conservative government, especially in its first two terms from 1979 to 1987, with 'efficiency', typically construed as short-term cost-limitation, pursued

[4] Torben Beck Jørgensen and Lotte Andersen, 'An Aftermath of NPM: Regained Relevance of Public Values and Public Service Motivation', in The Ashgate Research Companion to New Public Management, edited by Tom Christensen and Per Laegreid (Farnham, Surrey: Ashgate, 2011), p. 336. The works they cite in support of this view are John Stewart and Kieron Walsh, 'Change in Management of Public Services', Public Administration 70, no. 4 (1992): pp. 499–518; Robin Butler, 'Reinventing British Government', Public Administration 72, no. 2 (1994), pp. 263–70; John Greenaway, 'Having the Bun and the Halfpenny: Can Old Public Service Ethics Survive in the New Whitehall?' Public Administration 73, no. 3 (1995): pp. 357–74.
[5] Gerard C. Maas and Frits K. M. Van Nispen, 'The Quest for a Leaner, Not a Meaner Government', in Research in Public Administration, Vol. 5., edited by James L. Perry (Stamford: JAI Press, 1999), pp. 63–86.
[6] Ezra Suleiman, Dismantling Democratic States (Princeton NJ: Princeton University Press, 2003).
[7] Christopher Pollitt, Managerialism and the Public Services, 2nd edn (Oxford: Blackwell, 1993), pp. 177–87.

in a single-minded way at the expense of other values. But Pollitt and others argue that from about 1990 (and perhaps associated with the ostensibly milder style of Conservatism pursued by the government of John Major, Thatcher's successor, and the public service management policies followed later by Tony Blair's 'New Labour' regime), the emphasis started to switch to a new 'quality' agenda alongside that of cost control *simpliciter*.[8] Indeed, Pollitt originally reserved the term 'New Public Management' for the later era.[9] So we need to pay careful attention to what happened to cost control at different points in the thirty-year period we are examining here, to see what signs there are of varying emphasis over time.

4.2 Running Cost Reductions: Hard Questions, Soft Facts

While the notion of NPM as a movement originally motivated by the desire to pursue efficiency by cost-cutting is a 'fact' often referred to (and for some the same applies to the idea that NPM in the UK morphed into a 'quality' phase later on), there is a remarkable dearth of empirical evidence about the extent of any such cost reductions. Nor does this lack of convincing evidence about cost savings seem to be a uniquely British phenomenon. Almost twenty years ago, Christopher Pollitt pointed out how flimsy were the empirical underpinnings of the claims for greater efficiency associated with NPM,[10] even in major evaluations of management changes in Australia and New Zealand.[11] At about the same time, Alasdair Roberts questioned the dramatic cost savings then being attributed to the UK's executive agencies programme by those campaigning for the introduction of similar 'performance based organizations' in the USA in the mid-1990s (including David Osborne and the 1993 Clinton–Gore National Performance Review that we referred to in the first chapter). Those campaigners claimed the creation of the agencies had produced operating cost reductions of 3 to 5 per cent a year with no loss of service quality.[12] Roberts pointed out that those dramatic claims were not

---

[8] Such a change was said to be reflected in developments such as the 1991 Citizen's Charter, which set out quality standards for various aspects of public service performance, the introduction of new audit and inspection systems across the public sector, and the targets/league tables approach to handling quality in public services, which reached its apogee under New Labour after 1998. See Pollitt, *Managerialism and The Public Services*, p. 177 and Christopher Pollitt, 'Managerialism Revisited', in *Taking Stock: Assessing Public Service Reforms*, edited by B. Guy Peters and Donald Savoie (Montreal: McGill-Queens University Press, 1998), p. 54.

[9] Pollitt, *Managerialism and the Public Services*.

[10] Pollitt, 'Managerialism Revisited', p. 54.

[11] Christopher Pollitt, 'Justification by Works or by Faith? Evaluating the New Public Management', *Evaluation* 1, no. 2 (1995): pp. 133–54.

[12] Alasdair Roberts, 'Performance-Based Organizations: Assessing the Gore Plan', *Public Administration Review* 57, no. 6 (1997): pp. 465–78. We return to this subject in Chapter 7.

based on *actual* cost reductions but rather on unverifiable claims made by the agencies themselves about savings from *planned* increases in costs, which of course the managers involved had good reasons to exaggerate, and that the reported numbers on what happened to actual operating costs pointed to a very different story. More recently, the UK's National Audit Office pointed out in a review of government efficiency programmes since 2004 that the calculation of the baseline against which efficiency savings were assessed was the responsibility of each department, and the licence to craft such counter-factual baselines allowed impressive-sounding 'savings' to be claimed even while actual spending sharply increased.[13] That highly creative approach to 'cost-saving' accounting was not entirely new, in that it extended the traditional tactic by spending departments of claiming 'fairy gold' from projected future cost savings—a term Hugh Heclo and Aaron Wildavsky took from financial-control parlance in their classic account of how the UK Treasury operated in the early 1970s.[14]

Nor has the evidence gap on putative NPM cost savings been greatly closed in work done since Pollitt's and Roberts' comments in the 1990s, as shown by Rhys Andrews' systematic review of statistical testing of efficiency claims.[15] Most of the studies Andrews found focused on the effects of competition on productive efficiency (rather than the effects of other reforms in public management) and even there he found equal chances of positive and nil effects, though positive and nil effects far outweighed negative ones. As we shall see in Chapter 7, much the same applies to studies of the cost-cutting effects of the creation of executive agencies in the 1990s. There were some studies in the 1990s on the effects of privatization of public utilities on productivity and efficiency[16] and there have been some survey studies as well.[17] But it is still remarkable that what might be thought of as the most basic question about NPM reforms—did they succeed in their avowed goals of increasing efficiency, cutting costs, improving productivity in public and government services outside the domain of utility privatization?—has still not really

---

[13] National Audit Office, *Progress with VFM Savings and Lessons for Cost Reduction Programmes.* (HC 291, 2010): pp. 14 and 20.

[14] Hugh Heclo and Aaron Wildavsky, *The Private Government of Public Money: Community and Policy Inside British Politics* (London: Macmillan, 1974).

[15] Rhys Andrews, 'NPM and the Search for Efficiency', in *The Ashgate Research Companion to New Public Management,* edited by Tom Christensen and Per Laegreid (Farnham, Surrey: Ashgate, 2011), Chapter 19.

[16] Paul Cook and Colin Kirkpatrick, *Privatisation Policy and Performance: International Perspectives* (London: Harvester Wheatsheaf, 1995).

[17] For example, António Afonso, Ludger Schuknecht, and Vito Tanzi, 'Public Sector Efficiency: An International Comparison', *Public Choice* 123, nos. 3–4 (2005): pp. 321–47; Sabine Kuhlmann, Jörg Bogumil, and Stephan Grohs, 'Evaluating Administrative Modernization in German Local Governments: Success or Failure of the "New Steering Model"?', *Public Administration Review* 68, no. 5 (2008): pp. 851–63.

been answered in spite of decades of research and writing on the subject. At the time of writing, the latest (2011) edition of a well-known cross-national analysis of public management reforms across a set of European and OECD countries by Christopher Pollitt and Geert Bouckaert included OECD data on levels of public employment and public spending as a proportion of GDP, but no systematic indicators of operating costs or productivity. Indeed the authors noted that 'availability of evidence of efficiency gains is patchy and incomplete',[18] and that could be considered something of an understatement.

Part of the reason why all the investment in cross-national studies has not been able to take us very far in answering the basic question of whether or how far NPM reforms succeeded in cutting costs is that the data needed to answer that question are not to be found in the sort of convenient cross-national datasets that many comparative scholars of politics and government rely on. So if the question can be answered at all, it can only be through one or a set of single-country studies. And even that sort of data inevitably comes with all the built-in problems associated with trying to draw meaning out of runs of frequently changed administrative numbers, as we saw in Chapter 3. That makes the 'consilience' method that we mentioned in the first chapter (of putting evidence together from several sources, no one of which is perfect on its own) the only real way to get to grips with the question of what happened to overhead costs during the NPM era.

As well as those data problems, there are of course tricky conceptual issues to be considered as well. Even the apparently common-sense notion of 'running costs' or 'administration costs' turns out to be surprisingly plastic and indeed was radically reinterpreted over the thirty years we consider here, as we show later. Moreover, the much-used and rhetorically important term 'efficiency' is a notoriously slippery concept in practice. For example, economists conventionally distinguish between 'Pareto efficiency' (the extent to which anyone could be made better off by measures that would make no one else worse off), 'allocative efficiency' (the extent to which resources in an economy are applied to their highest value uses), and 'productive efficiency' (the extent to which any given set of goods and services are produced at the lowest feasible cost). And that notion of 'productive efficiency' overlaps with a common engineering definition of efficiency as input per unit of output.

Advocates of managerialist reform under NPM used the term in a variety of ways too, reflecting their various objectives, but broadly seem to have been more concerned with productive efficiency in government than with efficiency in its other senses. Indeed, in practice, the term was often taken (as

---

[18] Christopher Pollitt and Geert Bouckaert, *Public Management Reform: A Comparative Analysis—New Public Management, Governance, and the Neo-Weberian State*, 3rd edn (Oxford: Oxford University Press, 2011), p. 140.

in successive UK 'Efficiency Reviews' and the 1993 Clinton–Gore National Performance Review in the USA) to mean simply cost reduction or at least containment.

Applying the consilience approach by looking at two different—though related—administrative data sources, this chapter looks at evidence of change in 'efficiency' in the sense of what happened to reported running costs (calculated according to the original definition of such costs that was developed in the early NPM era) in UK central government. It puts that into perspective by looking at the paybill of the civil service—that is, the costs of employing those central government staff classified as civil servants—over the same period. We compare the trajectory of these two sets of costs and look at them both in absolute terms (corrected for price inflation by dividing nominal costs by the 2012–13 GDP deflator series) and relative to total public spending. Since civil service paybill was a substantial component of running costs, comparison of these two series allows us to investigate the changing balance between 'staff' and 'other' costs.

4.3 The Concept of Running or Administration Costs in UK Central Government and How it Changed

The introduction of the concept of running costs in UK central government in the mid-1980s (they were first defined in 1986[19] and renamed 'administrative expenditure' for no obvious reason after 1997) was an important early NPM development, though administrative costs had been reported at local-government level well before that (and curiously, as we shall see in Chapter 7, local and central government administrative costs never seem to be compared, certainly not on a routine basis). Running costs were a key part of a more 'managerial agenda' because they were intended to bring together into a single budget all the main costs of running government departments. Up to that time, costs had been reported for the whole of central government under separate heads (e.g. property services costs and civil service paybill). Non-staff costs were controlled by different bureaucratic players in the form of common service departments that provided many of the bureaucratic factors of production, such as offices, computing, and printing services.[20] For instance, superannuation payments were the responsibility of the Paymaster General's Office, printing of HM Stationery Office, publicity services of the Central

---

[19] Running costs were first officially defined in *Supply Estimates 1986–87: Summary and Guide* (Cmnd 9742, 1986), p. 29.

[20] A decreasing fraction of these costs was reported under 'Common Services' in *The Government's Expenditure Plans* White Paper annual editions until 1986.

Office of Information, while the Central Computer and Telecommunications Agency supplied IT services across government.

That older system of dispersed responsibility for the various aspects of running costs had been justified on the grounds that common-services agencies handling each element (such as accommodation or information technology) had greater specialist expertise and that would lead to lower costs or better outcomes (or both) than putting responsibility in the hands of less specialist managers. Nevertheless, by the late 1970s and early 1980s, an increasing proportion of 'common service' costs were charged to individual departments, as early steps in the process of devolving financial responsibility to the users of the services.[21] This process culminated in the new running costs regime of the mid-1980s. That new system chimed with prime ministerial and ministerial concerns (and the dismay of advisers with a business background) that no one was effectively responsible for the overall running costs of any department, or could even say what those costs amounted to, as well as with the desire of the Treasury to find new weapons with which to control costs. (Indeed the running cost system was officially said to have been introduced because of Treasury concerns about such costs outrunning inflation in the early 1980s and it was explicitly intended to create pressures to reduce such costs.[22]) Bringing responsibility for running costs together was intended to both enable and require departmental managers to monitor and act upon such costs as a whole, against financial targets for which they could be held accountable. It was also intended to enable those managers to trade off the different aspects of costs, for example in spending more on staff costs and less on accommodation costs or vice versa.

Departmental running costs were reported in the UK Treasury's *Public Expenditure Statistical Analyses* (PESA) and their predecessors since 1986. But for reasons noted in Chapter 3 there were numerous discontinuities in the running or administration cost data reported over that period. Those data breaks—discussed in Chapter 3 and listed in Appendix 2—reflect a mixture of minor adjustments (some of them reflecting organizational dynamics in the form of the Treasury's eternal cat-and-mouse game with departments looking for ways to 'game' the spending-control rules), attempts to rationalize particular anomalies (by excluding or including certain organizations or types of spending),[23] and more generally the emergence of a way of conceptualizing running costs that differed radically from the original mid-1980s framework.

---

[21] For instance, computing and telecommunications costs were charged to departments from 1978 and the Property Services Agency began to charge departments for accommodation in 1983.

[22] See *Summary and Guide to the 1986–87 Supply Estimates* (Cmnd 9742, 1986), p. 15; and *The Government's Expenditure Plans 1986–87 to 1988–89, Part II* (Cmnd 9702-II, 1986), p. 26.

[23] For example, civil service superannuation payments were included in running costs from 1993.

Arguably one of the most obvious flaws in the way the running-costs system was originally set up in the mid-1980s was that central government departments differed widely from one another according to whether the organizations responsible for the final delivery of services were administratively located within the central department (as had traditionally applied to prison and custodial services) or outside it (as had traditionally been the case with schools and hospitals). As a result of that, administration costs relative to total spending for each department varied enormously for reasons that had much more to do with whether the front-line delivery happened to be located inside or outside the department than with how efficiently or otherwise it was managed. And during the 2000s the older conception of administration costs as reflecting whatever it cost to staff and operate a department, however its service-delivery arrangements were constituted, came to be steadily replaced by a new distinction between 'front-line delivery' (whose staff and operating costs were counted under 'programme expenditure' rather than 'administration costs') and 'back-office' costs that reflected a new and narrower definition of 'administration costs'. A major turning point in this reconception of administration costs came in a high-level review of public sector efficiency chaired by Sir Peter Gershon, a prominent business leader, in the mid-2000s,[24] which was packaged as 'releasing resources to the front line', and used as a reason to reclassify the costs of allegedly 'front-line' staff out of administration costs. This was not a one-off event, however, since such reclassifications continued and indeed gathered pace during the 2010s, as we noted in Chapter 3.

Whether this reconceptualization of administration costs as the costs of whatever is not deemed to be 'front line' in an organization, was really more robust than what preceded it, is debatable. After all, the distinction between precisely what counts as 'front line' and 'back office' in public services can be every bit as precarious, changeable, and contestable as the notoriously difficult distinction between 'tail' and 'teeth' in military operations (is the medical corps 'tail' or 'teeth' or a bit of both?). For example, if policy attention swings away from orthodox service provision by specialist bureaucracies towards various forms of 'citizen engagement' and 'community empowerment' (as it has done from time to time), the 'front line' for that engagement and empowerment activity may turn out to be in what might otherwise be regarded as 'back office' central units. As Jean Monnet, the founder of the European Union, memorably remarked of the idea of 'modernization'—'the front line' is arguably as much a state of mind as a state of nature.[25] And

---

[24] See Peter Gershon, *Releasing Resources to the Front Line: An Independent Review of Public Sector Efficiency* (London: HMSO, 2004); *Public Expenditure Statistical Analyses 2005* (Cm 6521, 2005), p. 57.

[25] Jean Monnet, *Memoirs*, trans. Richard Mayne (London: Collins, 1978), p. 259.

basing the notion of administration costs on a slippery distinction between front-line and back-office work is obviously vulnerable to gaming by managers adept at finding reasons why more and more aspects of their organization's operations should be counted as 'front line'. One of our interviewees who had run several agencies over the period recalled numerous pre-budget talks with those who handled the organization's accounts as to how much of staff costs could be plausibly shifted out of the category of administration costs into programme spending, and that seems likely to have been a fairly general response.

Still, the move towards a 'front-line/back-office' basis for classifying administration costs plainly had politician-appeal because it chimed with rhetoric about concentrating resources on 'front-line services', and understandable criticisms about the tendency of the central core of departments under the old regime to respond to pressures for spending reductions by automatically passing the cuts down the line. In addition, the move to a new way of counting administration costs could also be said to link with business management ideas about how to conceive 'overhead' cost; reclassifying staff out of administration cost into programme spending conveyed the impression that administration costs were being cut sharply, and at the same time service-delivery departments were to some extent sheltered from the effects of targets for reducing administration costs.

4.4 Administration or Running Costs Over Time: Do the Facts Fit the Stereotypes?

Those changes in what was conceived as running or administration costs are important background for understanding Figure 4.1, which shows what happened to reported running costs over the period. To be more precise, what that figure shows are adjusted outturn data for the gross and net running costs over the fiscal years 1980–81 to 2009–10 of the UK's civil central government departments (i.e. excluding defence, for which the concept of running costs is perhaps particularly problematic, and for which running costs were calculated differently and in some years not reported at all). Net running costs as shown in Figure 4.1 denote running costs after subtracting fees or charges paid to departments for their services (for instance for providing passports, criminal records checks, etc.), while gross running costs represent the full administrative costs of departments without subtracting any payments made for services. But those gross costs—arguably the most telling indicator for assessing the extent of cost-cutting within departments—were only publicly reported for part of the period covered by Figure 4.1 (fiscal years 1980–81 to 2003–04), which is why that series is incomplete.

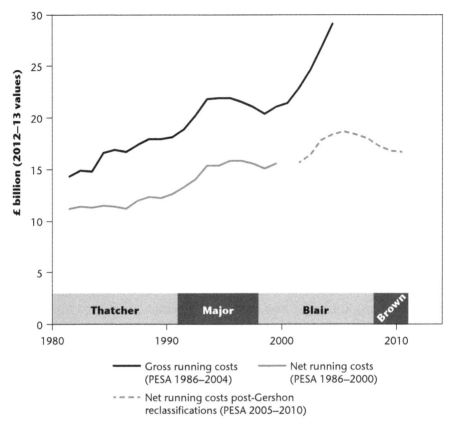

Figure 4.1. Running Costs of UK Civil Departments in Real Terms (£ billion 2012–13 values) 1981–2010

Source: Calculated from data in annual editions of *Public Expenditure Statistical Analyses* (PESA) 1986 to 2010, from tables showing 'running costs' or 'administrative expenditure' for central government. That publication was originally entitled *The Government's Expenditure Plans* and became the *Public Expenditure Statistical Supplement* (and variants), before settling on its current title in 1997. In this chapter we use PESA as the title for the whole series, cited by date of publication. Real terms costs were calculated throughout this chapter by dividing nominal costs by the 2012–13 GDP deflator series.

The outturn data represented in Figure 4.1 were adjusted in two ways. First, the numbers are shown in constant-price terms to take account of price inflation over the period. Second, the numbers are shown with the effects of the frequent administrative reclassifications (of the various types we discussed in Chapter 3) taken out so that the trend can be inspected on a like-for-like basis as far as possible. As described in Appendix 3 at the end of this book, we recalculated running costs after each classificatory change into the earlier basis of classification, using the information reported for the same years in different PESA editions. So what Figure 4.1 represents is running costs as that term was defined in the mid-1980s (before running costs started to morph into a concept of 'back-office' costs, as noted earlier). The reason for ending the series at the financial year 2009–10 was that the method described in Appendix 3 could not be applied to costs after that date, since it depended on the classifications being internally consistent within each edition of PESA. That ceased to be the case from 2011, after which time reclassifications and actual spending changes could no longer be distinguished.

Even so, the broken line on the right-hand side of Figure 4.1 (net costs for financial years 2000–01 to 2009–10) is not directly comparable to the line on the left-hand side of the figure, because in that case we could not apply the overlapping-series method of comparison (for the simple reason that no overlapping reports of net costs were provided at that time),[26] and no gross running cost numbers were reported for the later years. We discussed the classificatory changes that lie behind this major data break in Chapter 3, but the analytic consequence of that data break is that it is only possible to make fairly crude comparisons over the whole period, whereas we can put more weight on comparisons within the series taken separately (that is, for net costs for the periods 1980–81 to 1998–99 and 2000–01 to 2009–10, and for gross costs from 1980–81 to 2003–04).

As can readily be seen, Figure 4.1 does not in fact show any sharp real reduction in those costs during the 1980s when (as we noted earlier) cost-cutting is often claimed to have been the be-all and end-all of the then prevailing version of NPM. Net costs were fairly flat from 1980–81 to 1985–86 though gross costs rose sharply in 1983–84. But thereafter both those series of costs tended to rise markedly over the remainder of Margaret Thatcher's tenure as Conservative prime minister, which ended in late 1990, and in the early years of her successor, John Major.

Indeed, with reclassification changes removed by re-basing reported data back to the original definition of running costs, civil departments' reported gross and running costs rose by about 50 per cent in real terms from 1980–81 to 1992–93 (and net costs by a slightly smaller proportion). After that, as Figure 4.1 shows, reported running costs fell briefly under John Major, before rising again in the early years of Tony Blair's New Labour government elected in May 1997.[27]

---

[26] Net administration costs were not reported in, and could not be calculated from, PESA 2001 to PESA 2004 inclusive. Since PESA 2005 only net administration costs were reported.

[27] Oliver James' study of agencification in UK central government reached a similar conclusion over a shorter timescale, showing that central government administrative costs rose by some 17 per cent in real terms from 1988–89 to 2000–01, though James did not correct for reclassification effects as Figure 4.1 does. See Oliver James, *The Executive Agency in Whitehall: Public Interest Versus Bureau-Shaping Perspectives* (Basingstoke: Palgrave Macmillan, 2003) and Oliver James and Sandra Van Thiel, 'Structural Devolution to Agencies', in *The Ashgate Research Companion to New Public Management*, edited by Tom Christensen and Per Laegreid (Farnham, Surrey: Ashgate, 2011), p. 218.

So Figure 4.1 indicates that NPM changes were associated with a substantial rise, not a fall, in running costs over the twenty years from 1980 to 2000, and although there were some cost reductions independent of reclassification effects in the later years of John Major's premiership, running costs did not fall back even to 1990 levels, let alone to the level of the late 1970s (supposedly the 'bad old days' of poor cost control before NPM). The New Labour story shows a similar dynamic, with a rise in reported running costs followed by a decline that left absolute costs higher at the end of the period shown in Figure 4.1 than they had been at the outset of the Labour government in 1997. However, no information was given about gross costs after 2004, and it is very notable that those costs ceased to be publicly reported at an interesting point in their evolution, when they were rising vertiginously. So it is not possible to tell how much we should add to the reported net administrative costs to include the extra costs that were offset by increased fees and charges after that date.

The analysis in Figure 4.1 raises at least three questions. One is how far the picture changes when we express those costs as a ratio of total government spending, and whether that would be a better performance indicator than absolute cost levels. Figure 4.2 therefore shows two relevant measures of public spending in real terms, namely Total Managed Expenditure (TME, public spending including welfare payments and debt interest) and Departmental Expenditure Limits (DEL, public spending on goods and services, i.e. not including welfare benefits and debt interest). Figure 4.3 shows

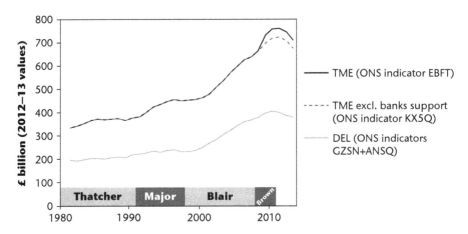

Figure 4.2. UK Public Spending: Total Managed Expenditure (TME) and Department Expenditure Limits (DEL) in Real Terms (£ billion 2012–13 values) 1981–2013

Source: Calculated from Office of National Statistics *Public Sector Finances Supplementary Tables* (May 2013). A discontinuity due to income from the sale of mobile phone licences in 2000–01 was removed.

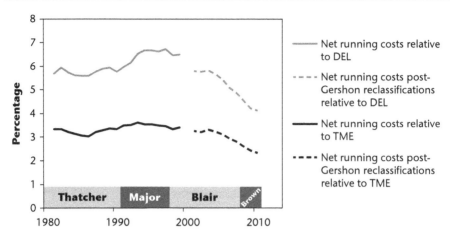

Figure 4.3. Net Running Costs of UK Civil Departments as a Percentage of Departmental Expenditure Limits (DEL) and Total Managed Expenditure (TME) 1981–2010

the net running cost figures as a percentage of TME (excluding the support extended to banks following the 2008 financial crisis) and to DEL over the same period. The figure gives a picture similar to that of Figure 4.1 for the early NPM period, with running costs noticeably higher relative to both TME and DEL in the early 1990s than they had been a decade earlier, and then falling from about 1993. For the later period, after the data break in 2000, Figure 4.3 shows that net costs relative to TME and DEL fell after 2003 as total public spending rose sharply.

For that post-2000 period, Figure 4.3 presents the more dramatic picture, but it is of course debatable whether absolute running costs or such costs relative to total spending are the more meaningful measure of administrative performance. After all, given that the biggest drivers of increasing overall public expenditure were rising costs of welfare and pension provision and of spending on education and health (where the relevant delivery units were outside the central departments), it is not obvious that the writing of larger cheques at the centre should need commensurately more administrative resources, particularly in a digital age. Indeed, focusing exclusively on administration costs relative to spending leads to the ironic conclusion that the way to cut such costs is to spend more. It seems hard to argue convincingly that a 1 percentage point fall in relative reported running costs over a period when TME increased by over 50 per cent in real terms should be counted as a strong performance.

Second, it might be asked whether the aggregate picture presented in Figure 4.1 might be skewed by the behaviour of one or two big departments, and thus mask what might have been early NPM successes in cost-cutting elsewhere. It is true, as mentioned earlier, that there were wide variations

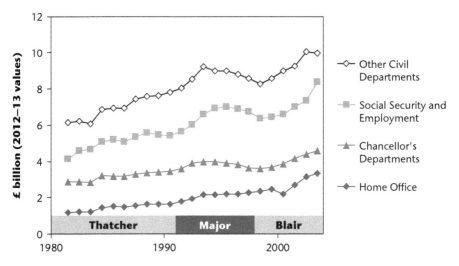

Figure 4.4. Gross Running Costs of Selected Civil Departments and Groups in Real Terms (£ billion 2012–13 values) 1981–2004

in the ratio of total expenditure to administrative spending among different departments, given that 'administration costs' depended on whether the main service provision element in the policy domain was administratively counted as inside the department or outside it. But even so, when we break down the costs among a set of departmental groups, Figure 4.4 shows that gross administration costs rose in real terms in all of those groups from 1980 until about 1993, and then fell in all of them except the Home Office group, to greater or lesser extents, until about 1999, before rising again in the early 2000s. So while the Home Office group (which included all prison and immigration staff costs at that time) seems to have exerted a continuous upward pressure on costs, that department was not the only driver of the real-terms increase in Figure 4.1. A similar pattern was exhibited by all the large departmental groupings shown in Figure 4.4, suggesting that we can neither attribute the initial rise, nor the mid-1990s fall, to any one particular major department or group.

Third and perhaps more fundamentally, it might be questioned whether some of the measures associated with NPM amounted to changes in modes of control[28] that would change the balance between what is categorized as 'running costs' relative to 'programme costs'. For example, the introduction of internal market systems in which previously monolithic systems were broken up into purchaser and provider units might mean more running costs in

[28] Mahmoud Ezzamel, 'Corporate Governance and Financial Control', in *Perspectives on Financial Control*, edited by Mahmoud Ezzamel and David Heathfield (London: Chapman & Hall, 1992).

central government (in establishing and regulating systems of competition or rules of the game), in the expectation that such competition would in time drive down programme costs. On the other hand, the establishment of arms-length bodies with delegated budgeting arrangements (as, for example, when some large museums became non-departmental public bodies having been previously parts of government departments)[29] might be expected to transfer 'running costs' into the category of 'programme costs'.

Such questions are undoubtedly important, but they cannot be definitively answered from the data presented in the four figures above. Nevertheless, it can be argued, as indicated in the examples above, that such shifts could be expected to cross the running-programme costs boundary in both directions, and it is not clear how far they would cancel each other out. Further, if the available data shows (as it does) no real-terms reduction in either running costs or programme costs over a period of decades, that observation casts a sizeable measure of doubt on the idea that what was gained on the running-cost swings might have been lost on the programme-cost roundabouts, or vice versa.

4.5 Payroll Costs and Staffing Numbers: Did They Cause the Rise in Running Costs?

Until 2004 the running costs considered above included essentially the entire paybill costs of the civil service. Separating out this element of the costs can help us to see whether or how far the running cost increases we identified earlier were driven by civil service pay, and provides another way of testing whether claims of cost reduction through managerial or other measures are observable over a generation.

Of course, debate often focuses on the relative pay of public servants relative to private sector workers, and whether those working for government are overpaid or underpaid relative to what might be argued to be their private sector counterparts. And there are also interesting questions about pay relativities, since over the period considered here there seems to have been a weakening of what was once referred to as a 'double imbalance' pay pattern in the public sector (comprising relatively well-paid lower bureaucratic ranks while those in the higher ranks earned substantially less than their counterparts in the private sector[30]) as lower ranks were removed or outsourced, and

---

[29] Brian Hogwood, 'The 'Growth' of Quangos: Evidence and Explanations', *Parliamentary Affairs* 48, no. 2 (1995): pp. 207–25.

[30] See Maivor Sjölund, *Statens Lönepolitik 1986–1988* (Stockholm: Publica, 1989); Christopher Hood and Martin Lodge, *The Politics of Public Service Bargains* (Oxford: Oxford University Press, 2006), pp. 71–6.

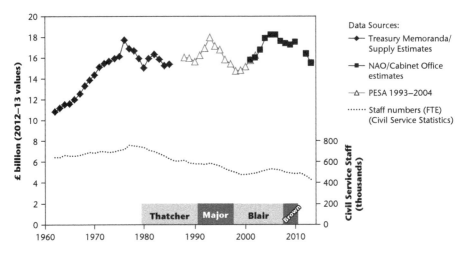

Figure 4.5. UK Civil Service Paybill in Real Terms (£ billion 2012–13 values) 1962–2013

Source: Data sources for Figures 4.5 and 4.6 were (i) *Memoranda of the Chief Secretary to the Treasury on the Supply Estimates*, annual editions, (ii) *Public Expenditure Statistical Analyses*, annual editions (corrected for reclassification changes as shown in Appendix 3), (iii) National Audit Office *Managing Staff Costs in Central Government* (HC 818, 2010-12) and (iv) the final two data points were a personal communication from the Cabinet Office. Staff numbers (full-time equivalent, FTE) were from *Civil Service Statistics*, annual editions. Costs include superannuation and National Insurance contributions.

some top civil servants began to be paid substantially more than the prime minister. But instead of focusing on comparisons of pay rates between the civil service and other organizations or relativities within the civil service, our focus here is simply on what happened to total paybill over time and how far it shaped the overall running cost increases noted earlier. After all, the whole point of giving managers greater freedom under NPM reforms (e.g. to hire fewer staff at higher pay rates, to use bonus schemes, etc.) was that it allowed managers in principle more choice over how to use labour resources most effectively. So how were those freedoms reflected in changes in the total paybill changed over three decades?

To explore that issue, Figure 4.5 shows a set of indicators of reported staffing costs (in constant-price terms) of the UK civil service in the years such figures were published and also includes staff numbers for the whole civil service.[31] As with the running-cost data discussed in Section 4.4 (and as

---

[31] These numbers cover the whole civil service, not including the Post Office but including the so-called industrial staff. (Industrial or blue-collar civil servants were mainly employed by the Ministry of Defence in, for instance, naval dockyards, as well as more generally in maintenance and cleaning roles.) Such staff formed over a quarter of the total civil service in 1975 but dwindled to below 4 per cent by the mid-2000s, after which they were no longer reported separately. Unlike the running costs shown earlier, the paybill costs include the civilian staff of the Ministry of Defence.

described in Appendix 2), these data do not come in a conveniently continuous series, so some tricky issues of interpretation arose in trying to make sense of them. But they have the advantage of providing an almost continuous series extending over fifty years.

Putting the various data series together, Figure 4.5 shows that civil service paybill started to fall in the mid-1970s after more than a decade of steady increases, moved up and down during the Thatcher premiership, but finished higher in real terms in 1992–93 than it had been in 1979–80. The paybill then fell noticeably in the latter years of John Major's premiership before starting to rise again during the early years of New Labour. During the Blair government the real-terms costs were briefly up to the level they were at before the NPM era, before starting to fall after the financial crisis in 2007–08. Overall, we come to the rather less-than-dramatic conclusion that total civil service staff costs were about the same in real terms in 2012–13 (about £16 billion in 2012–13 values) as they had been over thirty years earlier, despite three decades of outsourcing and much-hyped NPM initiatives, plus a fall of over a third in civil service staff numbers.

We must therefore conclude that the increase we observed in running costs over the whole period cannot plausibly be explained by increased civil service staffing costs. From 1987–88 to 2003–04—the longest period for which we can make a like-for-like comparison—the paybill costs of civil departments rose 19 per cent, while the 'non-paybill' portion of the gross running costs of the same departments more than doubled. That 'non-paybill' component included consultancy fees and costs of public finance initiatives and outsourcing contracts (the reporting of such costs tended to be highly opaque),[32] and of course such costs included the pay of those working for outsourcing companies, who in some cases were ex-civil servants formerly employed 'in-house'.[33]

As with the running costs discussed in Section 4.4, we can also express these paybill costs relative to total spending (TME). Figure 4.6 shows this ratio, which fell as a proportion of total spending throughout this time. But how far those reductions can be counted as an effect of NPM policies in containing cost rises is debatable, since as the figure shows, civil service payroll costs had been falling (albeit unsteadily) as a proportion of total spending since the early 1960s—long before the NPM era as it is conventionally dated.

---

[32] A report by the Institute for Government estimated that £51 billion was paid by central government to private providers in 2013 (though we cannot tell what proportion of that was classed as running costs). Gavin Freeguard and Ian Makgill, *Government Contracting: Public Data, Private Providers* (London: Institute for Government, 2014), p. 9.

[33] For instance, *The Report of the Commissioners of Her Majesty's Inland Revenue for the year ended 31st March 1994* (Cm 2665, 1994), p. 5, noted that 1900 staff were transferred to the IT contractor EDS between 1994 and 1996.

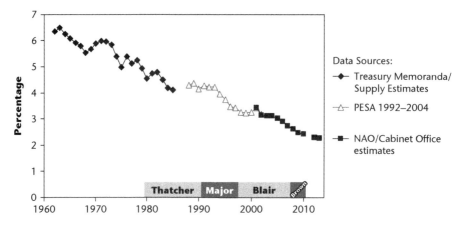

Figure 4.6. UK Civil Service Paybill as a Percentage of Total Managed Expenditure 1962–2013

6. Conclusions

All the numbers used in the figures shown in this chapter are based on administrative numbers that fall well short of some putative 'gold standard' of perfect validity and reliability, for reasons that we discussed in Chapter 3, when we showed there were at least five major classification changes in UK central government running-cost data over thirty years and many other smaller changes. Indeed, it is remarkable that in what is claimed to be an era of 'managerialism' and cost-consciousness, comparison of costs over time was rendered so laborious as to be impossible without hundreds of hours of fine-print analysis.

Nevertheless, when we apply the consilience principle and consider the pattern emerging from the payroll cost numbers as well as those for administration costs, a fairly consistent pattern emerges, and we show that in Table 4.1, which comprises a summary scorecard of how the numbers explored in this chapter relate to the claims made for the ability of managerialism and related changes to cut government's running costs in the medium- and long-run, as discussed in Chapter 1.

As Table 4.1 shows, the conclusion we can draw about the extent to which government 'cost less' over the thirty years considered by this book depends (a) on whether 'cost less' is taken to refer to absolute reductions in operating costs (in constant prices) or reductions relative to the total of spending; (b) on whether reported running costs or paybill costs are the most meaningful measure of what government cost to run; and (c) on what time period is being considered.

Table 4.1. An Overall Assessment: Did NPM Cut Government Costs and if so by How Much?

	'Early NPM' 1980–81 to 1990–91	'Middle NPM' 1990–91 to 2000–01	'Late or post-NPM' 2000–01 to 2009–10[a]	Whole period 1980–81 to 2009–10[a]
Percentage Change in Real Terms Costs (2012–13 values)[b]				
Net Running Costs of Civil Government Departments	19	17[c]	7[d]	[about 50][d]
Gross Running Costs of Civil Government Departments	32	21	n/a[d]	n/a[d]
Civil Service Paybill (including MoD civilian staff)	2	−7	11	10
Percentage Change in Cost/TME				
Net Running Costs of Civil Government Departments/ TME	9	−3[c]	−28[d]	[about −30][d]
Gross Running Costs of Civil Government Departments/ TME	16	−7	n/a[d]	n/a[d]
Civil Service Paybill/TME (including MoD civilian staff)	−10	−20	−29	−49
Percentage Change in Staff Numbers				
Civil Service Staff Numbers	−20	−16	1	−32
Percentage Change in Real Terms TME				
Total Managed Expenditure	13	21	57	114

Notes to the table.

a. The end date of 2009–10 was chosen because consistent data on administration costs were not available after financial year 2009–10, and the civil service paybill was unavailable for 2010–11.

b. The precise percentage changes depend on the GDP deflator series used to correct for inflation. The annual GDP deflator series published by the Treasury since 2012 resulted in a lower apparent rate of inflation over this period than if earlier deflator series are used, and hence larger real-terms increases.

c. This series ended with financial year 1998–99.

d. As discussed above and in Chapter 3, gross administration costs were not available after 2004, and net costs reported after 2000 were calculated on a very different basis. Therefore the percentage change over the whole period cannot be calculated for gross costs, and can only be estimated approximately for net costs.

As the table shows (reflecting the analysis in Section 4.4), reported running costs of the civil departments rose substantially in constant-price terms in each of the periods shown in the table, though at a declining rate. But those costs fell relative to total government spending in most of the sub-periods, and so far as can be determined, fell over the period as a whole. We have already raised the issue of whether or how far that fall in running costs relative to total spending should be counted as 'good performance', given that much of the rise in programme spending consisted of higher transfer payments from central government to individuals or other organizations—how much more does or should it cost to write cheques for larger amounts? If all government had done was to write bigger cheques, we could draw an analogy with a petrol (gas) filling station operating in a period of steeply rising prices. It is hard to see why there would be extra cost of selling the fuel (until in the extreme case the pumps can no longer display the price, or extra security measures are needed to prevent drivers absconding without paying). The filling station might well have to pay its employees more to reflect increased living costs, of which fuel is a component, but that should be taken care of by calculating real-terms prices. In a case like that, absolute (real-terms) operating costs seem to be a more telling metric of performance than costs relative to revenue. Of course this example is an extreme case and we do not suggest the analogy is exact, but it shows the drawbacks of putting all the weight on relative cost measures.

By contrast, the table shows that civil service paybill costs rose and fell over the period as a whole, ending up only slightly above what they had been at the beginning (in constant-price terms) despite a reduction of one-third or so in the staffing of the civil service. Civil service average pay also fell relative to UK average earnings.[34] And those staffing costs fell more sharply relative to total government spending than did net running costs. As we noted earlier, this observation implies that the 'non-staff' component of running costs rose sharply over the period, which can most plausibly be attributed to a rise in contracting-out and consultancy costs. Such costs can reflect contracts 'locked-in' over many years, sometimes by a predecessor or parent department, as several of our interviewees pointed out, and therefore not under the direct control of current managers.[35]

The overall conclusion from this analysis—running counter to the strong claims made by both the advocates and critics of managerialism concerning outsourcing, IT changes, and other developments—must therefore be that UK central government both cost more and less in the period from 1980 to 2010, dependent on whether we put more weight on absolute numbers or relativities. Indeed, we might even also conclude that government cost much the same, if it is civil service staffing costs that are to be taken as the most significant measure of cost. The fact that non-staff costs rose so sharply at the same time that civil servant numbers were falling suggests that it takes more to cut running costs in government than cutting numbers of civil

---

[34] Average UK per capita pay rose 358 per cent (in cash terms) between 1980–81 and 2009–10, while per capita civil service pay rose 345 per cent (a 4 per cent difference) over the same period in which the civil service shifted towards higher grades and far fewer 'industrial' staff. UK earnings from Gregory Clark, 'What Were the British Earnings and Prices Then? (New Series)', *Measuring Worth* (2014, <http://www.measuringworth.com/ukearncpi/>).

[35] It is notable that the Conservative–Liberal coalition government elected in 2010 enacted a number of stringent measures to contain and reduce IT and consultancy costs but, as noted in Chapter 3, because of data breaks we have not been able to determine the effects of those efforts on administration costs since 2010.

servants. And contrary to stereotype, it appears to be the time of the Margaret Thatcher 'Iron Lady' Conservative government, often said, as noted earlier, to have been a period of all-out cost-cutting in the public sector, in which running-cost performance, both in absolute terms and relative to total spending, was the least impressive.

5

Collecting Taxes

Central and Local Government Taxation Compared

. . . Plucking the goose . . . to obtain the largest possible amount of
feathers with the smallest possible amount of hissing.[1]

5.1 Taxation as a Key Test of the Power of Managerialism and IT Developments

Chapter 4 looked at what happened to whole-of-government running costs at central level in the UK over time. The advantage of starting with a big-picture, whole-of-government approach is that it puts together all of the various (civilian) departments, so the overall number is unaffected by all the many transfers of functions among central departments and agencies during the period that we discussed in Chapters 2 and 3.

But there is a potential downside to that big-picture approach as well. Staying at that level of aggregation risks masking variety among high and low performers, and would not pick up any notable cost-cutting successes in some departments and services that might be overshadowed by poor or mediocre performance elsewhere. Advocates and defenders of the efficiency reforms that took place over the period covered by this book might well argue that we need to delve below that aggregate level to find the areas in which the energy put into the many bureaucratic makeovers did in fact result in government costing less. Indeed, that was precisely the reaction we got from a number of the senior civil servants we interviewed for this study when we presented them with the aggregate numbers shown in Chapter 4. 'Disaggregate!' they said.

---

[1] A comment on 'the art of taxation' traditionally attributed to Jean-Baptiste Colbert, Minister of Finance under King Louis XIV of France, 1619–83.

Readers will recall that in Chapter 4 we did disaggregate a set of departmental groups and that the analysis did not show up very marked differences in running-cost performance. But those departmental groups still involved putting a number of organizations together (to take account of frequent shifts in departmental responsibilities over time) and that analysis might therefore fail to pick up important instances of individual departments and agencies whose running-cost performance was much better than the aggregate numbers for government as a whole. Accordingly in this chapter we turn from running and paybill costs for government as a whole to concentrate on the costs associated with tax collection in central government over the thirty years considered by this study, and we also make some comparisons with costs of local authority tax collection over the whole period.

So why pick on taxation? The reason is that tax collection (like payment of welfare benefits) can be argued to be a policy domain in which the big changes we discussed in the opening chapter might be expected to have particularly dramatic and transformative effects. After all, in the case of taxation, there is a more obvious bottom-line metric for management to focus on (of maximizing revenue collected per unit of resource and of managing financial risks) than applies in other more nebulous fields of public management, such as justice, foreign affairs, or security, where the 'bottom line' can appear much more polyvalent and elusive. That is not to deny that there are numerous problems with the cost-to-yield metric (discussed below), since it is sensitive to tax rates and to 'gaming' by reducing effort on, for instance, costly compliance and enforcement activities.

In principle too, the collection of taxes (involving as it does financial and accounting transactions with tens of millions of individuals and millions of organizations in the UK)[2] seems to be a domain of government activity that offers particularly rich scope for creative applications of modern IT by managers as society moves from the quill pen era to the digital age, and the factory offices of an older era involving thousands of clerks working on cumbersome paper processes are replaced by ever more powerful IT systems. So if there are indeed success stories in cost-cutting arising from new managerialism or IT transformations over these three decades, tax collection is one of the domains in which we might most expect to find such stories. Accordingly, this chapter begins by sketching out a brief account of what happened to UK central government tax administration over three decades, and then moves to examining what happened to the costs of central tax collection. It goes on to look at what happened in the field of local tax administration over the same period and what happened to collection costs in a more decentralized

---

[2] *Business Demography 2012* (Office for National Statistics Statistical Bulletin, 2013), p. 4, reported between 2.1 and 2.4 million 'active enterprises' in the UK from 2003 to 2012.

operation without the massive IT projects that characterized central government tax collection, and, as in Chapter 4, concludes with a scorecard and overall assessment.

5.2 The Development of Central Government Tax Administration Over Three Decades: An Overview

Over most of the thirty years or so covered by this book, most central government tax collection activity in the UK was conducted by two organizations. One was the Board of Inland Revenue, which was responsible for 'direct taxes' on organizations and individuals, such as income tax, capital gains tax, corporation tax, and inheritance taxes. The other was the Board of Customs & Excise, which was responsible for 'indirect taxes' on goods or transactions, such as import duties and sales taxes.[3] These organizations, both of which assumed their modern form in the nineteenth century as a result of mergers of separate tax departments, though originating long before that, were formally constituted as boards of civil servants (known as Commissioners). Tax policy was ultimately set by the Treasury and Chancellor of the Exchequer (the finance minister), who steered financial legislation through Parliament. But the tax boards were part of that policy process and they had some autonomy in management from the Treasury and Chancellor of the Exchequer, reflecting the view that ministers should not be directly involved in individual casework decisions.

Given that distinction between policy-setting and individual casework, the tax departments constituted a partial model for the executive agencies—semi-autonomous and separately managed delivery bodies within the ambit of central departments, as mentioned in Chapter 2—that became widely adopted in UK central government in the 1990s and were often seen as part of the managerial transformation of government. The tax departments were also pioneers in the use of quantitative performance indicators, both at the organizational level in the form of measuring cost relative to tax yield, and within the organization (in the form of caseload measures) long before such indicators came to be adopted more widely across central government. So the record of what happened to operating costs in these organizations is particularly interesting for this study.

Toward the end of the period considered in this book, the two central tax departments were merged into a single body, Her Majesty's Revenue and

---

[3] In addition, the Post Office, a public corporation during the period covered by this book, operated counter services for collecting some licence taxes (such as vehicle and TV licences) and the BBC, also a public corporation, operated its own enforcement regime for the TV (originally radio) licence tax which funded its operations.

Customs (HMRC) in 2005. That organizational change, arguably the logical conclusion of the nineteenth-century mergers of tax departments, had been mooted before, and the proposal was taken up again by a parliamentary committee (the Treasury Select Committee) in 2000. The Committee argued that merging the two departments would 'improve compliance with taxation, reduce businesses' compliance costs and *reduce the Government's revenue collection costs*'[4] [our emphasis]. The merger was carried out after a 2004 review by the then Permanent Secretary of the Treasury (Sir Gus, now Lord O'Donnell), which also concluded that integration of the two departments could produce substantial cost savings and other benefits. Indeed, the new merged organization was set an apparently impressive target to cut some 16,000 of its workforce (then numbering more than 98,000 people) within three years, and to make 'efficiency savings' of some £500 million over that period. At the time of its creation HMRC presided over an administrative empire comprising almost 900 properties in 300 locations around the UK, with two or more buildings in many towns and cities. Much was made of the cost savings that could be realized from a programme of rationalization and disposal, with savings of annual running costs expected to be of the order of £100m by 2011.[5] So here too tax collection presents an important case study for exploring the savings achieved by management changes.

Tax structure and policy changed over these three decades in several ways. As far as direct taxes were concerned, some important new revenue streams developed, particularly taxation of the North Sea oilfields, which began to come on stream in the late 1970s. And the method of collection shifted from assessment by tax bureaucrats on the basis of returns submitted to a later system of self-assessment by taxpayers themselves calculating how much they were obliged to pay. That change was applied to individual income tax in 1996[6] and to corporation taxes in 1999 (nearly twenty years after the first field tests for self-assessment of corporation tax had taken place[7]). Moreover, the use of the tax administration to provide welfare benefits in the form of tax credits to low-income workers and pensioners—a scheme originally planned and then discarded in the 1970s after a change in government[8]—made a major change to the clientele and method of operation of the Inland Revenue

---

[4] Treasury Select Committee, *The Merger of Customs & Excise and the Inland Revenue* (HC 556, 2003–04), p. 10.
[5] *HM Revenue & Customs Annual Report 2005–6 and Autumn Performance Report 2006* (Cm 6983, 2006), p. 44.
[6] This shift from bureaucratic assessment to self-assessment, following a pattern long adopted in the United States, had been mooted at least as far back as the 1970s. See *Report of the Commissioners of Her Majesty's Inland Revenue for the year ended 31st March 1977* (Cmnd 7092, 1978), p. 25.
[7] *Report of the Commissioners of Her Majesty's Inland Revenue for the year ended 31st December 1983* (Cmnd 9305, 1984), p. 45.
[8] *Report of the Commissioners of Her Majesty's Inland Revenue for the year ended 31st March 1974* (Cmnd 5804, 1974), p. 19.

in the early 2000s. As far as indirect taxes were concerned, a number of new taxes were introduced—insurance premium tax, air passenger duty, and landfill tax, for example, all of which began in the 1990s—and a few disappeared (such as the car tax [a purchase tax on new vehicles] in 1992), but the big indirect tax staples over the period continued to be Value-added Tax (VAT), oil taxes, and excise taxes, for example on fuel, alcohol, and tobacco.

Information technology developments, one of the big changes in government that we discussed in Chapter 2, also figured large in the world of tax administration over this period, and were justified by claims of cost-saving as well as improved capability. In the late 1970s, just before our starting point for this study, there were precisely four computers in the Customs and Excise Department and six in the Inland Revenue Department—all of them mainframe machines huge in physical size but puny in processing power by today's standards and only able to be programmed through inflexible and unforgiving systems of clerical entry of punched cards or paper tape for batch-processing. Towards the end of our period, in the mid-2000s, the by-then-merged HMRC department was reported to have over 100,000 computer screens and over 250 major IT systems (updated by more than 1200 releases every year), accessed by about 75,000 users.[9] So anyone working in tax administration over the thirty-year period covered by our study would have seen a dramatic transformation in office technology and working methods, even though the move away from paper-based systems linked to mainframe machines was much slower than numerous critics thought it ought to have been.

In the domain of indirect taxes, the then Customs and Excise Department began the period covered by this book with a relatively new tax (VAT, introduced in 1973) that, in contrast to income tax, had been introduced for the computer age from the outset.[10] It was therefore designed around a central computer system in the South of England (which kept records of registered VAT traders, issued tax return forms, handled the receipt of tax payments through cheque sorting equipment, issued repayments and provided statistics) linked to some seventy or so offices in the main towns and cities that were responsible for enforcing the tax and acting as a point of contact with local traders.[11] Microcomputers began to appear in the local offices in the 1980s, for collection of statistics, casework records, and the like.[12]

[9] *HM Revenue & Customs Annual Report 2005–6 and Autumn Performance Report 2006* (Cm 6983, 2006), p. 44.

[10] Dorothy Johnstone, *A Tax Shall be Charged: Some Aspects of the Introduction of the British Value Added Tax* (London: HMSO, 1975), p. 17.

[11] *Report of the Commissioners of Her Majesty's Customs and Excise for the year ended 31 March 1974* (Cmnd 5789, 1974), p. 109.

[12] *Report of the Commissioners of Her Majesty's Customs and Excise for the year ended 31 March 1984* (Cm 9391, 1984), pp. 12 and 15.

As far as direct taxes are concerned, the then Board of Inland Revenue had developed plans in the early 1960s for bringing its staff into nine large clerical offices supported by the early computers of those days, to computerize the 'Pay as You Earn' (PAYE) system of tax deduction at source by employers on the basis of tax codes issued by the Inland Revenue, originally developed during the Second World War as an elaborate paper-based system, and (along with VAT) one of the main tax innovations of the twentieth century. But as a result of expenditure cutbacks and hold-ups while developments such as self-assessment and tax credits were considered, by 1980 only one such centre out of the nine that had been originally planned had actually come into existence (the optimistically named 'Centre 1' at East Kilbride in central Scotland, which opened in 1968, but in fact was destined to remain the one and only such centre). Even that operated in a way that meant, as one report put it, 'effectiveness is limited by the inability of staff to communicate directly with the computer, on which taxpayers' records are held'.[13] And even by the early 1980s such a system was already technologically obsolete, since computer technology had by then changed to screens and keyboards instead of punched cards and paper tape. In the 1980s screen and keyboard technology was introduced in the regional tax offices (albeit not without strikes and even litigation over whether civil servants were contractually obliged to use the new technology)[14] and was described by the department as 'a massive project *which will bring large savings in our administrative costs*' [our emphasis] as well as providing a better service to taxpayers.[15] In the mid-1990s the IT systems of the department (along with some 2000 of its staff) were turned over to a private contractor, EDS (Electronic Data Services), in a major and controversial £1.78bn ten-year outsourcing deal, which meant that the department's IT office was to move from its previous role of delivering IT services to 'managing the delivery of IT services' (and slim down radically in the process). The overall move was '*expected to enable the Department to make savings of 15-20 per cent in the costs of IT support*'[16] [our emphasis].

Given this recurrent drum-beat of anticipated cost savings from IT makeovers, as well as the cost savings later anticipated from restructuring the tax bureaucracy, did the results match the expectations? In Section 5.3 we turn to exploring how reported outcomes on tax collection costs compared to these

---

[13] *Report of the Commissioners of Her Majesty's Inland Revenue for the year ended 31st March 1980* (Cm 8160, 1981), p. 22.

[14] *Report of the Commissioners of Her Majesty's Inland Revenue for the year ended 31st December 1983* (Cmnd 9305, 1984), p. 8.

[15] *Report of the Commissioners of Her Majesty's Inland Revenue for the year ended 31st December 1983*, p. 1.

[16] *Report of the Commissioners of Her Majesty's Inland Revenue for the year ended 31st March 1994* (Cm 2665, 1994), p. 81, paras 5.11 and 5.12. See also *Report of the Commissioners of Her Majesty's Inland Revenue for the year ending 31st March 1997* (Cm 3771, 1998), p. 28.

various plans and projects of running cost savings over the period covered by this book, before turning in Section 5.4 to consider how the tax collection costs of English local government changed over the same period.

5.3 Tax Collection Costs: Were Expectations of Big Savings Realized?

Figure 5.1 shows what happened from the mid-1960s to the late 2000s to the reported costs of collecting taxes in the Inland Revenue and Customs & Excise Departments, and following their merger in 2005, the single department, HM Revenue and Customs (HMRC). Whereas we started the analysis of running costs in Chapter 4 by examining absolute levels of costs and then looked at such costs relative to overall spending, in this case we start the analysis the other way round, using the traditional measure of cost-to-yield as an indicator of performance in tax collection. In Figure 5.1 'yield' is defined as net revenues and 'cost' defined as net administration cost.[17] The numbers were reported or obtainable in reasonably consistent form in the successive annual reports of Inland Revenue, Customs & Excise, and HMRC over the period shown in Figure 5.1, though the later HMRC figures were rather more opaque than the numbers provided by the separate tax departments prior to the financial year 2005–06, as we discussed in Chapter 3. The only substantial data break in this series is the point at which the costs and yields of National Insurance contributions began to be included in the overall cost-to-yield figures for the Inland Revenue in 2000.

Figure 5.1 shows that over the whole three decades from the start of the early NPM period in the 1980s to the early 2010s, there was indeed a noticeable overall fall in reported cost-to-yield of the two UK central government revenue departments. That observation suggests at first sight that efficiency in that sense may indeed have improved over this period, in line with the expectation that taking a more disaggregated approach might reveal successes in cost-cutting that would be masked by a whole-of-government approach and that taxation is a domain that lends itself particularly to the sort of cost-cutting that managerialism and IT developments can deliver.

Figure 5.1 also shows how that cost-to-yield performance varied over the thirty-year period. In the early days of NPM, from the early 1980s to the early 1990s, the costs of the Inland Revenue as a percentage of revenue did not show much evidence of a clear downward trend. There was a slight fall in the overall reported costs of collection in the early 1980s, but those numbers

---

[17] Comprising staff costs, including superannuation, plus other administration costs and capital expenditure, less fees and charges.

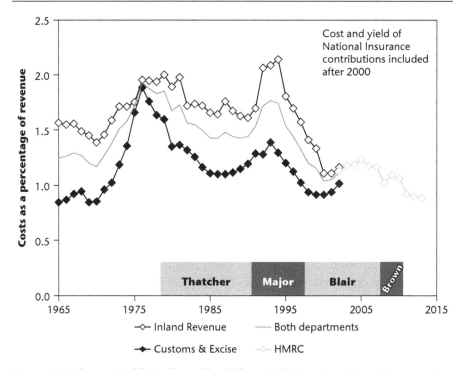

Figure 5.1. Cost-to-Yield for Centrally Collected UK Taxation (Net Administration Costs as a Percentage of Net Revenues) 1965–2013

Sources: Figures 5.1 to 5.3 were derived from successive Inland Revenue, Customs and Excise, and HMRC *Annual Reports*. HMRC costs were departmental expenditure limits (DEL) including allowance for depreciation, adjusted for the transfer of staff to the UK Border Agency (created in 2009 as an executive agency of the Home Office). DEL was used in the analysis as it was consistent with HMRC's published cost/yield figures for 2006 to 2009. After 2009, HMRC reported only unit costs of collection for individual taxes and of payment for individual benefits.

were no lower than they had been in the supposedly less-cost-conscious mid-1970s, and by 1993–94 had risen well above those mid-1970s levels. By contrast, for the Customs & Excise, Figure 5.1 shows a long-term process of cost reduction predating the NPM period and arguably continuing in the early NPM period. That cost reduction was followed by a rise in costs relative to yields in the later 1980s and early 1990s (probably reflecting the economic downturn of that time), followed by a further period of reduction to below 1970s levels (but not to below those of the pre-NPM era of the late 1960s, before VAT was introduced in 1973).

Now there are some very well-known problems about the validity of the cost-to-yield ratio as an indicator of tax administration performance. Factors entirely extraneous to management can have a big effect on such ratios, notably economic prosperity or otherwise that affects the levels of incomes and profits subject to taxation, the rates at which taxes are levied and the level of complexity imposed on the tax bureaucracy by politicians through legislation. For example, cost reductions achieved by new technology or new methods of management might be wiped out by the legislature writing extra complications into the tax code, analogous to the development of more powerful brakes leading motorists to drive closer to the vehicle in front.[18] There might well be a political logic in such a legislative response to cost savings.

We certainly cannot dismiss that possibility. But the problem for analysis is that there is no standard measure of 'legislative complication' that we can use to take account of such legislative change. And just from casual observation, it seems clear that over the period taken here there were changes going in opposite directions in terms of expected impacts on collection costs. For example, changes such as introduction of self-assessment for income tax, abolition of tax offsets, and doubling of VAT rates would be expected to reduce collection costs or increase revenues, while introduction of a variety of tax credit schemes and some new taxes might be expected to have the opposite effect on collection costs. So it is not easy to make even a qualitative assessment of the likely net effect of such changes.

Such problems are well understood and have been long discussed. Indeed in the 1970s, the Inland Revenue considered (but never adopted) alternative performance indicators for tax collection that would be less subject to such shortcomings, such as numbers of tax officials relative to taxpayers, and tax department costs relative to total income subject to tax.[19] And although looking at cost to yield over a thirty-year period ought to wash out the differences that short-term fluctuations in the economic cycle make to such costs, it does not necessarily wash out the effects on cost to yield of changing tax rates or levels of legislative complication.

Accordingly, to put the apparent productivity gains shown in Figure 5.1 in perspective, we need to examine what happened to the reported costs and yields separately over this period. Those numbers are shown respectively in Figures 5.2 and 5.3, in constant 2012–13 prices by dividing nominal values by the GDP deflator series. To aid comparison of costs before and after the formation of HMRC in 2005, in Figures 5.2 and 5.3 we show the total costs and revenues of the former tax departments prior to the merger.

Figure 5.2 shows that (just like the overall administration costs of civil departments discussed in Chapter 4) absolute costs of tax collection rose

---

[18] An example of the so-called 'risk compensation' hypothesis in which some or all of the potential risk reduction effect of safety improvements is consumed instead as performance increases (see for example, John Adams, 'Risk Homeostasis and the Purpose of Safety Legislation', *Ergonomics* 31 (1988): 407–28). It is of course possible that there could be an analogous 'cost compensation' effect, with cost reductions consumed by the legislature as increases in complexity, and indeed such a point was suggested to us by several individuals we interviewed.

[19] *Report of the Commissioners of Her Majesty's Inland Revenue for the year ended 31st March 1978* (Cmnd 7473, 1979), p. 12.

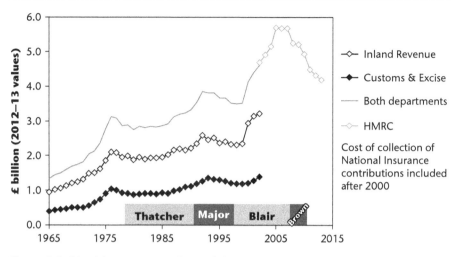

Figure 5.2. Net Administration Costs of the Tax Departments in Real Terms (£ billion 2012–13 values) 1965–2013

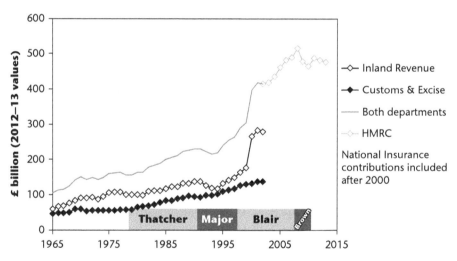

Figure 5.3. Net Revenues of the Tax Departments in Real Terms (£ billion 2012–13 values) 1965–2013

generally in real terms throughout the early NPM period of the 1980s and the start of the middle NPM period in the early 1990s, even though that period was often portrayed by critics of managerial reforms as an era of a particularly harsh 'slash and burn' approach to costs in the bureaucracy. But, also in line with our observations in Chapter 4, Figure 5.2 also shows that the absolute level of those costs began to fall after 1993 under John Major's government, in spite of the frequent stereotyping of that government as less resolute than the 'Iron Lady' Thatcher government it replaced.

Now if we look at Figures 5.2 and 5.3 together, we can see that much of the overall downward slope of the cost-to-yield ratios after 1975–76 in Figure 5.1 was due to revenues rising faster than costs rather than to absolute falls in real costs. Similarly, the sudden drop in direct tax revenue in the early 1990s recession was responsible for a sharp increase in the Inland Revenue's cost-to-yield ratio. What that means is that there is strikingly little evidence of cost reductions—whether relative to revenues or in absolute real-terms costs—by either the Inland Revenue or the Customs & Excise Department in the early NPM period. Both cost-to-yield ratios and absolute costs fell notably in the middle period, from the early 1990s to 2000. But just as with the running costs of all civil departments shown in Figure 4.1 in Chapter 4, the absolute level of costs in the tax departments was still markedly higher in 2000 than it had been in the mid-1980s. And that is in spite of massive investment in IT that, as we showed earlier, was expected and claimed to have the effect of cutting costs and improving efficiency (as well as to enable different sorts of functions to be performed, of course).

Comparing the periods before and after the formation of HMRC in 2005 is complicated by the changing responsibilities of the tax departments (for instance the inclusion of National Insurance contributions costs in 2000, and the creation of the UK Border Agency resulting in transfer of former Customs staff to the Home Office in 2009). We can be reasonably sure that costs continued to rise steeply in the first years after the merger and began to fall after 2008 (revenues levelled off at the same time, due to the economic downturn). The final years shown in Figure 5.2 may provide some support to the various strong claims that we noted earlier to the effect that the merger of the two formerly separate tax departments into HMRC would substantially cut the costs of tax collection, but as with the administration costs discussed in Chapter 4, reclassifications and far from transparent reporting conventions make it difficult to compare that most recent period with earlier years.

5.4 Other Studies of Tax and Welfare Performance

The picture shown here is broadly compatible with productivity studies of UK tax collection and welfare payments conducted by Patrick Dunleavy, Leandro Carrera, and their colleagues, albeit over a different period and using different methodology. On the welfare side, Dunleavy and Carrera calculated total factor productivity for delivering the UK's main welfare benefits since the late 1980s by dividing total weighted outputs by all factor inputs.[20] Their results suggested that the productivity of the welfare-payment system fell rather than increased in the period up to 1992–93, then rose over the rest of John Major's premiership, fell during the first six years of Tony Blair's New Labour government, and thereafter rose modestly, but still remained below the 1988 numbers. The overall picture they present is that 'across two decades of rapid technological progress, the delivery of welfare benefits got no more efficient', whereas (as we suggested earlier) it might have been thought that welfare payments would be a field particularly ripe for cost-cutting through the application of managerial methods linked to IT developments.

Leandro Carrera, Patrick Dunleavy, and Simon Bastow applied a similar method to UK tax productivity for the years 1997–98 to 2007–08, in this case focusing on labour productivity.[21] Over that decade, they found a trendless pattern over the first three years, a downward productivity trend over the four years from 2000–01 to 2004–05, and a sharp increase in productivity over the final three years 2004–05 to 2007–08. That analysis suggests that some productivity increases took place in tax administration, but in contrast to their study of UK welfare benefits, did not cover the period back to the 1980s when NPM was often said to be single-mindedly focused on cutting costs.

Putting such evidence together with our running-costs based analysis, the early NPM-era picture seems to show little sign of major cost reductions in tax collection. Absolute costs for tax collection follow a broadly similar track to the running costs of the civil departments as a whole shown in Chapter 4 over the period taken here, suggesting that tax administration was not in fact more tractable to the cost-cutting potential of managerialism than other policy domains. It is true that there was a dramatic fall in cost-to-yield ratios from the early 1990s to 2000, which brought the cost-to-yield ratio for Customs and Excise roughly back to the level it had been in the pre-VAT era of the late 1960s, and left the corresponding ratio for the Inland Revenue rather lower than it had been in the pre-NPM era. But how much credit for those changes should be attributed to management depends on how much of the fall in the cost-to-yield ratios over the final seven years shown in Figure 5.1 is attributable to overall economic buoyancy, as discussed earlier. It also depends on how much is attributable to

---

[20] Carrera and Dunleavy used data from the Department of Work and Pensions from 1998 to 2008 and matched that with public data about caseloads for the period going back to 1988; see Patrick Dunleavy and Leandro Carrera, *Growing The Productivity Of Government Services* (London: Edward Elgar, 2013) and 'Government productivity in UK social security has not grown across two decades', *British Politics and Policy Blog* (2011) <http://blogs.lse.ac.uk/politicsandpolicy/government-productivity-in-uk-social-security-has-not-grown/> (accessed October 2014).
[21] Leandro Carrera, Patrick Dunleavy, and Simon Bastow, *Understanding productivity trends in UK tax collection*, LSE Public Policy Group Working Paper (London: LSE PPG, 2009).

policy changes affecting collection costs, such as the shift from bureaucratic assessment to self-assessment of income tax in 1996.

5.5 How Central Government Tax Collection Compared with Local Government Tax Collection

Even though taxes collected at subnational level in the UK were only about 12 per cent of the total UK tax revenue during the period covered by this book, a remarkably low proportion compared with many other advanced democracies,[22] not all taxes were collected at the central level. At the start of the period covered by our study, the main local tax was a tax on real estate owned by individuals or organizations within each municipality. Local authorities set the rate of taxation (subject to often stringent constraints imposed by central government) and collected the tax. But central government produced periodic valuations of all properties in the country (in the form of an estimate of the rental value of each property), which constituted the tax base.

Towards the middle of the period covered by this book, a historic change was made to this system. Legislation introduced by Margaret Thatcher's Conservative government in 1989 for Scotland and in 1990 for England and Wales replaced domestic rates in England, Scotland, and Wales (not Northern Ireland) with a poll tax or 'Community Charge', levied on individuals rather than on real estate,[23] and replaced local authority discretion in setting business rates with a uniform, centrally set business rate. The poll tax, a political initiative apparently intended to create more winners than losers, led to widespread protests and became so politically unpopular that in 1990 it led to the ousting of Margaret Thatcher as leader of the Conservative Party. After that, in 1993, it was replaced throughout Great Britain by another property-based tax, called Council Tax, which differed from the older rates system in that it was based on capital values of real estate (which was grouped into a series of bands) rather than estimated rental values.

But the centralized system of business rates introduced by the Thatcher government remained, not just in centralized rate-setting but also in the pooling of the revenue from such rates for redistribution from the centre, both of which were still in operation at the time of writing. And apart from the short and politically unhappy life of the poll tax, the basic administrative structure for local tax collection consisted of central government assessing

---

[22] OECD, *Government at a Glance 2013* (Paris: OECD Publishing, 2009), Table 3.17.
[23] See David Butler, Andrew Adonis, and Tony Travers, *Failure in British Government: The Politics of the Poll Tax* (Oxford: Oxford University Press, 1994).

property values[24] and local government carrying out billing and collection, plus the administration of a complex system of reliefs.

Curiously, there seemed to be no practice or tradition of comparing costs of tax collection between the two levels of government, and they almost seem to have operated in parallel universes. Parliamentary committees, think tanks, and other overseers did not appear to apply or press for such comparative benchmarking, and indeed the two levels of government tended to use quite different performance metrics to assess their operations. Cost-to-yield was the dominant performance measure used for the central government departments, while 'rates of local tax collection' (the amount of tax collected as a percentage of that owed) was the dominant one for local authorities. There may have been a plausible logic behind this difference in performance metrics, since, as one of our interviewees pointed out, the total potential tax take can be estimated much more accurately for a property-based tax than, for instance, can the potential yield of income tax be estimated across the national economy.

Even so, a comparison of what happened to costs of tax collection at central and local level is instructive, because there was no real equivalent of central government's 'great leap forward' massive IT projects at the local level: each local authority managed its own revenue collection system (our interviewees indicated that there was a wide variety of different in-house and contracted-out arrangements for revenue collection). So a comparison of the two can in principle tell us something about the cost payoffs of centralized management and big IT systems for tax collection.[25]

Accordingly, we explore here what happened to the reported costs of local tax collection in England over the three decades covered by this study. In the years before the introduction of the poll tax in England, local tax collection costs were reported in local government financial statistics simply as 'cost of rate collection', putting together domestic and business rate collection, in a table alongside 'General Administration'. When the poll tax was introduced in the early 1990s, the cost reporting categories split into 'Community Charge preparation', 'Cost of non-domestic rates collection', 'Community Charge collection', 'Council Tax preparation', and the administration costs of various reduction schemes. After the replacement of the poll tax by Council Tax, as noted above, the reporting categories changed further, eventually (by 2012–13) including: 'Council Tax collection', 'Council Tax discounts for

---

[24] At the time of writing no general revaluation had been carried out on the housing stock in England or Scotland since 1993 (governments kept postponing it because of the political unpopularity such a revaluation was expected to bring about), though such a revaluation was carried out in Wales in 2005.

[25] See David Collingridge, *The Management of Scale: Big Organizations, Big Decisions, Big Mistakes* (London: Routledge, 1992).

prompt payment', 'Council Tax discounts locally funded', 'Council Tax benefits administration', and 'Non-domestic rates collection'.

It is not easy to decide exactly which of the various categories of reported costs used at the end of this period should be used to compare either with the costs of collecting local rates before 1990, or with the costs of collecting central government taxes shown earlier in this chapter. And one substantial cost did not appear in local government accounts at all over this period, namely the cost of local property valuations, which were carried out by a central government body, the Valuation Office Agency (earlier part of the Inland Revenue department) and paid directly by central government.

In contrast to the practice of the central tax departments, we found no overall assessment of the total cost of collecting local taxes, so our analysis reflects several judgement calls and best estimates. This applies particularly to the issue of whether to use net or gross costs. Prior to 1990, the net and gross costs of collecting local rates were similar, and so no issues arose. However, a substantial income was recorded after the introduction of the Community Charge in 1990, causing the net and gross costs to diverge.[26] For non-domestic rates (NDR), the income was a grant from central government which covered almost the entire cost of collection, which means that gross costs should be used to assess the cost of collection in that case. For Council Tax collection, however, we were unable to pin down the precise source of the associated income from documentary or interview sources. The gross costs reflect the 'total cost of collection' in one sense—but there is an argument for allowing associated income (apart from government grants) to offset part of that cost, which would mean that net costs would be more appropriate. In the absence of more exact information, we show the gross costs of collection as the 'cost of local tax collection' in Figures 5.4 and 5.5, with dotted lines showing the effect of using net costs of Council Tax (and Community Charge) collection.

A second question is which other costs should be counted as 'costs of local tax collection'. In particular, should the costs of Council Tax benefit administration (CTBA) and the work of the Valuation Office Agency be included?

Council Tax benefit was a nationwide system involving payments to households whose combined income, savings, and investments were below

---

[26] In financial year 2012–13, for instance, over a third of the cost of Council Tax collection and almost all of the cost of collecting non-domestic rates (NDR) were offset by income. Council Tax income was approximately equally split between 'Sales, Fees and Charges' and 'Other Income'. Council Tax income was not a grant from central government, nor did it appear to be transfers between different types of local authorities (for instance, county councils did not directly 'pay' district councils to collect tax on their behalf—county councils reported essentially no expenditure on any aspect of local tax collection). Source: *Local authority revenue expenditure and financing England: 2012 to 2013*, Table RO6 <https://www.gov.uk/government/publications/local-authority-revenue-expenditure-and-financing england-2012-to-2013-individual-local-authority-data-outturn>.

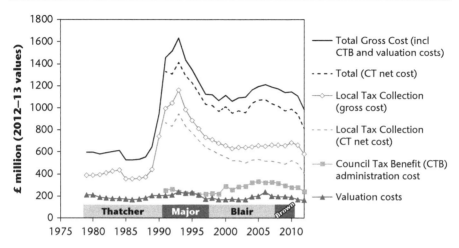

Figure 5.4. English Local Authorities' Total Tax Collection Costs in Real Terms (£ billion 2012–13 values) 1979–2012

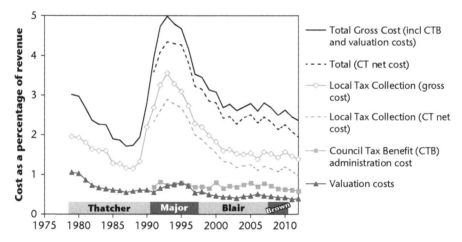

Figure 5.5. Estimated Cost-to-Yield of English Local Government Taxes 1979–2012 (CT = Council Tax)

Sources: Data for figures 5.4 and 5.5 are from annual editions of *Local Government Finance Statistics*, apart from the costs of valuations, which are from Inland Revenue and (from 1992) Valuation Office Agency Annual Reports. The effect on the calculations of using Council Tax (CT) net (rather than gross) costs are shown for reasons described in the text. Real-terms values were calculated by dividing nominal values by the 2012–13 GDP deflator series.

a certain level (replaced in 2013 by a devolved system of locally determined relief administration). Administering this benefit could certainly be argued to be a 'cost of the tax' in a general sense, in so far as it was part of the redistributive machinery associated with that tax. The Inland Revenue included the costs of administering Tax Credits in the calculation of overall cost-to-yield since their introduction in 1999–2000, and so the comparison with central government would favour including CTBA in the costs. On the other hand, CTBA was not reported as part of local tax collection costs until 2005 (being listed under social security administration costs), and had no exact counterpart in the pre-1990 domestic rates system.

As already mentioned, the costs associated with valuing the properties forming the tax base for Council Tax and non-domestic rates were met by central government, an arrangement dating back to 1950 when the Valuation Office took on this task. Those activities certainly formed part of the machinery for assessing local taxes, and therefore their inclusion in the total costs can be justified for comparing tax costs between local and central government. However, if our interest is in comparing the outcomes of the different approaches of local and central government, we could also argue that valuation costs were not the responsibility of local authorities, and therefore should not be included in our comparison, particularly when comparing change over time.

We therefore present the separate costs in disaggregated form in Figures 5.4 and 5.5, so that the effect of each can be determined. We also show the total of these costs, in effect the 'worst case' if all relevant costs are included. It is clear that the choice of which costs to include makes a substantial difference to the overall costs of local tax collection, and also to any comparison of pre- and post-1990 local tax arrangements.

Now if we compare the pattern of cost change shown in Figure 5.4 with the equivalent cost pattern for the central government tax departments shown earlier in Figure 5.2, there is a marked contrast between the two (regardless of the local tax costs metric that we choose). Whereas the central government tax collection costs showed a long-term increase in constant-price terms, broadly in a peak-and-rising plateau pattern, the corresponding local collection cost pattern is one of a previously fairly flat profile followed by a massive peak in the early 1990s (reflecting the costs of introducing first the poll tax in a context of massive resistance from poll tax protesters, and then quickly replacing it with the Council Tax), but then subsiding to a lower and relatively constant level. How much higher costs rose over the period as a whole depends, as Figure 5.4 shows, on which costs are included in the calculation. If CTBA and valuation costs are included, local tax collection costs markedly increased in the period since the 1980s. Even so, there was nothing comparable to the steep rise in central government tax collection costs in the early 2000s, since local government tax costs were relatively stable in real terms from about 2000 to 2012. So this comparison does not clearly show a big cost–saving payoff from all those major IT projects at central government level as compared with what happened at local government level.

As noted earlier, cost-to-yield ratios were not routinely reported for local government taxes at any point in the thirty-year period covered by this book (in sharp contrast to their salience at central government level). Data breaks associated with shifts from one tax regime to another introduce further complications and even reported revenue amounts vary from source to source, so any comparison can only be approximate and must depend heavily on judgement. But with those caveats, Figure 5.5 presents the cost-to-yield of local government taxes over the period, showing the same costs as Figure 5.4, each relative to total local tax revenue.

The overall cost-to-yield of local taxes is of course dominated by the one-off costs of replacing domestic rates with the poll tax in the early 1990s and shortly after that replacing the poll tax with Council Tax. In the early 1980s, the cost-to-yield of collecting the rates (domestic plus non-domestic) was somewhat under 2 per cent (ignoring costs of valuations), which is higher than the equivalent cost of collecting Customs & Excise taxes at that time, and about the same as the cost-to-yield of the Inland Revenue taxes. During the 1980s, as Figures 5.1 and 5.5 indicate, cost-to-yield fell both at central and local government level. And if we compare local and central taxes in the 2000s (after the massive disruption caused by the life and death of the poll tax), we find that costs were averaging about 1 per cent of revenue for central taxes and about 1.5 per cent for local taxes—but, as we have noted above, other costs were also involved for local taxes. If either (or both) of valuation costs or CTBA are included, local government taxes looked substantially more expensive to administer than central government taxation in the later years of this study.[27] On the other hand, the revenue from local government taxes rose much less steeply than central government taxes over most of this period, falling from about 15 to about 10 per cent of total tax revenues, relatively reducing the yield component of the cost-to-yield ratio for local taxation.

So overall, apart from the 1990s, when various major policy decisions affected both central and local government tax collection costs, there were no dramatic differences between central and local level. We might reasonably conclude that the decentralized system for collecting non-domestic rates and Council Tax by local authorities worked more or less as well as the centralized and arguably more IT-intensive central government tax collection system.

Of course these conclusions need to be qualified at least two ways. First, there may be other costs met by central government which should added to

---

[27] Council Tax benefit administration appears to have been a particularly expensive scheme to run. Administration costs were very high in the first few years, and continued to run at 8 to 10 per cent of the benefits distributed in most subsequent years (albeit falling somewhat in recent years), compared with, for instance, the costs of 1.55 pence per pound distributed in Tax Credits and 0.58 pence per pound distributed in Child Benefit in 2011–12 (HM Revenue & Customs *Annual Report and Accounts 2011–12* (HC 38, 2012–13), p. 11).

local tax collection costs. For instance, the enforcement activities carried out by the Department for Work and Pensions (and its predecessors) over centrally administered housing benefits were said by one of our interviewees to play a significant part in picking up local tax fraud as well, particularly since the introduction of Council Tax in 1993. However, the 'worth' of this activity to local government tax collection is hard to estimate.

Second, the taxes collected at central and local level were simply different, and we cannot exclude the possibility that one is somehow inherently more costly to collect than the other. Some local government officials who we interviewed suggested that local government taxes were probably less complex than central taxes to collect, although they also told us that internal benchmarking procedures showed a wide range of cost collection performance among different local authorities. In addition, there were substantial variations in the cost-to-yield ratios of different taxes at both central and local level. For local government, costs of non-domestic rates were only 0.5 per cent of revenue while Council Tax cost between 1.7 and 2 per cent since the mid-2000s. Some centrally collected taxes were relatively cheap to collect. In 2008–09, National Insurance contributions (NIC) cost 0.4 per cent, VAT cost 0.6 per cent, and some excise duties cost below 0.1 per cent of revenue. Income tax was made up of two taxes with very different cost profiles: Pay As You Earn (PAYE) income tax cost about 0.7 per cent in 2008–09 and self-assessed income tax cost almost 4.5 per cent.[28] So our comparators should arguably be particular taxes rather than the whole tax base, suggesting that the productivity measure applied by Carrera and Dunleavy, with weightings attached to each item, might be a more meaningful basis of comparison. But against that, the overall cost-to-yield ratios in central government were dominated by the taxes with the greatest volume, which in the late 2000s comprised income tax, NIC, and VAT together making up almost three-quarters of centrally collected revenue, and that would seem to be a fair comparison with local property taxes.

5.6 Conclusion

Table 5.1 offers a summary scorecard similar to the one we presented at the end of Chapter 4, showing what happened to tax collection costs both over the whole thirty years covered by this book and within particular sub-periods. As the table shows, the analysis of this chapter provides at best only partial support for the idea that cost-cutting effects of NPM changes might be particularly

---

[28] Data for 2008–09 from HM Revenue & Customs *Departmental Autumn Performance Report 2009* (Cm 7774, 2009), p. 32. Subsequent editions did not report PAYE and self-assessment ratios separately.

Table 5.1. An Overall Assessment: What Happened to Central Tax Collection Costs Compared to Central Government as a Whole?

	'Early NPM' 1980–81 to 1990–91	'Middle NPM' 1990–91 to 2000–01	'Late or post-NPM' 2000–01 to 2009–10	Whole period 1980–81 to 2009–10
Percentage Change in Real Terms Costs (2012–13 values, GDP deflator)				
Tax collection costs	25	25	−5	48
Civil department net administration costs	19	17	7	50
Difference (percentage points)	6	8	−12	−2
Percentage Change in Real Terms Costs (2012–13 values)				
Tax department staff costs	12	8	−4	15
Civil service staff costs	2	−7	11	10
Difference (percentage points)	10	13	−15	5
Percentage Change in Cost /TME or (for tax collection costs) Cost/Yield				
Tax collection cost/yield	−11	−31	−14	−48
Civil departments net administration costs /TME	9	−3	−28	−30
Difference (percentage points)	−20	−28	14	−18
Percentage Change in Staff Numbers				
Tax department staff	−8	−5	−18	−28
Civil service staff	−20	−16	1	−32
Difference (percentage points)	12	11	−19	4

Cells showing differences between tax departments and the whole of central government administration costs (from Table 4.1) are shaded according to the following key: Dark grey: tax departments are over 5 percentage points 'worse' (in terms of cost-cutting) than central government as a whole; Light grey: tax departments are about the same as central government; Unshaded: tax departments are over 5 percentage points 'better' (in terms of cost-cutting) than central government as a whole.

apparent in areas of government activity that seem most susceptible to 'bottom-line' management and the transformative effects of bold IT initiatives. Reported cost-to-yield in tax collection certainly fell markedly over the period considered here, and indeed as the final column in Table 5.1 shows, the fall in the cost-to-yield ratio for the revenue departments was greater than the fall in civil department net administration costs/TME over the whole period.

On the other hand, absolute administrative costs of tax collection in constant-price terms rose by a very similar percentage to that of all civil departments over the same period, and much the same picture applies to staff costs and numbers. Moreover, the fact that (aside from the massive disruption and huge cost spike occasioned by the poll tax debacle of the early 1990s) the decentralized local government tax collection system with far less emphasis on great-leap-forward IT developments seems to have produced fairly similar cost-to-yield outcomes, suggests that centralization and massive IT projects may not have been an automatic route to cost-cutting.

So we have to conclude that there is some, but only some, evidence from the data considered here for the hypothesis that tax collection organization presents a particular success story in cost reduction that is masked by the government-wide numbers we presented in the previous chapters. As with Chapter 4, whether that hypothesis is accepted or rejected turns largely on whether the primary emphasis is placed on the absolute level of costs (in constant price terms) or on costs relative to revenue or total expenditure. To probe further into the issue of whether the cost performance we reported for UK central government in Chapter 4 was distinctive or out of line with what can be observed elsewhere, we look further outside 'Whitehall' in Chapter 7 to see whether there are marked differences between UK central departments and other administrative units. But before turning to that issue, Chapter 6 explores the other side of the 'performance equation', examining indicators of whether government 'worked better' in terms of perceived consistency and fairness over three decades.

6

Consistency and Fairness in Administration

Formal Complaints and Legal Challenges

> . . . the better the situation of the French became, the more
> unbearable they found it . . .[1]

6.1 Grappling with Administrative Quality

As was discussed in the first chapter, managerial reforms in government and IT developments over the period covered by this book were frequently justified as a way of making the public services more customer-focused, business-like, and effective. But as we have already noticed, the many critics of those developments typically claimed that important aspects of administrative quality, specifically the 'rule-of-law' focus often associated with Max Weber's analysis of bureaucracy—careful framing and application of rules, consistency, and fairness in case-handling and fitting cases into categories—would tend to suffer as a result of more emphasis on efficiency and cost-cutting. Who was correct? This chapter turns to examining that question.

Chapters 4 and 5 showed how slippery the apparently common-sense notion of administrative or running 'cost' is in government, and how much effort consequently has to go into reconstructing consistent numbers for such costs over three decades. When it comes to indicators of administrative quality in terms of consistency, fairness, and careful attention to framing and applying rules, the problem is compounded further. Quite apart from the sort of data continuity issues we discussed in Chapter 3, evaluating what happened

---

[1] Alexis de Tocqueville, *The Ancient Regime and the French Revolution*, trans. Arthur Goldhammer, edited by Jon Elster (Cambridge: Cambridge University Press, [1856] 2011), pp. 156–7.

to administrative quality in government and public services is more theoretically and methodologically challenging, for at least five reasons.

One is that while 'cost' is in principle a generic concept that can be applied across government and public services, the indicators of performance used in many evaluation studies (such as waiting times for medical care or levels of achievement on school test scores) are typically service-specific, precluding comparisons across policy domains, and not directly focused on the 'Weberian' aspects of bureaucratic quality that interest us here. Another is that while cost is in principle a concept not susceptible to obsolescence and therefore just as applicable to the 2010s as it was to the 1910s or the 1810s, the specifics of what government did and how it worked in many fields changed radically over the three decades taken here. Those changes reflect social and technological change, some of which has been discussed in the previous chapters, and that can make once-standard indicators obsolete. For example, how can we meaningfully compare the letter or telephone response times that were central to many kinds of government work thirty years or so ago with today's era of email, texts, interactive websites, smartphone apps, and the like?

A third challenge is to identify indicators that directly reflect what government does and how it conducts itself according to the 'Weberian' qualities we are interested in here, rather than broader social trends for which government may or may not be responsible. After all, some indicators of performance that are often stressed in the literature on development and which may well be salutary in focusing government's attention on things that really matter, such as mortality rates, tend to be rather indirectly related to government performance. They may reflect changes in social behaviour or the broader environment (such as changes in diet or decisions to quit smoking made decades ago) for which government responsibility can be at best tenuous. If obesity rates go up or down, is that because whatever government does has made us fatter or thinner, or does it stem from broader social trends over which government has relatively little control? Opinions on that will differ according to our worldview, including our assessment of how much social engineering government ought to do and how effective its efforts at such social engineering can be. The famous US political scientist Robert Putnam strongly dismissed the use of such outcomes as a measure of government performance. His argument was that that focusing on items such as changes in health or longevity rather than intermediate outputs such as treatment episodes or numbers of cases handled runs into severe causal attribution problems, since government may have little power to affect such outcomes:

> To include social outcomes in an assessment of government performance is to commit the 'Massachusetts Miracle Fallacy': only a modest part of the praise for

the affluence of New England in the 1980s (and a similarly modest portion of the blame for the subsequent recession) was realistically attributable to state government, despite 1988 presidential campaign rhetoric to the contrary.[2]

Putnam is here focusing on the use of social outcome indicators for credit-claiming and blame attribution, and perhaps underestimates the beneficial effect that such indicators may have on keeping politicians and bureaucrats focused on devising effective policies for shaping such outcomes; but in any case such indicators do not help us to focus on the rule-of-law aspect of bureaucracy that is of central interest here.

Fourth, the validity of many possible performance indicators is hotly contested, and often raises issues about gaming and fiddling of performance numbers by managers or officials to make them fit better with the political demands of the day. Such behaviour is arguably characteristic of all bureaucracies to some extent. It was much discussed in the days of the Soviet Union, whose centrally planned economy incentivized managers of the state-owned companies to find creative ways of meeting their production targets (for example by making goods heavier than they needed to be when such targets were set in tons),[3] and similar issues were commonly raised during the heyday of the 'targets' regime of Tony Blair's New Labour government in the early 2000s.[4] Opinions about the extent of such gaming and fiddling differ too: like the extent of the informal or black economy, such behaviour will obviously be exaggerated by opponents of the relevant programmes or governments and played down by their supporters, and its extent is hard to assess objectively by evaluators and researchers.[5] But clearly we need to be cautious about putting too much weight on indicators of performance which governments have both political motive and bureaucratic opportunity to shape in their favour.

Fifth, some issues relating to quality of government and public services that are undeniably important do not readily lend themselves to even approximate

---

[2] Robert Putnam, *Making Democracy Work: Civic Traditions in Modern Italy* (Princeton: Princeton University Press, 1994). See also Richard Boyle, *Measuring Public Sector Productivity: Lessons from International Experience* (Dublin: Institute of Public Administration, 2005), p. 5.

[3] Maurice Dobb, in *Socialist Planning: Some Problems* (London: Lawrence & Wishart, 1970), p. 34, cites examples from *Pravda* in 1968 of roofing iron, yarn, paper, and glass all being thicker than necessary because of plan-targets based on weight. A contemporary cartoon shows a factory meeting its tonnage target by producing a single giant nail <https://i.imgur.com/zL6ntxH.jpg>.

[4] R. Gwyn Bevan and Christopher Hood, 'What's Measured is What Matters: Targets and Gaming in Healthcare in England', *Public Administration* 84, no. 3 (2006): pp. 517–38; Christopher Hood, 'Gaming in Targetworld', *Public Administration Review* 66, no. 4 (2006): pp. 515–20; Christopher Hood and Ruth Dixon, 'The Political Payoff from Performance Target Systems: No-Brainer or No-Gainer?', *Journal of Public Administration Research and Theory* 20 (Suppl 2) (2010): i281–i298.

[5] See Steve Kelman and John Freidman, 'Performance Improvement and Performance Dysfunction: An Empirical Examination of Impacts of the Emergency Room Wait-Time Target in the English National Health Service', *Journal of Public Administration Research and Theory* 19, no. 4 (2009): pp. 917–46.

measurement. For example, there were numerous and well-publicized inci-
dents of serious public service failures in the UK over the period taken here
(including scandals over child and elder abuse; standards in some schools,
hospitals, and care homes so low as to amount to human rights abuse; racism
and abuse of power by police).[6] Such failures certainly do touch on important
rule-of-law issues, but the problem is that we do not have a satisfactory metric
to directly assess the overall level of such shortcomings or accurately track
changes over time so that we could say that the incidence of such failures
rose, fell, or stayed about the same as in other time periods.

In the light of those issues, and to focus on the rule-of-law aspect of government that academic critics of 'New Public Management' reforms have often
claimed to have been sacrificed to cost-cutting considerations, we look primarily here at the incidence of formal complaints (to ombudsmen and other
official complaint-handling bodies) and legal challenges to government in
the form of applications for judicial review. Such indicators have at least five
advantages for our analytic purpose here. First, they are generic rather than
policy-domain specific. Second, they are relatively technology-free. Third,
they relate directly to how government conducts itself, rather than to changes
in society for which government may or may not be responsible. Fourth, they
can be traced in a reasonably consistent and measurable form over three decades and are not readily 'gameable' because they are not directly controlled
by civil servants, ministers, managers, or service providers whose jobs, career
prospects, or chances of re-election may depend on what the numbers say.
Fifth and most important, they relate more directly to the rule-of-law aspect
of administration that we mentioned earlier than any other available indicators, including survey indicators such as the 'satisfaction with government'
series that we discussed in Chapter 2, expressions of 'trust' in particular professions or institutions, or alternative possible measures of satisfaction with
government such as 'voting with your feet' by emigration or immigration.
Certainly, cases in which large numbers of people flee their countries as a
result of government oppression or economic mismanagement are not far
to seek in this or any other age. But since people emigrate for many reasons,
of which unhappiness with government is only one, and published figures
do not allow us to take account of that, they are not a sufficiently direct test
of the rule-of-law qualities of government for our purposes here (and indeed
seem most appropriate only for extreme cases of government failure, such as
dramatic economic collapse, civil war, or genocide).[7]

---

[6] See for example Anthony King and Ivor Crewe, *Blunders of Our Governments* (London:
Oneworld Publications, 2013).

[7] For the record, the Office of National Statistics Long-Term International Migration data (based
on data from the International Passenger Survey) indicated that between 100,000 and 200,000
British citizens emigrated each year from 1980 to 2012 with no upward or downward trend over

It is of course true that indicators of formal complaints and judicial review applications will tend to be biased toward the negative (focusing on a small minority who register active dissatisfaction with what government does rather than the majority that does not) and 'negativity bias' is a much-discussed phenomenon in politics, media, and human affairs more generally.[8] We will take that 'negativity bias' issue into account when we assess these indicators later, but several countervailing considerations need to be kept in mind. First, as with our exploration of what government cost in Chapters 4 and 5, we apply the 'consilience' method of looking across a range of indicators (complaints as well as litigation, outcomes as well as numbers lodged) rather than focusing on one alone.

Second, it is the direction of travel rather than the absolute level of complaints and litigation that is at issue here. The observation that such indicators reflect negativity bias would not of itself lead us to expect anything other than a consistent level of negativity, if that is considered to be a constant in human affairs. But if we see a marked *change* (up or down) in complaints and litigation lodged or upheld, that cannot itself be explained by inherent negativity bias.

Third, in contrast to, say, expressing satisfaction or otherwise with government performance in an opinion poll, which typically involves an anonymous encounter and takes only a few minutes, these indicators reflect considerable cost to and commitment by those involved. Complainants at least have to track down the relevant outlet for their expressions of dissatisfaction, they are identified rather than able to remain anonymous, and have to put effort into framing a relatively plausible and coherent complaint. When it comes to judicial challenges to government actions, complainants additionally have to accept exposure to the full rigour of proceedings open to the public and the media, plus (in an adversarial justice system, at least) hostile cross-examination by high-powered lawyers aiming to find the slightest chink of inconsistency or factual incorrectness in their accounts and all the other stressful features of formal courtroom proceedings.

---

time. Corresponding immigration statistics reflected a sharp increase of non-British citizens migrating to the UK over that period, particularly since the mid-1990s (although there was no overall trend in the incidence of return by British citizens). But we do not know whether or how far perception of government or public service performance figured in the migration decisions of those individuals.

[8] See for example Christopher Hood, *The Blame Game* (Princeton: Princeton University Press, 2011), pp. 9–14; Howard Bloom and Douglas Price, 'Voter Response to Short-Run Economic Conditions: The Asymmetric Effect of Prosperity and Recession', *American Political Science Review* 69 (1975): pp. 1240–54; R. Kent Weaver, 'The Politics of Blame Avoidance', *Journal of Public Policy* 6, no. 4 (1986): pp. 371–98; R. Kent Weaver, *Automatic Government: The Politics of Indexation* (Washington, DC: Brookings Institution Press, 1988); Stuart Soroka, 'Good News and Bad News: Asymmetric Responses to Economic Information', *The Journal of Politics* 68, no. 2 (2006): pp. 372–85.

So what happened over the thirty years considered here to the incidence of complaints and judicial challenges (lodged and upheld) against UK central government, as a proxy for perceptions of its 'rule-of-law' performance? Sections 6.2 and 6.3 delve into those issues, and, as with Chapters 4 and 5, the final section reflects on the general pattern and provides an overall assessment.

6.2 Formal Complaints to Ombudsmen and Other Complaint-Handling Bodies

Starting with the incidence of complaints to ombudsmen or similar high-level complaints-handling bodies, the two ombudsmen bodies which dated sufficiently far back to include all three decades covered by this study were the Parliamentary Commissioner for Administration (the 'Parliamentary Ombudsman') and the Health Service Commissioner (HSC). The Parliamentary Ombudsman might be considered to be the 'senior' ombudsman, both in the sense of having been established in 1967 as the first of many subsequent ombudsmen type bodies (it was copied in modified form from a Swedish institution originally established in the early nineteenth century) and because it was empowered to accept complaints about any public body or government department named as within its jurisdiction even if that body also fell under the responsibility of another ombudsman.

Six years after the creation of the Parliamentary Ombudsman in 1967, another UK-level ombudsman, the Health Service Commissioner, was created for the National Health Service in 1973. Since then, up to the time of writing both offices were held by the same person (now known as the Parliamentary and Health Service Ombudsman [PHSO]) and latterly combined their reports into a single document. After that, numerous other ombudsmen or complaint-handling bodies were created—for example, for local government in 1974, for taxation and for the devolved administrations in the 1990s—and some of those subsequent changes, particularly after devolution to Scotland and Wales in 1999, affected the jurisdiction of the PHSO. Figure 6.1 shows the incidence of complaints over the three decades covered by this book to those two 'original' ombudsmen. In the case of the Parliamentary Ombudsman, the three main topics of complaint throughout the period concerned tax, welfare, and employment benefits—all issues that tap directly into the perceived fairness and consistency with which government bodies framed and applied rules and handled cases. In Chapter 7 we will come back to what happened to the level of complaints to ombudsmen for English local government and for Scottish devolved government.

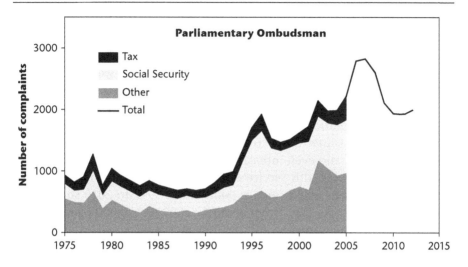

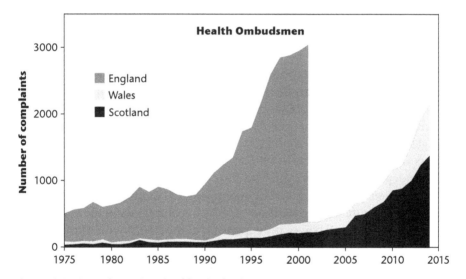

Figure 6.1. Complaints Received by Ombudsmen 1975–2014

Sources: Annual reports of the Parliamentary Ombudsman, the Health Service Commissioner, the Scottish and Welsh Public Service Ombudsmen and a personal communication from the office of the Parliamentary Ombudsman.

As the breaks in Figure 6.1 indicate, neither of those ombudsmen reported wholly comparable data over our whole time period. In the case of the Parliamentary Ombudsman's Office, a series of data breaks in the early 2000s (discussed in Chapter 3) reflected a major shake-up in the way the organization conceived of and handled complaints.

The Health Service Commissioner (HSC) also changed how complaints were reported. Before 2002, as Figure 6.1 shows, the numbers of complaints were rising steeply, having more than tripled since 1990. Even though we cannot trace the overall number of complaints after 2002, we can show the levels of health complaints in Scotland and Wales on a consistent basis over the whole period, because those complaints were recorded separately before as well as after devolution. As was the case for England, Scottish and Welsh health complaints started to increase steeply after 1990 and that rate of increase continued, and even intensified, for Scotland and Wales after 2002. Further, the National Health Service's record of written complaints received by England and Wales health service bodies from 1997 to 2010 showed an increase of about 20 per cent (from about 120,000 to 150,000 complaints a year). That observation provides another indicator of increased levels of complaint, even though the percentage increase was far less than the three-fold increase in complaints received by the Health Service Commissioner from 1990 to 2003.

Now it is certainly true that some of this rise in the incidence of complaints can plausibly be put down to an expansion of the remit of the HSC over the three decades covered by this book. The office was originally created in 1973 to handle complaints about hospital and community health services, but after 1996 the HSC's jurisdiction was extended to cover complaints about general practitioners and about matters of clinical judgement,[9] and the latter came to account for the vast majority of all complaints.[10] But there were changes in the opposite direction too, for example in the form of a three-stage process in operation between 1996 and 2008 which involved locally convened independent review panels to hear cases after local resolution procedures had been exhausted, before the complainant could approach the HSC.[11] Moreover, as Figure 6.1 shows, the steep rise in complaints to the HSC began in the early 1990s, well before the expansion of the HSC's remit in the second half of that decade, so that expansion cannot plausibly account for the whole increase. We can therefore reasonably conclude that complaints to the HSC (and equivalents in Scotland and Wales) started to increase in the 1990s and continued to increase up to the end of the period covered by this book.

---

[9] Health Service Commissioner, *Annual report for 1996–97* (HC 41, 1997–98).

[10] Mary Seneviratne, in *Ombudsmen: Public Services and Administrative Justice* (London: Butterworths, 2002), p. 168, reported that by 2000, 80 per cent of complaints were at least partly concerned with clinical judgement, and the PHSO report *Listening and Learning: The Ombudsman's review of complaint handling by the NHS in England 2011–12* (HC 695, 2010–12), p. 40, gave a figure of 98 per cent in 2011–12.

[11] Another oversight body, then called the Healthcare Commission, took over the administration of these independent local reviews in England and Wales from 2004 up to 2009, when the Commission was abolished and the complaints procedure reverted to a two-stage process, involving just local resolution procedures and the HSC. See Parliamentary and Health Service Ombudsman *Annual Report 2006–07* (HC 838, 2006–07), p. 27 and 2008–09 (HC 786, 2008–09), p. 21.

As far as the pattern of complaints to the Parliamentary Ombudsman is concerned, it seems plausible to attribute some of the reduction shown in Figure 6.1 after the peak of the early 2000s to the creation of other bodies to handle complaints that would previously have gone to the ombudsman, and two bodies in particular deserve to be considered. In the early days of the Parliamentary Ombudsman, complaints about tax administration always figured as one of the biggest parts of the office's workload, but from 1993 a separate Adjudicator's Office was set up to deal with tax complaints. Likewise, prior to the passage of a formal Freedom of Information Act (FOI, passed in 2002, but only coming fully into operation in 2005), the Parliamentary Ombudsman had considered complaints about disclosure and information provision under pre-FOI 'open government' policies, but after the FOI Act such complaints became the responsibility of a separate Information Commissioner, evolving from a body originally set up to handle complaints over data protection. Both of those bodies reported very big spikes in the number of the complaints they handled in the later 2000s,[12] which would certainly have mitigated or indeed reversed the fall shown in Figure 6.1 if those matters had still been the responsibility of the Parliamentary Ombudsman. So in this case it does seem plausible to argue that the creation of these alternative routes of complaint may partly account for the slower rate of increase of complaints to the Parliamentary Ombudsman in the 2000s than in the 1990s.

Taking such changes into consideration, it seems reasonable to conclude that complaints about government administration in general and healthcare provision in particular increased substantially in the NPM era of the 1990s, after having been relatively stable in the 1980s. The number of complaints apparently continued to increase in the 2000s, but data breaks in reporting in the early 2000s make comparisons after that date more difficult.

It could of course be argued that the reported rise in the incidence of complaints shown in Figure 6.1 says more about increased propensity to complain and protest on the part of the citizenry than about any real reduction in the rule-of-law quality of public administration in the care with which rules were framed or applied or cases handled. And again there is a mass of popular writing about the attitudes and behaviour of the so-called 'Me Generation' and 'Generation X' (commonly characterized as more self-preoccupied and

---

[12] The Tax Adjudicator reported the numbers of complaints *accepted* (numbers of complaints *received* were inconsistently reported), and those numbers showed the steepest increase between 2005 and 2007, when the number of accepted complaints almost tripled in two years (an increase attributed to the introduction of Tax Credits in 2003–04). That high level of complaints was subsequently sustained, and from 2007 to 2013 averaged over three times the annual average from 1994 to 2005. Data from the Information Commissioner on FOI complaints showed that such complaints ran at about 2500 per year from 2006 to 2008, and almost doubled to nearly 4500 in 2011, remaining at or above that level in 2012 and 2013. Sources: *Annual Reports* of the Tax Adjudicator and the Information Commissioner available on those organizations' websites.

less inclined to suffer in silence than their allegedly more stoical forebears), that might be thought to support such a conclusion.

We cannot wholly dismiss such an interpretation, but at least two pieces of evidence seem to suggest it is not the full story. One is to look at what happened to the proportion of complaints lodged that were taken to the next stage by the Parliamentary Ombudsman, which from the beginning operated a 'filtration' system that separated complaints that were taken further for formal investigation from those that were weeded out as frivolous or otherwise unsuitable for further investigation. If the rising tide of complaints shown in Figure 6.1 was indeed no more than a reflection of unreasonable or casual complaints by the 'Me Generation', we might expect the proportion of complaints proceeding to the next stage to fall proportionately. As Figure 6.2 shows, there was indeed a dramatic fall in the success rate of complaints passing through the first-stage filter to the second stage of formal investigation (from over 20 per cent at the start of our period to under 5 per cent by the end).

But there are two things that need to be noted about that. The first is that the two trends noted in Figures 6.1 and 6.2, namely the soaring rate of first-stage complaints and the plummeting rate of complaints getting through the filter to the second stage, do not cancel one another out: absolute numbers of complaints proceeding to the next round grew overall, if not quite proportionately to the increase in applications. Until a new process of reporting was introduced in the early 2000s, the success rate at the first stage varied between 15 and 25 per cent in the first twenty of the thirty years considered here, with no definite trend, suggesting there is no evidence of a sudden increase of 'frivolous' complaints at the point where complaints to the Parliamentary

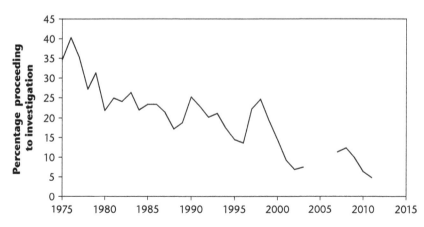

Figure 6.2. Complaints to Parliamentary Ombudsman Proceeding to Formal Investigation 1975–2011

Ombudsman began to soar in the early 1990s. The other point to note in weighing this information is that the data in Figure 6.2 only represent an indirect measure of the 'success' or non-frivolous nature of first-stage complaints, many of which were settled to the complainants' satisfaction without recourse to a full investigation. Indeed the Parliamentary Ombudsman introduced a new term 'intervention' in 2007 to reflect that fact.[13] 'Survival' may therefore be a better term than 'success'.

Another way of trying to determine whether the rising number of complaints shown by Figure 6.1 was just a reflection of a broader social trend towards more expression of dissatisfaction is to see how far it matches with other possible indicators of satisfaction or propensity to complain and litigate. As we noted in Chapter 2, such survey evidence as is available on satisfaction or trust with government over the period covered by this book shows no clear trend in either direction (some series show falls, others show rises, yet others show little change). We also examined what evidence was available on the changing incidence of public participation in anti-government demonstrations, which could be considered to be (ordinarily at least) a 'middle-level' of expression of dissatisfaction in countries like the UK, since it requires much more time, effort, and emotional commitment than a response to a survey.

Ideally we would like to have information about recent participation in demonstrations collected on a consistent basis over decades, so that we could tell whether such activity in the UK during the three decades considered by this book was at historically high or low levels compared with earlier decades (for example, nuclear disarmament or anti-Vietnam war protests of the 1960s) but such data do not exist.[14] However, the most consistent series available, a survey question asked by the British Social Attitudes Survey (BSAS) since 1986 ('Have you ever gone on a protest or demonstration about a government action which you thought was unjust and harmful?') reveals a pattern that does not match very clearly the incidence of complaints shown in Figure 6.1 either in timing or extent. (The same goes for other possible 'medium-cost' responses to an 'unjust or harmful' government action recorded in the BSAS surveys from 1986 to 2011, such as contacting an MP, signing a petition, or contacting the press. [15]) Most such indicators showed a rapid rise from 1986 to

[13] Parliamentary and Health Services Ombudsman, *Annual Report 2007–08*, (HC 1040, 2007–08), p. 10.

[14] Alasdair Roberts, in *The End of Protest: How Free-Market Capitalism Learned to Control Dissent* (Cornell: Cornell University Press, 2013) argued that free-market economies have over the past half century invented new strategies for discouraging protest, for instance by strengthening police forces, weakening the power of unions, and passing restrictive legislation. Therefore even if we could measure it, the level of protest does not only reflect citizen dissatisfaction.

[15] These indicators showed similar time courses to responses about 'participating in demonstrations and protests'. The most likely response was 'signing a petition' ('ever done' by 34–53 per cent of respondents), followed by 'contacting my MP' (replaced after 2000 by 'contacting my MP or MSP') (11–17 per cent), then 'going on a protest or demonstration' (6–12 per cent).

1991, and little or no fall since then. This pattern has commonly been interpreted as showing an increase in protest since the 1980s, but that interpretation is debatable.[16] Unlike many other survey questions, the question 'have you ever . . . ?' captures a lifetime of experience (averaging several decades), thus blurring the temporal information. We therefore analysed the BSAS data by age, and found that that the youngest age group (15 to 24 years)—who had the shortest 'lifetime experience' to look back on—showed two notable peaks in affirmative answers (in 1989 to 1991 and in 2002) but with levels of protest quite low outside those periods.

That is, whereas the incidence of first-stage complaints shown in Figure 6.1 markedly rose over the whole period and was at a much higher level at the end than at the beginning, BSAS data on participation in demonstrations suggests a more up-and-down pattern. Moreover, the timing of the incidence of protest activity as captured by the BSAS data by no means matched that of the complaints data shown in Figure 6.1. Whereas complaint levels seem to have been relatively stable in the 1980s and began to rise sharply in the mid-1990s, with evidence of a continuing increase in the 2000s, protest activity declined in the 1990s after reaching a peak in 1991 (attributed to the poll tax protests of that time), and likewise declined after a second peak in the early 2000s (around the time of the 2003 Iraq War).

Putting these pieces of information together, it is clear that the 'soar-away' pattern of complaints shown in Figure 6.1 has to be qualified to some extent in the light of the changing remit of the two main complaint-handling bodies, and it is also clear that survival rate of complaints in passing through the initial filter fell sharply over the period. But even allowing for such qualifications it seems hard to explain all the increase in complaints by these factors, or to see them as just part of a more general pattern of steadily rising citizen protest against government actions rather than more specific concerns about fairness and consistency in case handling.

6.3 Going to Law: Judicial Review

As we have already noted, making a formal complaint to an ombudsman or similar body about government decisions is a process that requires a degree of effort and determination, including sacrifice of anonymity and commitment of time, emotional engagement, and money, for example in costs of

---

[16] For the commonly held view that protest participation has increased, see Russell J. Dalton, *Citizen politics: Public Opinion and Political Parties in Advanced Industrial Democracies*, 6th edn (Los Angeles: Sage, 2013), pp. 55–6. Difficulties with this interpretation were discussed by Michael Biggs in 'Has Protest Increased Since the 1970s? How a Survey Question Can Construct a Spurious Trend', *British Journal of Sociology* (forthcoming, 2015).

correspondence, travel to attend meetings, and in some cases loss of earnings when time is taken off work to pursue such complaints. Challenging the decisions of government or public bodies in law courts is at least as demanding for the complainant if not more so. Not only does it involve loss of anonymity, substantial emotional commitment, and the obligation to frame a coherent complaint, but indeed requires the individual concerned to be prepared to appear in a public courtroom and face demanding, sometimes intimate, questioning from professional lawyers over the coherence and truthfulness of their story. On top of those emotional and intellectual stresses, the financial costs to individuals of taking this course can be far from trivial as well. While pursuing a formal complaint to an ombudsman is not necessarily free of financial costs, those costs are typically under the control of the complainants (for example in deciding how much to spend on their own travel or how much time to take off work as those costs arise in the course of complaint activity). In contrast, the costs of litigation against a public body can be open-ended, unless those costs can be covered by public funding (which was limited in various ways during the period considered here, and at the time of writing increasingly so) or from other sources, such as public-interest charities or 'no win, no fee' legal representation. Moreover, those costs tend to be high, since pursuit of judicial review ordinarily requires the services of highly paid professional lawyers, and even the brave (or desperate) who opt to represent themselves without legal advice are liable for court fees.[17] The financial risk can be considerable in that in an adversarial justice system of the kind represented by English law, those who lose their case risk being ordered to pay the defendants' costs as well as their own.[18] So this route to questioning the consistency and fairness of government decision-making was decidedly not for the faint-hearted.

Over the period considered here, there were two broad avenues available for legally challenging the decisions of government and public bodies by individuals who believed that they had been unfairly treated. One route lay through the UK's specialist administrative courts, taking the form of 'tribunals' intended to offer relatively quick justice in a range of domains, such as social security and child support, mental health, and immigration and asylum. This system of tribunals originated in the early twentieth century with the advent of the modern welfare state, has been subject to numerous

---

[17] Sarah Nason and Maurice Sunkin, 'The Regionalisation of Judicial Review: Constitutional Authority, Access to Justice and Specialisation of Legal Services in Public Law', *Modern Law Review* 77, no. 2 (2013): pp. 223–53 found that the number of litigants in person increased from 400 (19 per cent of all civil judicial review claims) in 2007 to 474 (22 per cent) in 2011. More than half of judicial review applications were estimated to be publicly funded (by legal aid) over the past few decades (Maurice Sunkin, personal communication).

[18] Ministry of Justice, *Applying for Judicial Review* (2013), Section 18.

reorganizations and reforms over the subsequent century, and at the time of writing was dealing with some 800,000 cases a year. But some of those tribunals, notably in employment, covered private and independent sector as well as government and public employment, and the various reorganizations and consolidations made it difficult to derive a consistent series of numbers of cases passing through tribunals, although there is some strong circumstantial evidence for a marked increase over the period.[19] So our analysis here focuses on the other and higher level avenue of litigation against government and public bodies in the UK, the system of judicial review, conducted by higher level administrative courts rather than the ordinary civil or criminal justice system. This is a system which focuses only on cases involving government and public bodies and for which consistent data can be assembled for the three decades being considered here.

That regime varied according to the different jurisdictions of the UK, with separate systems for Northern Ireland, Scotland, and England and Wales. Taken together, the sum of judicial review applications across the jurisdictions was only a small fraction of the number of cases going through tribunals. In this chapter we focus on the largest of those systems, that of England and Wales (we will come to comparisons with Scotland in Chapter 7). As with the Parliamentary Ombudsman complaints procedure discussed earlier, the judicial review system in England and Wales involves a two-stage process, and our analysis here focuses on the cases and outcomes of the first stage 'applications for permission to apply for judicial review'. If there was indeed increased perception of unfair or inconsistent case-handling by government and public bodies, it would be very surprising if it did not show up in increased volumes of such applications at both stages of the process.

Accordingly, Figure 6.3a shows what happened to the number of requests for permission to apply for judicial review in England and Wales. Three main conclusions can be drawn from the pattern indicated in Figure 6.3a. First, there was clearly no overall diminution in the incidence of attempts to pursue this 'high-cost' route of expressing dissatisfaction with government and public services: the only question is how much of an increase in dissatisfaction we can plausibly infer from this indicator. Second, a substantial part of the increase in applications for judicial review in England and Wales was accounted for by immigration or asylum cases, which increased dramatically for much of the period and especially so in the later 2000s (after immigration,

---

[19] For example, an average of 172,000 cases were lodged annually with Social Security Appeals Tribunals in the decade 1988 to 1997, while over 400,000 social security cases were received annually by the Tribunals Service from 2010–11 to 2013–14 (Sources: Office for National Statistics, *Social Security Statistics*, annual editions, and Ministry of Justice, *Annual Tribunals Statistics 2013–14*).

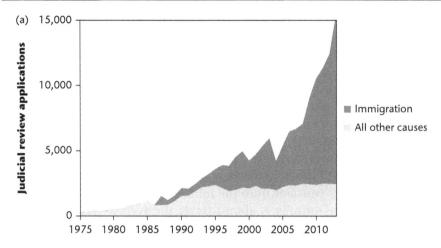

Figure 6.3a. First Stage Applications for Judicial Review, England and Wales 1975–2013

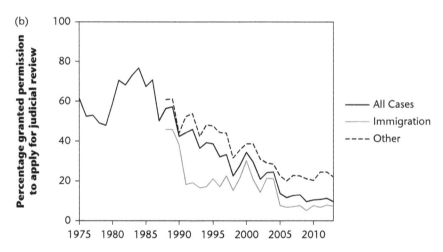

Figure 6.3b. Outcomes of First Stage Applications for Judicial Review 1975–2013

Sources: Annual editions of *Judicial Statistics* showed judicial review applications to 2011. Subsequent years' data were from *Court Statistics Quarterly* Jan–Mar editions (2012 figures were corrected according to a revision notice [Ministry of Justice, November 2013] and 2013 figures were corrected according to Ministry of Justice personal communication [2014]). The transient decrease in 2004 occurred when an alternative procedure ('statutory review') was introduced in 2003 for immigration claims but fell out of use after 2005 (Ministry of Justice, *Court Statistics Quarterly* [Jan–Mar 2014], p. 32).

the main subject in contention in applications for judicial review, dwarfing all other topics, was the administration of the criminal justice system). How far we should consider those immigration cases as a valid indicator of changing perceptions of the rule-of-law quality of UK public administration is a moot point: after all, as we have already noted, immigration pressures rose dramatically over this period, applicants often had no other recourse than to opt for judicial review, and in many cases were not themselves in a position to pay the financial costs of these actions.[20] But third, even if we set aside the immigration/asylum cases as a valid indicator of levels of dissatisfaction with the rule-of-law behaviour of the bureaucracy, Figure 6.3a shows that non-immigration applications for judicial review increased substantially over the period as a whole. In England and Wales, such applications rose sharply in the 'early NPM' era of the 1980s and early 1990s (a 'take-off' pattern rather similar in its timing to the marked rise in complaints made to the Parliamentary Ombudsman in the early 1990s as shown in Figure 6.1). They remained relatively constant from the mid-1990s to the end of our period, but even then were running at almost treble the average level observed in the 1980s.

As with the pattern of complaints to ombudsmen that we explored in Section 6.2, the question arises as to whether this increase in first-stage applications for judicial review represents a real deterioration in the rule-of-law behaviour of government and other public bodies (as many of the critics of NPM argued would be the inevitable price of giving managers more discretion and greater efforts to cut costs) or just some kind of generational shift in disposition to express dissatisfaction and disappointment through formal challenges. And as with the complaints to ombudsmen, there are other pieces of evidence that can shed some light on that issue.

One such piece of evidence on that point is the proportion of those increased numbers of first-stage applications for judicial review that got through to the next stage, after judicial decisions about their eligibility. Figure 6.3b shows those numbers for England and Wales, and indicates there was in fact a substantial decline in the proportion of non-immigration cases making it to the next stage, down from over 60 per cent in the late 1980s to about 20 per cent by the later 2000s.

However, as with the changing incidence of complaints made to the Parliamentary Ombudsman that got through the organization's filtration process to go to a further stage of investigation, the rate of decline in the percentage of non-immigration judicial review cases going to the second stage in England and Wales did not get steeper when numbers of initial applications shot up in the early 1990s, and the number of cases proceeding to the next

---

[20] Although not the main focus of this chapter, we note that the spectacular rise in immigration judicial review applications was more-or-less matched over much of the period by the increase in total immigration numbers, such that legal challenges remained between 0.5 and 1.2 per cent of total non-British immigration from 1990 to 2009 with no obvious upward trend. Only since 2010 have immigration judicial review applications exceeded 1.5 per cent of total immigration and by 2012 approached 2 per cent (immigration data from the *International Passenger Survey*, Office for National Statistics).

stage increased in absolute terms until the early 2000s. Further, as with the ombudsman data considered earlier, the data shown in Figure 6.3b do not take into account the number of cases settled before they proceed to a full hearing or investigation. Such cases were recorded in the official statistics as 'withdrawn' whether or not the settlement was in favour of the complainant. We might disregard that fact if we could safely assume that the pre-hearing settlement rate for judicial review was relatively constant over time, but for England and Wales, that settlement rate was estimated to have doubled between 1990 and the late 2000s,[21] suggesting that we may need to discount some of the apparent fall in judicial review 'success' rates over the last two decades of the period covered by Figure 6.3b.

Just as with formal complaints to ombudsmen, other factors may have affected the overall levels of judicial review applications. While few changes were made to the formal procedures (for instance, the three-month time limit dates from 1978, and much of the procedure current at the time of writing was codified in the Supreme Court Act 1981), the way in which applications were treated by the administrative courts became less restrictive during the 1980s and 1990s. The scope of judicial review increased over the period to bring more public bodies within its remit, and the criteria of 'unreasonableness' (of the action of the public body) and 'standing' or 'interest' (of the litigant) were progressively relaxed.[22]

Such factors may account for some of the rise in non-immigration applications in the 1990s, although there were also pressures in the opposite direction. First, distinctions between private and public law became more rigid, which would tend to limit the cases eligible for judicial review.[23] Second, far more cases began to be handled by the tribunal system mentioned earlier, whose relationship with the administrative courts became closer over the period. Many were brought together into a two-level Tribunals Service in 2006, which in 2011 became part of HM Courts and Tribunals Service, comprising fifteen tribunals or similar bodies. Many appeals regarding decisions of First-Tier tribunals were heard by an Upper Tribunal rather than proceeding to judicial review, a process designed to relieve the pressure on the administrative courts.[24] This development suggests that when complaints threaten

---

[21] See Varda Bondy and Maurice Sunkin, *The Dynamics of Judicial Review Litigation: The Resolution of Public Law Challenges Before Final Hearing* (London: The Public Law Project, 2009), p. 37.

[22] Paul Craig, *Administrative Law* (London: Sweet and Maxwell, 2008); Timothy Endicott, *Administrative Law, Second Edition* (Oxford: Oxford University Press, 2011).

[23] C. F. Forsyth, 'Beyond *O'Reilly V. Mackman*: The Foundations and Nature of Procedural Exclusivity', *The Cambridge Law Journal* 44, no.3 (1985): pp. 415–34.

[24] Lord Justice Robert Carnwarth (formerly Senior President of Tribunals): 'I see us developing a practical partnership in which we can relieve the Administrative Court of some of its burden in relation to specialist tribunals, and thus help it to concentrate on its central role as guardian of constitutional rights.' In 'Tribunal Justice—a New Start', *Public Law* 48, no. 1 (2009): pp. 1–15.

to overwhelm capacity, another route is created, as we saw with the proliferation of ombudsmen, so that instead of attempting to reduce complaints overall, an extra lane is added to the motorway to relieve traffic congestion, so to speak.

The level of litigation in general provides another relevant piece of information for assessing whether the pattern shown in Figure 6.3 is part of some general trend towards greater litigiousness in society rather than a specific change in perceptions of the rule-of-law performance of government and public bodies. As with the survey data on satisfaction, trust, and reported participation in demonstrations that we used to assess the distinctiveness or otherwise of the rise in ombudsman complaints in Section 6.2, we looked at available data on the changing incidence of various types of litigation to see whether the rise in judicial review applications was part of a wider trend. And as with that survey evidence, the picture that emerges from looking at other types of litigation over the thirty-year period covered by this study is a varied one, with sharp rises in some domains (such as motor claims and medical negligence cases) but not in others (such as employer liability).[25] For what that comparison is worth (and it should be borne in mind that the vast bulk of civil litigation consists of businesses chasing bad debts), it suggests that the pattern shown in Figure 6.3 is not reproduced in every other domain of litigation.

6.4 An Overall Assessment

Examining the rule-of-law indicators in Sections 6.2 and 6.3 and putting them together with the survey evidence discussed earlier (which, as we explained, is not directly focused on 'rule-of-law' performance but might reasonably be expected to reflect severe declines in that aspect of performance), we find a more nuanced picture than might be expected either by champions of the various government and public service makeovers in UK central government over the past thirty years, or by their critics. If evidence for government 'working better' would be provided by unambiguous decreases in formal complaints and judicial challenges relating to government actions, that is certainly not what we found. Table 6.1 comprises a summary 'scorecard' of

---

[25] See e.g. Richard Lewis, Annette Morris, and Ken Oliphant, 'Is there a Compensation Culture in the United Kingdom?', *Torts Law Journal* 14 (2006): pp. 158–75; Richard Lewis and Annette Morris, 'Tort Law Culture in the United Kingdom: Image and Reality in Personal Injury Compensation', *Journal of European Tort Law* 3, no. 2 (2012): pp. 230–64; and Paul Fenn, Stephen Diacon, Alastair Gray, Ron Hodges, and Neil Rickman, 'Current Cost of Medical Negligence in NHS hospitals: analysis of claims database', *British Medical Journal* 320, no. 7249 (2000): pp. 1567–71. Data on compensation claims since 2007 were available from the Compensation Recovery Unit via the gov.uk website.

Table 6.1. Did Government Work Better? A Scorecard of Indicators of Citizen Response

	'Early NPM' 1980–81 to 1990–91	'Middle NPM' 1990–91 to 2000–01	'Late or post-NPM' 2000–01 to 2010–11	Whole period 1980–81 to 2010–11
Attitude Survey Responses		Opinions mostly worse or unchanged over the period as a whole (see Chapter 2)		
Complaints to ombudsmen (Parliamentary Ombudsman and Health Service Commissioner [HSC])	Complaints stable or falling	Complaints rose sharply	Data on complaints limited, suggest continuing rise for HSC, falling off for Parliamentary Ombudsman	Complaints to Parliamentary Ombudsman approximately doubled, HSC increased five-fold
Complaints to Parliamentary Ombudsman proceeding to a 'statutory report'	20–25 per cent of applications reported, little overall trend	Proportion of cases reported fell sharply to below 15 per cent	Proportion of cases proceeding to report continued to fall	Proportion of cases undergoing statutory report decreased from over 25 per cent to under 10 per cent
Judicial review applications (England and Wales)	Total applications tripled from low baseline	Immigration cases rose sharply; non immigration applications rose more slowly;	Immigration cases rose dramatically; non-immigration applications levelled off	Immigration applications rose more than ten-fold; Non-immigration applications tripled
Non-immigration judicial review applications 'granted permission to apply'	Proportion fell from over 70 per cent to under 50 per cent; absolute numbers rose	Proportion fell to under 40 per cent; absolute numbers rose	Proportion fell to 20–25 per cent; absolute numbers levelled off	Proportion fell from over 70 per cent to 20–25 per cent; absolute numbers rose overall

what the two types of indicators examined in this chapter point to, together with the survey responses discussed earlier. Table 6.1 is presented in a broadly similar form to the scorecards about cost performance that we presented in Chapters 4 and 5, but is mostly expressed in qualitative scores indicating direction of travel rather than raw numbers.

We find no evidence from these indicators that government 'worked better' over this period. Perhaps more contestable would be the question as to whether the observed pattern is more consistent with the view that government performance, viewed through the lens of citizens' responses considered here, got clearly worse over this period or did not change markedly. Pessimists looking for evidence to support the former conclusion would have to put more weight on changing incidence of complaints or litigation rather than on survival rates. The argument for that would have to be that individuals showed an increasing tendency to challenge government through those higher-stakes mechanisms. From this perspective, falling survival rates for litigation and some kinds of complaints may simply reflect governments and bureaucracies finding ways to limit spiralling challenges (as they undoubtedly attempted to do in some cases) rather than the application of standards about the seriousness of challenges that were consistent over time.

The case for the 'null hypothesis'—that government worked neither appreciably better nor worse over this period—would have to rest on the argument that (a) a rising incidence of complaints may be partly accounted for by a tendency to broaden the remit of complaint-handling bodies, particularly in the early expansive phases of their lives and to make complaints processes more accessible, and (b) while both complaints and litigation show a noticeable increase, survival rates for judicial review dived as the numbers of judicial review cases went up, and for the period during which consistent data are available, the same seems to have applied to complaints to the Parliamentary Ombudsman. That pattern might be argued to reflect an increasing propensity to complain or litigate on the part of (a minority of) the population rather than clear evidence of a striking increase in well-justified challenges But we noted earlier that complaints or legal actions may be settled to the complainants' satisfaction before reaching the second stage of the process, and that there is some evidence at least for a sharp increase in the pre-hearing settlement rate for judicial review from 1990 to the late 2000s.

As far as periodization or temporality is concerned, the idea we have referred to earlier of the first NPM phase of the 1980s as being particularly characterized by 'slash-and-burn' attitudes to traditional bureaucracy with scant concern for due process and careful case handling, to be replaced by greater emphasis on quality later, only partly fits with the data presented here. It is true that the biggest proportionate rise in non-immigration judicial review applications (for England and Wales) took place over this time, but complaints to ombudsmen did not take off dramatically in this decade. It is also true that in the subsequent two decades, supposedly more characterized by concerns about quality of administration, the increase in non-immigration judicial review applications tended to slow and level off, but complaints to ombudsmen soared, particularly in the 1990s. So the indicators we have taken here only partly fit those stereotypes.

Overall, these indicators do not support a 'worked better' interpretation, as the advocates of government makeover that we discussed earlier might have hoped and expected. Though it is debatable whether they more convincingly support a 'worked worse' or a 'worked about the same' interpretation, the 'worked worse' interpretation seems on balance more plausible, for indicators that bear directly on the rule-of-law aspects of government activity.

7

Comparative Perspectives on Performance

Nothing good comes out of Whitehall[1]

7.1 Four Kinds of Comparison

Previous chapters have focused on the performance of UK central government departments over thirty years of attempts at modernization and managerialist reform initiatives taking place alongside other social and technological developments. As we have seen, running costs (but not civil service paybill) rose substantially in constant price terms over that period, while the volume of formal complaints and litigation relating to the rule-of-law performance of government increased markedly as well. So far, so bad for those advocates of reform and modernization who hoped to see those initiatives bring down the cost of running government while satisfying citizens' expectations of fair and consistent administration. But these findings leave open at least two important questions. One is whether the outcomes analysed in Chapters 4–6 would have been even worse in the absence of all that reform and modernization activity—a counterfactual proposition about how the UK would have performed if it had taken a different path over the past three decades. The other question is whether those outcomes reflect some general late twentieth/early twenty-first century administrative condition, or whether there are notable variations among types or levels of administration.

Neither of those questions can be answered definitively. But in this chapter we aim to throw some light on them and to put our findings into perspective by exploring four kinds of comparison, namely:

- *The UK with other countries.* If it is correct to argue, as we suggested in Chapter 1, that the UK was a 'vanguard state' or 'poster-child' case of

---

[1] Words spoken by a character in the BBC 'Yes Minister' series (Jim Hacker's wife Annie) at the end of the episode 'The Whisky Priest' by Antony Jay and Jonathan Lynn, broadcast on 16 December 1982.

managerial public service reforms, does the UK's performance stand out from that of other (supposedly 'rearguard' or non-poster-child) states, on such international comparative data relating to administrative quality and productivity as are available?

- *UK ministerial departments with other types of delivery bodies within central government, such as the once much-hyped executive ('Next Steps') agencies.* If such agencies were intended to create more scope and incentives for managers to achieve efficiencies and serve 'customers' better, can we observe any marked difference between the two kinds of bodies, on such data and studies as are available?

- *Central government with (English) local government.* Reforms aimed at a more 'managerial' approach to public administration took place at both of these levels of government over the period examined by this book, but it has often been remarked that the two levels of government have traditionally had rather different cultures and institutional styles, and we have already compared central and local tax collection performance in Chapter 5. Extending that analysis, can we say that those different cultural and institutional styles were associated with marked variations in performance between the two levels of government over that period?

- *UK central government with the Scottish government departments before and after devolution of legislative and oversight powers over those departments to a Scottish Parliament in 1999.* Again, it is often said that (even before legislative devolution) Scottish administration has traditionally had a culture and operating style very different from that operating in 'Whitehall', so can we observe major differences in performance between UK and Scottish government over our period?

In exploring these four types of comparison, this chapter also shows some of the built-in limits of such comparison. In a world made entirely for the convenience of social science evaluators, it would of course be readily possible to make all of those comparisons from standard documentation, and indeed after decades of advocacy of benchmarking in management and public services, we might expect such comparisons to be routinely made throughout government. In practice, as we shall see, none of those sorts of comparisons are problem-free for various reasons (some of which we have discussed in previous chapters), though there is something that can be drawn out of the comparison in almost every case. So this is precisely the kind of analysis for which it is important to apply the 'consilience' principle that we discussed in the first chapter—meaning a careful assessment of whether a set of data sources, each of which is less than perfect as a measure when taken on its own, point to the same conclusion when they are taken together. And, as we shall see, there is indeed a certain consilience that emerges from this analysis.

As we will show, the kinds of comparison that are possible vary across these four types. Where there is a choice between comparison of performance in terms of *levels* and *trends*, we generally opt for trends as constituting the more meaningful test. By levels we mean relating indicators of cost or of administrative consistency and fairness to demographic or resource factors, such as population served or total expenditure. By a trends analysis we mean comparing the slopes of the observable changes over time, to assess how far those indicators moved in the same direction or at the same rate for UK central government and our control cases.[2]

7.2 International Comparisons

If the UK was an international trailblazer of public service reforms over recent decades, is that status reflected in commensurate performance according to such cross-national studies and performance indicators as are available? When it comes to international comparisons, there are no established cross-national datasets on government running costs over time, government ministries are not routinely benchmarked against their counterparts in other countries on cost and quality indicators, and indeed Chapters 3 and 4 showed how laborious it is to trace reported running costs in a reasonably consistent form over time even in a single country. As far as tax collection is concerned, as mentioned in Chapter 5, the OECD has published comparative data on tax collection costs since the mid-2000s, drawing on data provided by revenue bodies or extracted from their general reports, with the UK in the late 2000s ranking in the bottom third of thirty-two OECD countries.[3] But that ranking—as the OECD itself pointed out—does not take into account the very different tasks faced by revenue administrations across the OECD, for example, as between those revenue departments that in effect provide welfare benefits as well as collecting taxes (as in the UK's various tax credit systems developed since the late 1990s), and as between more and less complicated tax systems.

More broadly, some efforts have been made to compare public sector productivity cross-nationally. Perhaps the best-known example, which we

---

[2] A now classic example of that sort of analysis is a comparative over-time study of reported wait times for hospital operations as between England and Scotland in the early 2000s by Carol Propper and her colleagues, which showed very different slopes in the way performance changed over time by the two countries, even though the direction of travel was the same, with a downward slope in both cases. Carol Propper, Matt Sutton, Carolyn Whitnall, and Frank Windemeijer, 'Incentives and Targets in Hospital Care: Evidence from a Naural Experiment', *Journal of Public Economics* 94 (2008): pp. 318–35.

[3] OECD, *Government at a Glance* (OECD: Paris, 2011).

referred to in Chapter 4, is António Afonso, Ludger Schuknecht, and Vito Tanzi's comparison of the performance and efficiency of the public sectors of twenty-three OECD countries a decade or so ago, across a variety of performance indicators in 1990 and 2000. In that study, the UK emerged as a middle ranking performer for the indicator 'administration' (being ranked fifteenth of the twenty-three countries in the study for both performance and efficiency on this indicator in 2000).[4] Contrary to the idea that the UK's international poster-child status might be reflected in exceptional performance, the UK was toward the middle of the pack for most of the indicators used in this study—neither a star performer nor an obvious problem case.

A comparative study of public sector performance in twenty-two developed democracies sponsored by the Social and Cultural Planning Office of the Dutch government in 2004 reached rather similar conclusions as far as the placing of the UK is concerned. It placed the UK in a middle-ranking position on performance relative to levels of expenditure on education, health care, and law and order; in an upper-middle position in a 'quality of public administration' league based mainly on survey data from World Competitiveness Reports; and compared five types of rankings that placed the UK between thirteenth and sixteenth out of twenty-two, with the exception of the World Bank Governance rankings in which the UK was rated third at the time of that study.[5]

It is true that none of these studies involve a long-term over-time analysis of developments in government productivity and most tend to be 'snapshot' studies, often rather flimsily based on 'expert rankings' (in the case of the World Bank, different indicators are used for each round of governance rankings, making over-time comparison problematic),[6] and even after decades of work on such studies, commentators tend to stress the tentative nature of the comparisons.[7] But for what these limited data are worth, the UK does not look like a stark outlier on most of them (either at the top or the bottom),

---

[4] António Afonso, Ludger Schucknecht, and Vito Tanzi, 'Public Sector Efficiency: An International Comparison', *Public Choice* 123 (2005): pp. 321–47, Tables 1 and 2 and Figure 2. The administration indicator estimated 'red tape, quality of the judiciary, corruption and the size of the shadow economy' in 2000. On the composite indicators of public service as a whole, the UK ranked towards the bottom in performance (with only four other countries scoring lower) but towards the top in efficiency (with fourteen countries scoring lower). Efficiency was estimated by dividing the performance score by a normalized indicator of public spending for each category and country. The UK's performance ranking was almost unchanged between 1990 and 2000. The administration indicator was not given for 1990 so we cannot track deterioration or improvement on this item.

[5] Bob Kuhry and Evert Pommer, 'Performance of the Public Sector', in *Public Sector Performance: An International Comparison of Education, Health Care, Law and Order and Public Administration* (The Hague: SCP, 2004), Chapter 7, pp. 271–92, Table 7.3.

[6] Christiane Arndt, 'The Politics of Governance Rankings', *International Public Management Journal* 11 (2008): pp. 275–97.

[7] For example, Richard Boyle, *Measuring Public Sector Productivity: Lessons from International Experience* (Dublin: Institute of Public Administration, 2006), p. ix.

suggesting that its commonly perceived emphasis on managerial public service reforms was not obviously associated with exceptional performance (high or low) in international perspective.

7.3 Comparisons between Policy Departments and Delivery Units

When it comes to comparing semi-autonomous bodies focused mainly on service delivery within central government with core ministerial departments (which are assumed to focus more on policy formulation—albeit with certain responsibilities for implementation and delivery), the analysis in Chapter 5 of administration costs reported for the tax departments can be taken as a partial test of the difference that distinction might make, since those departments had operated since the nineteenth century with some autonomy from direct ministerial control. As we saw in that chapter, even though it might be thought that tax collection might be particularly fertile ground for cost-cutting managerialism allied with new information technology, the trajectory of absolute running costs in the tax departments appeared to differ very little from that of other central government departments and of government as a whole. As we saw, however, running costs relative to tax collected fell markedly over some of the period, particularly as direct tax revenue soared in the boom that preceded the financial crash of 2008.

In principle, the executive agencies that were spun out of central departments in the 1990s as delivery units to be managed at arms-length from the departmental hierarchy (a development we noted in Chapter 2), might provide an equally good test of whether cost performance might be different when an organization is at least partly insulated from the traditional operating style of core ministerial departments, in which, as we noted in Chapter 2, senior civil servants have been compared to 'courtiers' clustered around ministers, constantly moving into new positions within the square mile or so of the 'Whitehall village' and typically preoccupied with high policy and machinery of government issues rather than with the nitty-gritty of service delivery. Indeed, the original report that led to the creation of those agencies indicated that savings of 5 per cent or more might be achieved as a result of liberating managers from that sort of culture through agencification.[8]

But in spite of the massive rhetorical hype about performance measurement and managerialism that accompanied the creation of scores of 'Next Steps' executive agencies two decades ago, it is all but impossible to compare the

---

[8] Kate Jenkins, Karen Caines, and Andrew Jackson, *Improving Management in Government: The Next Steps* (London: HMSO, 1988), p. 16.

cost and performance of those agencies with that of core ministerial departments over time, because of data churn and discontinuities of the kind we discussed in Chapter 3. In line with what we noticed about the lack of systematic evidence about cost-cutting in government in Chapter 4, Oliver James and Sandra van Thiel argue that exactly the same applies to the effects of 'agencification' as an aspect of managerial reforms.[9] Although there were batteries of performance indicators applied to executive agencies from the outset in the late 1980s, churn in those indicators combined with their agency-specific nature (meaning an absence of matching numbers for central departments) makes comparison on administrative quality (specifically of the rule-of-law type) effectively impossible.

Even on the cost side, where we might expect it to be more feasible to make comparisons between agencies and departments, a combination of data breaks and over-time inconsistencies of the kind we discussed in Chapter 3, together with the fact that running costs reported in *Public Expenditure Statistical Analyses* did not distinguish between executive agencies and their parent ministerial departments,[10] meant the overall *levels* of administrative spending could not be feasibly compared as between those executive agencies and core ministerial departments. What could be done, though, was to take whole departments together with their associated agencies, and compare the *trends* in running costs of those departments with a lot of agencies and those with few or none.

That is done in Figure 7.1, which compares what happened to reported running costs in agency-heavy departments (those in the social security and employment domains, with over 85 per cent of their staff in agencies) as against less agency-heavy departments, including a group of departments (comprising foreign affairs; overseas aid; culture, media and sport; and the Northern Ireland Office) with less than 40 per cent staff in agencies. The graph shows costs relative to 1989–90, which was taken as a baseline because it was the financial year in which rapid 'agencification' began in central government, and runs from 1980–81 to 2002–03. After that point, as explained in Chapter 4, gross costs were no longer reported and a large (unspecified) number of staff was removed from administration costs, making a consistent series impossible to reconstruct with any confidence.

Contrary to the idea that more agencies might lead to tighter control of running costs as a result of more focused management, Figure 7.1 suggests precisely the opposite outcome—that running costs rose faster in the

[9] Oliver James and Sandra van Thiel, 'Structural Devolution to Agencies', in *The Ashgate Research Companion to New Public Management*, edited by Tom Christensen and Per Laegreid (Farnham: Ashgate, 2011), Chapter 14, pp. 209–22.
[10] As well as the difficulty of identifying valid comparators of absolute costs, given the wide range of functions carried out by both agencies and departments.

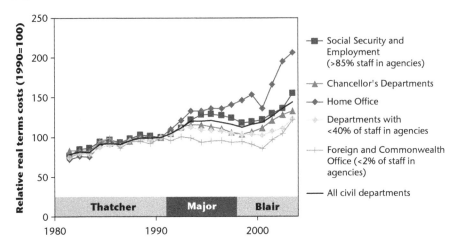

Figure 7.1. Relative Gross Running Costs of 'Agency-Heavy' and 'Agency-Light' Departments 1980–2004. Costs Shown in Real Terms Relative to 1990 (=100)

Sources: Annual editions of *Public Expenditure Statistical Analyses* (PESA), with reclassification effects removed as described in Appendix 3. Departments with less than 40 per cent of staff in agencies were Department of Health, Foreign and Commonwealth Office, Overseas Development Administration, Northern Ireland Office, and Department for Culture, Media and Sport. The majority of the Chancellor's Departments' running costs were from the Inland Revenue and Customs & Excise Departments, both working on 'Next Steps lines' from 1993. The largest component of the Home Office's running costs was the Prison Service, which became an agency in 1993.

agency-heavy departmental groups. Similarly, the general fall in running costs from about 1993 to 1999 that we described in Chapter 4 seems to have occurred in almost all civil departments (other than the Home Office), regardless of their proportion of staff in agencies. Departmental groups with a high proportion of their staff in agencies were therefore not obviously more 'business-like' in terms of holding down running costs than either departments with few agency staff or the same departments prior to 'agencification', and indeed it could be argued that they were less so at least in the early 1990s.

We can also look at what happened to civil service employment within and outside agencies, taking staff numbers as a proxy for costs (albeit an imperfect proxy, as we have seen). Executive 'Next Steps' agencies were first created in the late 1980s at a time when total civil service numbers were falling from their mid-1970s peak of over 750,000 full-time equivalent (FTE) staff. Executive agency staff remained civil servants, but staff numbers within and outside agencies were reported separately in *Civil Service Statistics* (CSS) during the 1990s and early 2000s. As Figure 7.2a shows, the number of civil servants in agencies (including those organizations defined as 'working on Next Steps lines'—which in practice meant mainly the tax departments) increased slightly between 1993 and 1998, while the

(a)

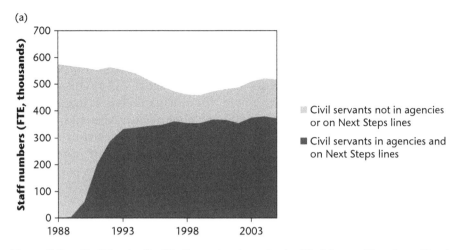

Figure 7.2a. Civil Service Staff in Executive Agencies (or Working on Next Steps Lines) and in the Rest of the Civil Service 1988–2002

(b)

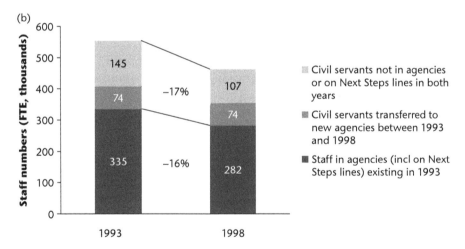

Figure 7.2b. Estimated Changes in Agency and Non-Agency Civil Servants between 1993 and 1998

Source: Civil Service Statistics, annual editions. Full-time equivalent (FTE).

number of civil servants not working in such agencies (i.e. remaining in the core ministerial departments) halved. But the difference between the two groups was not as extreme as this graph suggests, since additional agencies were 'carved out' of the parent departments during this time. The new agencies employed some 74,000 civil servants by 1998, about half of them in the ambit of the Ministry of Defence. Assuming that the new agencies

135

employed existing civil servants (who had previously carried out the functions of those agencies within departments) we concluded that the 16.4 per cent reduction in total civil servant numbers between 1993 and 1998 was shared approximately equally pro rata between civil servants within and outside the Next Steps agency framework (Figure 7.2b). This analysis is complicated by the fact that some of the calculated fall in agency staff numbers was due to the disappearance of some twenty agencies (15,000 staff) from the CSS lists.[11] But if we consider only agencies continuously existing from 1993 to 1998, we found a fall in agency staff numbers of 10.5 per cent over this time, and a corresponding fall of 14.4 per cent in the 'non-agency' staff of departments that did not create any new agencies during the period.

This evidence is certainly limited, but on the 'consilience' principle, it chimes with what other independent scholars of executive agency performance have concluded. The dramatic claims about achievable cost savings in agencies were not matched by any consistent and systematic recording of cost over time, and the same went for other performance indicators. In a study published a decade ago Colin Talbot found that agencies did not supply data that made direct calculation of their running costs possible, but concluded that agencies did not achieve cuts in running costs 'anywhere near the 5 per cent per annum savings suggested in the report'.[12] A little earlier Oliver James reached a similar conclusion, in a survey comprising an aggregate analysis of government running costs, a detailed study of the Benefits Agency and a survey of the seventy-two executive agencies that existed both in 1995–96 and 1997–98. The agencies' costs in his study showed a fall of 4.6 per cent in real terms over that two-year period but total central government running costs (which included those of agencies) fell by 5.9 per cent over the same period, indicating that agencies 'were associated with lower improvements in economy than central government as a whole'.[13] Such conclusions are consistent with the longer-term picture given in Figures 7.1 and 7.2, and run clearly against the proposition that separately run agencies would display either markedly lower or less rapidly rising running costs than core ministerial departments.

---

[11] Some agencies were closed or privatized while others were merged or reabsorbed into the parent department. Agencies whose direct successors could be identified as agencies were included in the 'continuously existing' category.

[12] Colin Talbot, 'Executive Agencies; Have They Improved Management in Government?', *Public Money and Management* 24 (2004): pp. 110–11. We note that the Next Steps Report itself did not define a timescale for the cost savings to be made (see Jenkins, Caines, and Jackson, *Improving Management in Government*, p. 16).

[13] Oliver James, 'Evaluating Executive Agencies in UK Government', *Public Policy and Management* 16 (2001): p. 30.

7.4 Comparisons between Central Government and Local Government in England

A third type of comparison is to explore the record of English local government relative to that of UK central government. As noted earlier, both levels of government were exposed to 'managerial' reforms over the period, although it can be claimed that a number of aspects of modern public service managerialism started earlier in local government (in respect of developments such as performance indicators, management boards, outsourcing, and cost-centre accounting). And if we compare central government as a whole (including agencies as well as core departments) with local government, both were dominated by service-delivery activity. But still it is often claimed that the two levels of government comprise rather different cultures and institutional traditions, and advocates of local government[14] often declare that local government can be more efficient than central government to the extent that its revenues (taxes and charges) are raised from local people and more effective in administration than central government in so far as it has better knowledge of local conditions.[15] If such claims are true, we might expect to find indicators that show a marked difference between local and central government in terms of operating costs and quality of administration.

Readers will recall that we compared the collection costs of (English) local and (UK) central taxes in Chapter 5. That comparison indicated that, apart from a heady period in the 1990s, when tax collection costs at both central and local government level were affected by major policy decisions, tax collection costs did not look dramatically different as between central and local levels of government either at the beginning or at the end of our period. Here we add to that analysis by comparing what happened to overall administration costs in UK central government (again taking core departments and agencies together) and local authorities in England over the period covered by this book, to see whether the observed pattern indicates a marked difference in slopes of levels of such costs between the two levels of government.

Once again, the data available for such comparisons are less than perfect. Local and central government provide very different services, making comparisons of service quality problematic. And though there are standard accounting conventions for local authorities, the definition of administrative costs (or its variants, as we discuss below) has varied over the thirty-year period considered in this book (reflecting changes in the way local government

---

[14] Such as George W. Jones and John Stewart, *The Case for Local Government* (London: Allen & Unwin, 1983).

[15] George W. Jones, *The Future of Local Government: Has it One?*, Public Management and Policy Association Report (London: CIPFA, 2008), p. 3.

was managed and organized), with at least one significant data break. The way administrative spending was counted in local government is also not directly comparable with the conventions for recording administrative costs in central government (which themselves changed markedly over time, as we showed in Chapters 3 and 4).

Until 1994, local authorities in England reported the costs of what was termed 'general administration',[16] comprising the administrative support supplied by local authorities' central support services (such as legal, financial, IT, and HR services)[17] to 'users', the latter consisting of functional departments within the authority (for example in education), direct service organizations (DSOs) such as schools, and indeed other central support service units. The category of 'general administration' also originally covered the cost of the strategic management of the local authority itself. But in 1994, in one of the many data breaks of the kind we discussed in Chapter Three, the Audit Commission recommended separation of the 'corporate core' (defined as those parts of the authority with overall 'responsibility for statutory and strategic functions and of ensuring value for money in service provision') from the other administrative support services. So at that point the term 'general administration' disappeared from the revenue tables,[18] and the costs of 'administration and support services' (later 'management and support services') and the 'corporate core'[19] were thereafter reported separately.

Accordingly, what we show in Figures 7.3 and 7.4 are reported figures for the gross central administrative expenditure of English local authorities, defined (after 1994) as the sum of 'administration and support services' plus the 'corporate and democratic core'. We chose gross rather than net figures because throughout the period considered here, central services provided to their various users were reflected by a system of 'recharges' whereby the service providers 'recharged' their users the cost of the services provided.

Figure 7.3 shows English local government gross administrative expenditure (as defined above) as a percentage of total local government spending and UK central civil departments' gross administration costs relative to total central (civil) government expenditure—that is, the *levels* of local and central

[16] *Local Government Financial Statistics*, annual editions.

[17] In 1994, the breakdown of 51,000 central support service staff was Finance (48%), IT (26%), Legal (15%), and Personnel (11%). Audit Commission, *Behind Closed Doors: The Revolution in Central Support Services* (London: HMSO, 1994).

[18] Although not, oddly, from the Capital Spending tables, where it persisted until 2010.

[19] 'The corporate core is composed of the elected members, assisted by a small corps of senior officers'. (Audit Commission, *Behind Closed Doors*, p. 4). Called 'Corporate and Democratic Core' at the time of writing, the relative net cost of this function rose from 0.5 per cent to 1.2 per cent of total local authority spending between 1993 and 2003, and fell over the past decade to about 0.8 per cent of total local authority spending (about £1.5 billion in 2011–12). This function includes councillors' expenses (estimated to be about £200 million in 2011 <http://www.dailymail.co.uk/news/article-1357034/Councillors-payouts-soared-local-services-face-savage-cuts.html>).

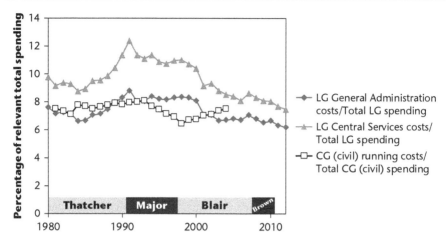

Figure 7.3. Gross Administration Costs of UK Central Government (CG) and English Local Government (LG) Relative to Total Spending 1980–2012

government administration costs (relative to the spending for which each was responsible). Figure 7.4 compares the *trend* in gross central and local administration expenditure in constant-price terms over the period they were both available.

Figure 7.3 shows that reported gross administration costs in local govern-ment varied more over this period as a proportion of total spending than did gross administration costs in central government. The former touched almost 9 per cent of total spending in 1990 before falling back to just over 6 per cent, whereas central government administration spending for the period for which we have gross figures stayed within a narrower range of 6 to 8 per cent from 1980 to the mid-2000s.

Of course we are not exactly comparing like with like here, in that what was classed as administration costs at the two levels of government was not identical, and we should be careful about making too precise comparisons. As we saw in Chapter 4, central government administration costs (as originally defined) covered the whole of the civil service, including prisons, job centres, tax offices etc., as well as the costs of running Whitehall departments, while local government 'general administration' included central services supplied to functional departments and DSOs as well as the costs of the corporate core. While not wholly different, the local government administration costs covered rather fewer functions than did the central government costs. So a more accurate comparison might be to include local tax collection costs, 'unallocated costs' (e.g. pension administration), and services to the public such as registration of electors. This combination of categories was desig-nated as 'Central Services' in *Local Government Financial Statistics* since 2005.

We calculated a consistent time series of such costs and found that including these functions added between 20 and 40 per cent to the local authority administration costs, as shown in Figure 7.3.

More to the point, perhaps, regardless of whether 'General Administration' or 'Central Services' expenditure were compared with UK central government administration costs, Figure 7.4 shows that English local government exhibited similar real-terms increases in administration costs during the 1980s and 1990s. For the decade of the 2000s, the scope for comparison is more limited, because central government stopped reporting gross administration costs after 2003–04, but Figure 7.4 indicates that administration costs rose steeply for both central and local government, albeit at slightly different times.

Turning from comparisons of administration cost to comparisons of the rule-of-law quality of administration, as explored in Chapter 6, Figure 7.5 compares complaints received by the Parliamentary Ombudsman against central government with those complaints received by the three Local Government Ombudsmen (LGO) for England over the period covered by this study. It is important to stress that the respective ombudsman bodies had different remits, and different practices over what was counted as a 'complaint' for reporting purposes. In particular, while the Parliamentary Ombudsman retained the 'MP filter' (that is, the formal requirement that all

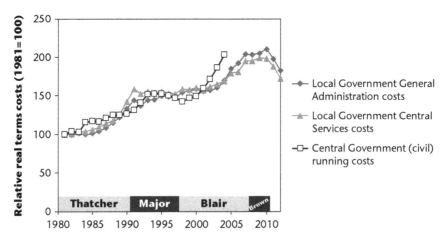

Figure 7.4. Relative Administration Costs in UK Central Government and English Local Government 1981–2012 (1980–81=100).

Sources for Figures 7.3 and 7.4: Local Government Finance Statistics, PESA, and ONS Public Sector Finances Supplementary Tables (for central and local total spending). Local Government General Administration spending was reported until 1994, when it was succeeded by Central Administration and Support Services plus Corporate and Democratic Core. Central Services include (in addition to General Administration) Local Tax Collection, Central Services to the Public, and Non-Distributed Costs. Council Tax Benefit Administration was excluded from these totals. Real-terms costs were calculated by dividing nominal values by the 2012–13 GDP deflator series.

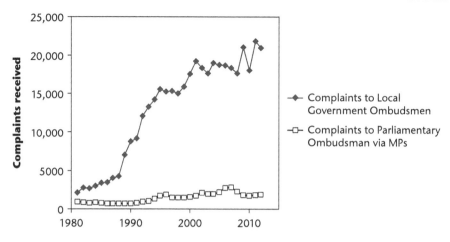

Figure 7.5. Complaints Received by Local Government Ombudsmen and Parliamentary Ombudsman 1981–2012

Sources: Annual Reports of the Local Government Ombudsmen and the Parliamentary Ombudsman.

complaints should be channelled through MPs) throughout the period, as mentioned in Chapter 6, the comparable 'councillor filter' for the LGO was removed in 1988.[20] Such institutional differences mean that it is the slopes of these complaints trajectories rather than the absolute levels which are important in this comparison. And what Figure 7.5 shows is that complaints to the LGO rose ten-fold over a period when complaints to the Parliamentary Ombudsman rose only two-fold.

If we look behind these numbers, we noted in Chapter 6 that the vast bulk of the increase in the rise in complaints to the Parliamentary Ombudsman about central government in the early 1990s concerned 'employment and benefits' matters. In the case of local authorities, the rising numbers of complaints were not so concentrated on any single topic, but housing and planning together accounted for 60 to 70 per cent of complaints to the LGO from 1984 to 2000. In both cases, the ombudsmen's methods of working changed over this period, as we discussed in Chapter 6, with an increasing emphasis on resolving complaints without the need for formal reports. The proportion of complaints formally reported on by the LGO decreased substantially more than those reported on by the Parliamentary Ombudsman. Nevertheless, the vast majority of LGO reports found evidence of maladministration while only about half of cases reported on by the Parliamentary Ombudsman found such evidence.

---

[20] From 2008–09 the LGO also began to report 'complaints and inquiries' together, so that the last four data points in Figure 7.4 are not strictly comparable with the previous ones, but this formal change did not cause an obvious discontinuity.

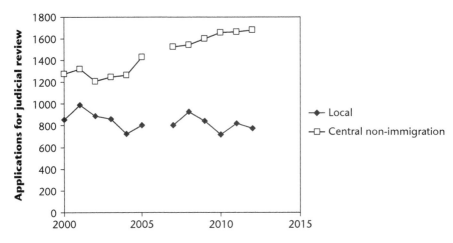

Figure 7.6. English Judicial Review Applications Concerning Central Government and Local Authorities, 2000–2012

Sources: Numbers of local judicial review applications 2000–2005 were kindly supplied by Lucinda Platt (personal communication). Applications 2007–2012 were from Ministry of Justice, *Court Statistics Quarterly* (January to March 2013), Table 4.3.

So even if we allow for substantial uncertainty in this kind of comparison and ignore entirely the relative levels of complaints about the two levels of government and focus entirely on the slopes of increase, the five-fold difference in the rate at which complaints to the ombudsmen rose in the two cases does not convincingly support the suggestion by local government advocates (as noted earlier) that greater knowledge of local conditions will automatically lead to better quality administration.

We get a somewhat different picture from the levels of judicial review (in England), although it should be noted that our data covered only the 2000s, since the relevant official data source (*Judicial Statistics*) only reported local and central government numbers separately for a small part of the thirty-year period covered by this book. Lucinda Platt and colleagues made an exhaustive search of English court records for the first half of the 2000s and found that judicial review applications regarding local government bodies ran at about 850 per year, or roughly 40 per cent of the total of non-immigration cases.[21] In December 2013, however, a dataset of all English judicial review applications since 2007 was published by the Ministry of Justice. Figure 7.6 combines those two series and shows that applications concerning central government (non-immigration cases)—the majority of which related to the criminal

---

[21] Lucinda Platt, Maurice Sunkin, and Kerman Calvo, 'Judicial Review Litigation as an Incentive to Change in Local Authority Public Services in England and Wales', *Journal of Public Administration Research and Theory* 20 Supplement 2 (2010): pp. i243–i260.

justice system, as noted in Chapter 6—rose about 50 per cent between 2000 and 2012, while local government cases showed no overall trend.

Now of course this comparison of costs and complaints only comprises local government in England (only one part of the UK, albeit 80 per cent of the population), and it is possible that comparison of equivalent metrics in the other countries of the UK would yield different results. But this analysis does not support the view that there was a very marked difference between the trajectory of administration costs in central and local government, while complaints (but not judicial review applications) rose much more sharply for local than for central government.

7.5 Comparison between Whitehall and the Devolved Administration in Scotland

A fourth and final way of exploring whether or how far there were different performance records across different parts of government is to compare the UK trends in running costs and citizen responses with those applying to the government of the UK's devolved countries. Here we use Scotland as our comparator for this analysis, and the administrative level we look at is the set of government departments and agencies in Scotland that comes between local government and 'whole of UK' government departments (such as defence, tax, social security) with responsibility and offices throughout the UK.

Scotland had the highest population of the UK's 'devolved countries' at the time of writing (somewhat over 5 million, or 8.4 per cent of the UK) and has had a well defined devolved administrative level of government, separate from that of the rest of the UK, that long pre-dated the re-establishment of the Scottish Parliament in 1999. The Scottish administration consisted of a set of organizations traditionally clustered in Edinburgh (but more recently subject to policies of dispersion within Scotland). A few of those organizations dated back to the time before the union of the Scottish and English parliaments in 1707 but many developed out of or around the Scottish Office created in 1885 and were further consolidated from a set of Edinburgh-based boards into more standard-issue government departments in a major reorganization in 1939.[22] Over the thirty-year period covered by this book, the number of civil servants working at this level of administration in Scotland increased by about one-third, as shown in Figure 7.7 (in sharp contrast to the picture for the UK as a whole, for which civil service numbers fell by about

---

[22] See, for example, John S. Gibson, *The Thistle and the Crown: A History of the Scottish Office* (Edinburgh: HMSO, 1985); James G. Kellas, *The Scottish Political System*, 3rd edn (Cambridge: Cambridge University Press, 1984), pp. 29–40.

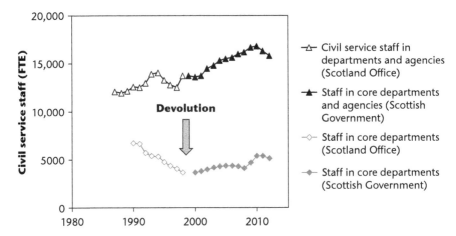

Figure 7.7. Civil Service Staff in Scottish Departments and Agencies 1984–2012

Sources: Pre-devolution staff numbers were from *Civil Service Statistics*, and post-devolution were from the Scottish government *Quarterly Public Sector Employment Statistics*.

one-third over the same period, as we noted in Chapter 2). Much of that growth took place outside the core Scottish departments.

Moreover, as we noted at the outset, it is often said that (even before legislative devolution in 1999) Scottish administration had its own distinctive culture and operating style very different from that operating in 'Whitehall', or UK government more generally. It tended to operate closer to the point of service delivery than departments or agencies with UK-wide responsibilities, was not dominated (as UK central government has traditionally been) by Oxbridge-educated elites with a London- or South-of-England-dominated mindset, and concentrated mainly on domestic service-delivery functions rather than the traditional 'high politics' issues of foreign affairs, intelligence, and defence. Other distinctive cultural characteristics have been claimed as well. So were those cultural and institutional differences associated with marked variations in performance on cost and administrative quality as between UK and Scottish government over our period?

Starting with administration costs, we begin by comparing *levels* of such costs between the Scottish administration and the UK central civil departments, and then go on to what is probably a more meaningful comparison of the *trends* of administration cost changes over time.

Comparisons before and after devolution are complicated by the fact that Scottish agencies and core departments were statistically bundled together as a single unit pre-devolution for reporting of administration costs, but after devolution in 1999 only the administration costs of 'core' departments were reported, and there appeared to be no duplicated reporting that allows

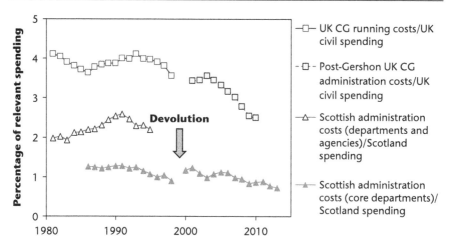

Figure 7.8. Net Administration Costs of Scottish and UK Civil Departments Relative to Scottish and UK Civil Spending 1981–2013

pre- and post-devolution Scottish administration costs to be directly compared. Comparison with the UK is complicated further by the data break in UK administration costs in the early 2000s discussed in Chapters 3 and 4, and the fact that the UK government reported only net administration costs after 2004.

Accordingly, Figure 7.8 shows the net administration costs of (i) the Scottish departments and agencies and (ii) the Scottish core departments only, each expressed as a proportion of the spending for which the Secretary of State for Scotland was responsible (before devolution in 1999) and the total spending of the Scottish government (after devolution). These ratios were compared with the net administration costs of the UK civil departments divided by UK total civil spending. This is admittedly a fairly crude comparison, since the responsibilities of the Scottish administration differed from those of UK central civil departments, as already explained.

As Figure 7.8 shows, the UK administration costs as a proportion of total UK civil spending consistently and markedly exceeded the Scottish comparator over the whole period (although, as already explained, we were unable to calculate the ideal comparison, that of Scottish core departments plus agencies post-devolution[23]). Similar differences appeared when we calculated administration costs relative to population rather than to total spending. But

---

[23] Agencies' running costs were no longer centrally reported after devolution, and can only be found in the separately published annual reports of each body. Missing editions and inconsistencies in reporting conventions made it in practice impossible to compile cost figures comparable with pre-devolution data.

before making very much of this comparison of ratios, we also need to look at *trends* in what it cost to run these two levels of government—did those costs rise or fall at markedly different rates?

For such a comparison, the longest comparable series available prior to devolution included the gross administration costs of departments and agencies (including UK civil departments and executive agencies). After devolution we can only compare net administration costs of Scottish core departments with net UK civil administration costs. These series are shown in Figure 7.9. When we concentrate on trends rather than levels, the rates of change in administrative spending showed little difference between the Scottish departments and central civil UK departments. As can be seen, after an initial rise, both levels of government underwent running cost cutbacks in the mid-1990s. Post devolution, administrative spending in both Scotland and the UK rose in real terms until the mid-2000s, and then started to fall. So

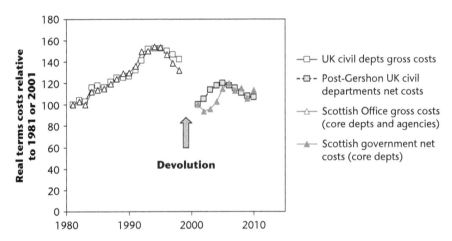

Figure 7.9. Relative Administration Costs of Scottish and UK Civil Departments 1980–2010. Gross Costs Relative to 1980–81 (=100) Prior to Devolution, and Net Administration Costs Relative to 2000–01 (=100) Post-Devolution

Sources for Figures 7.8 and 7.9: Before devolution in 1999, the three available data-series on the costs of Scottish departments were (a) the PESA series reporting 'gross running costs of Scottish departments and agencies' (alongside the running costs of all other UK departments, and subject to the same types of reclassifications as the UK data) (b) data reported in successive editions of *The Government's Expenditure Plans: Report of the Secretary of State for Scotland*, which allowed consistent series of costs of 'core departments' and agencies to be determined separately for the financial years ending 1990 to 1995. After devolution the two available data-series were (a) running cost figures for the small part of the former Scottish Office that was renamed 'the Scotland Office' and retained as a UK department after devolution; (b) running cost figures for the 'core' Scottish departments reported in the Scottish Executive (later 'government') *Core Departments' Resource Accounts* (later the *Scottish Government Consolidated Accounts*). Scottish total spending before devolution was the expenditure within the responsibility of the Secretary of State for Scotland, and after devolution was total Scottish government expenditure. UK civil spending was Total Managed Expenditure exclusive of defence.

any major difference between the two levels of government in terms of running costs lies in levels rather than trends.

Turning to the quality of administration issue that we explored in Chapter 6, it is perhaps worth noticing that, according to the most comparable annual surveys available over a run of years (the British Social Attitudes Survey since 1983 and the Scottish Social Attitudes Survey since 1999), the Scottish goverment apparently elicited a substantially higher level of trust from its citizens between 2000 and 2012 than did the British government over the same period, although the questions were slightly different.[24] Against that, the proportion of survey respondents who 'almost never' trusted politicians to tell the truth appeared to be very similar in Scotland and England, being between 50 and 60 per cent in the later years of our period and following similar gradually increasing trends.[25] But if there was any higher level of trust in Scottish government as against that of the UK, was it reflected in indicators more directly related to the the perceived fairness and consistency of administration that concerned us in Chapter 6—that is, the incidence of formal complaints and legal challenges?

For the first item we can make rough comparisons of the numbers of complaints about government bodies in the two administrations. A Scottish Parliamentary Ombudsman was created in 1999, and that office was merged with that of the Scottish Public Services Ombudsman in 2002. The number of complaints about 'bodies of the Scottish Executive or devolved administration' were recorded separately by the Public Services Ombudsman, which can be compared with the number of complaints about UK government bodies received by the UK Parliamentary Ombudsman that we analyzed in Chapter 6. Accordingly, Figure 7.10 shows the number of comparable complaints per million population received by these two offices.

As Figure 7.10 shows, Scottish complaints about government bodies per million population were running well below the UK level until about 2008. But we have to be cautious about putting too much weight on this 'levels' comparison because the rules and remits of the two ombudsmen were different in relation to what counted as a complaint (for example, in Scotland some phone calls were classed as complaints), what issues could

---

[24] The Scottish Social Attitudes Survey asked: 'How much do you trust the Scottish Government to work in Scotland's long-term interests?', and an average of 61 per cent of Scottish citizens answered 'most of the time' and 'almost all of the time' from 2000 to 2012. The British Social Attitudes Survey (BSAS) asked: 'How much do you trust British governments of any party to place the needs of the nation above the interests of their own political party?' and only 22 per cent of British citizens answered 'most of the time' and 'almost all of the time' to that question over the same period. In both cases the answers were stable over time, showing no upward or downward trend. Disaggregating the BSAS data by region, we found those living in Scotland showed no systematic differences from the rest of Britain in their trust of the British government.

[25] British Social Attitudes Survey indicator 'MPSTRUST' reported since 1995.

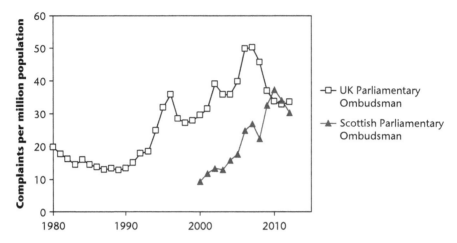

Figure 7.10. Complaints about Scottish Executive (later Government) Bodies and UK Government Bodies to the Scottish and UK Parliamentary Ombudsman 1980–2012

Sources: Annual Reports of the Scottish Public Services Ombudsman and the Parliamentary and Health Service Ombudsman.

be complained about and by what procedure, by the fact that the two levels of government provided different services (for instance, over tax and social security, mostly not handled by the devolved government at this time), and also the fact that Scots could still complain to the UK Parliamentary Ombudsman about bodies with UK-wide responsibility. It is therefore dangerous to read too much into differences in levels. But what we can more meaningfully compare is trends in the pattern of complaints (keeping in mind that the precise jurisdictions of the two ombudsmen varied from time to time over the period shown, as we noted in Chapter 6). And here it is notable that recorded complaints about Scottish government bodies rose sharply over the overall period since devolution and ended by running at about the same level per million population as comparable complaints to the UK Ombudsman. Similarly, when we looked at complaints to the Health Service Commissioner (and since devolution the Scottish Public Services Ombudsman) we find a very similar trajectory of complaints in Scotland and England, increasing from under twenty complaints per million people in 1990 to about one hundred per million population in the mid-2000s in both countries.

When it comes to the other measure of perceived consistency and fairness in administration that we explored in Chapter 6, namely applications for judicial review, Figure 7.11 compares requests for permission to apply for judicial review of government actions in England and Wales with their approximate equivalent, 'petitions initiated', in Scotland. Figure 7.11a

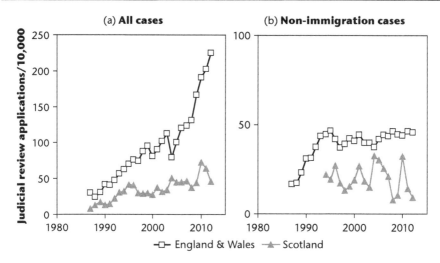

Figure 7.11. Judicial Review Applications Per 10,000 Population in Scotland and in England and Wales 1987–2012 (a) All Cases (b) Non-Immigration Cases

Sources: Annual editions of *Civil Judicial Statistics* (Scotland) and *Judicial Statistics* (England & Wales).

shows the jurisdictions on a per capita basis, showing judicial review applications per 10,000 population.

As can be seen, Figure 7.11a shows a difference in litigation levels between the two tiers of government that is consistent with the survey and complaint data we examined earlier. But we should note that the rules governing judicial review differed somewhat between the two jurisdictions (for instance Scotland did not have the category 'criminal judicial review' which made up about 3 per cent of English cases in 2012, and not all cases of judicial review in Scotland related to public law), so again a comparison of trends is arguably more meaningful than a comparison of levels. And here it is notable that per capita applications in England and Wales rose significantly faster than Scottish applications over this period, especially since 2005.

However, as we pointed out in Chapter 6, many of the applications in England and Wales were immigration cases and it is debatable how far we should consider those cases as a valid indicator of changing perceptions of the rule-of-law quality of UK public administration, given the special circumstances underlying the increase in that category of judicial review applications. Accordingly, Figured 7.11b shows the non-immigration cases per 10,000 population for Scotland between 1993 and 2012 and for England and Wales between 1987 and 2012. This figure shows that the number of non-immigration cases showed no overall upward or downward trend since 1993, in both jurisdictions, though England and Wales had a consistently higher per capita level of applications.

As in previous sections, we should sound a note of caution about what can be drawn from this analysis, and the picture is even more nuanced than applies to previous sections. As far as costs are concerned, a *levels* comparison showed that Scottish departments had overall lower running costs than UK central departments, but a *trends* analysis did not show up striking differences. On levels of formal complaint to ombudsmen as an indicator of the perceived fairness and consistency of administration, over most of the period considered a *levels* comparison showed that the Scottish administration elicited lower levels of complaints relative to population than applied to the UK level of government, but a *trends* analysis indicated that Scottish complaints increased rapidly, and indeed reached similar per capita levels as complaints to the UK ombudsman by 2008. Similarly, a *levels* comparison of applications for judicial review showed that the incidence of such applications was higher over the whole period for England and Wales than for Scotland. A *trends* analysis showed that the incidence of such applications had risen faster in England and Wales than in Scotland over the period, but that difference in trends disappeared if we consider only non-immigration cases.

So the conclusion we draw from this final comparison depends heavily on the weight we put on comparisons of levels relative to trends and how we interpret these results given the different remits and responsibilities of the two levels of government. It may be that the most judicious conclusion when looking at these performance indicators as a whole is the famous 'Scottish verdict'—that is, not proven. But if, as we have argued, a 'trends' comparison is more meaningful than a 'levels' comparison in such a case, the comparison shows up more similarities than differences.

7.6 Conclusion

This chapter aimed to put UK central government performance into comparative perspective on matters of running cost and administrative quality, taking advantage of such limited opportunities for comparison as are available. Given the counterfactual possibility mentioned at the outset, that performance could have been even worse in the absence of the attempts to modernize and introduce managerial reforms, it aimed to see if comparisons between entities said to be different in their emphasis on 'managerialism' suggest any notable differences in performance (UK central government compared with governments elsewhere that have not acquired the same vanguard-state or poster-child reputation for managerial reforms, core ministerial departments compared with executive agencies intended to give greater scope for creative management of service delivery).

More generally, and by comparing entities with different traditions and cultures (UK central government compared with English local government and with Scottish administration before and after devolution) this chapter aimed to find out whether the performance record we traced out for UK central government in Chapters 4–6 represented some general administrative condition of recent decades, or whether marked differences could be detected across different levels and types of government administration.

As far as the three within-UK comparisons are concerned (ministerial departments/executive agencies, central government/local government, UK or English government/Scottish government), such data as are available suggests only limited variation in 'trend' comparisons, which we argued earlier to be generally more meaningful than 'levels' comparisons where bodies do not have exactly the same functions, or where counting systems vary. For the three comparisons where supposedly or stereotypically more reformist units can be compared with others (the UK as poster-child in comparative perspective, ministerial departments relative to executive agencies ostensibly designed to give freer rein to managers, and possibly the UK [or at least England] relative to Scotland), the possible conclusions range from 'not proven' to outcomes in which the supposedly more 'reformist' and 'managerial' units performed no differently or worse than their counterparts. In line with what we have done in Chapters 4–6, Table 7.1 below summarizes our conclusions, with some qualifying comments.

What the analysis of this chapter, summed up in Table 7.1, seems to suggest is that according to such limited documentary evidence as is readily available, the UK was not a remarkable outlier in cross-national studies of administrative efficiency, productivity, and performance, except perhaps on the World Bank governance indicators. When it comes to comparisons between core ministerial departments and delivery units, the analysis here, taken together with other studies, does not support the view that running costs were markedly lower or rose more slowly in executive agencies than in core ministerial departments (if anything, the evidence suggests that the opposite was the case). And in spite—or should that be because—of the plethora of (mostly short-lived) performance indicators associated with executive agencies, we simply do not have relevant indicators on which to base a comparison of administrative fairness and consistency in this case.

Comparing our cost and rule-of-law indicators across entities with different cultures and institutional traditions (UK central government as against English local government and against Scottish administration), we suggested that a levels comparison is less meaningful than a trends comparison in both cases, but we can compare the trends in those cost numbers over time, and when we do so, there is no clear at-a-glance difference between those cost slopes in either case. On the rule-of-law indicators we see a mixed picture,

Table 7.1. Four Types of Comparison Summarized

Level of Comparison	Running costs	Consistency and fairness of administration	Analytic significance	General comment
Cross–national studies	The UK was not obviously an outlier in such limited comparisons as are available on efficiency/ costs	The UK was not obviously an outlier on most of a limited number of international comparisons	No evidence that the UK's status as NPM vanguard state was associated with notably high or low performance	Comparisons limited and typically not conducted at the level of individual central government departments
Ministerial department–Executive agency	In an aggregate analysis, central departments were not higher on running costs than executive agencies	Unknown: comparable indicators were not available	Limited evidence suggests no better running-cost performance in agencies despite scope for managerialism	Cost data was available only on a highly aggregated basis and performance data very limited
UK central government–English local government	Administration cost *trends* for central and local government were similar, though *levels* differed	Ombudsman complaints rose faster for local than central government, but applications for judicial review rose faster for central government	Managerial reforms affected both levels of government and in both cases running costs rose on similar slopes and formal complaints rose	It is more meaningful to compare slopes rather than levels of administration costs, given different classifications
UK (or England and Wales)–Scotland	Administration cost *trends* for UK civil central government were not steeper than those in Scottish government, though *levels* (and responsibilities) differed	Ombudsman complaints higher for UK central government than for Scottish government, but Scottish complaints rose after devolution. Judicial review trends similar for non-immigration cases	No evidence that the supposedly more 'managerial' thrust of UK reforms resulted in markedly different running-cost performance between the two levels of government	There was a major data break on administration costs at the time of devolution to Scotland in 1999. Many relevant indicators only dated back a few years

with a marked long-term rise in formal complaints in all cases (albeit with varying slopes) and a degree of variation in judicial review that depended heavily on whether immigration cases against the UK government were included in the comparison. But when we put the emphasis on the slopes comparison, much of that analysis seems to support the 'shared administrative condition' interpretation that we mentioned earlier rather than indicating completely different paths and trajectories.

Clearly there is much more that could and should be done in deepening and refining such comparisons, not just as a matter of academic curiosity but as a matter of good governance and administration following what Jeremy Bentham called the 'tabular comparison' principle. Indeed, if Bentham could be brought back from the dead today, he might well be shocked by how little systematic comparison of central and local government administration costs over time had been carried out in the UK, given all the hype and inflated claims that have surrounded successive efficiency drives. And the notion that devolution would provide a kind of laboratory for natural experiments in policy and institutions as different approaches were applied in different countries of the UK is not easy to apply in the case of administration costs, given that there is no basis in the reported data for a before-and-after comparison of Scottish (central government) administration costs. Whether such analytic and research deficits can be remedied in the future remains to be seen, and we shall return to that issue in the final chapter.

8

Government Processes

More Focused and Business-like or Heading into Chaos?

. . . it's been the biggest cock-up ever . . .[1]

8.1 Three Claims About Changing Process

As we have seen in the earlier chapters, the managerial reforms in UK government over the thirty years that we have explored in this book were intended to make government more business-like in at least two ways. One was that it should become tightly focused on performance and delivery (for example by separating service-delivery from policymaking or regulation and by more closely specifying delivery standards). The other was that it should develop systems and practices that were intended to be closer to those used in private firms (for example, in moves both to enable and require active management and to use variable bonus systems to reward public servants). And as we have also seen, much has been, and continues to be, claimed—and denied—for this kind of approach.

In Chapters 4 and 5, we explored what actually happened to reported running costs over the period considered here, and in Chapter 6 we explored what happened to formal complaints and litigation as indicators of the perceived fairness and consistency of public administration. As we have seen, that analysis shows it is far from clear that thirty years of reform and managerial makeovers resulted in a government that worked better and cost less in such terms. But other lines of comment and criticism focus as much on what happened to *processes* within government—its inner workings—as on output or outcomes. Such concerns were directed at what happened to the way

---

[1] Sir Richard Mottram, then Permanent secretary at the Department of Transport, on the resignation of Martin Sixsmith, as reported in the *Sunday Times* (24 February 2002).

policy and legislation was crafted inside the government machine as much as on service delivery. This chapter accordingly turns to three of those issues.

One recurring line of criticism targeted a perceived decline in procedural standards in the bureaucracy that manifested itself in various ways. A powerful critique of that kind came from Sir Christopher Foster, an influential figure who has worked in and around British government for over four decades from his early days as a Treasury economist in the 1950s, and who in 2005 published a hard-hitting book titled *British Government in Crisis*.[2] As its title implied, the book argued that there had been a substantial deterioration in some of the important ways that UK executive government worked from the 1970s to the 2000s, in particular in the way that policy was made and legislation crafted. One of the people we interviewed for our study partly echoed this theme, telling us that a reduction in the use of Green and White Papers (official government documents respectively floating options and putting forward proposals for action) in the process of developing policy meant that legislation was less well thought out than previously. According to Foster, the resulting shortcomings of inadequate policy were then compounded by hastily drafted, late-stage amendments that were subject to little detailed scrutiny. That in turn tended to damage the overall coherence of legislation, for example by building in contradictions, definitional problems, and compliance issues, which along with other changes might help to account for the rise in judicial challenge that we noticed in Chapter 6.

Foster associated the deterioration he observed in the quality of legislation submitted to Parliament with developments that included fragmentation of the executive machine, poorer working relations between ministers and civil servants, less scrupulous attention to careful documentation of policy decisions ('sofa government'), poorer consultation with affected groups and between government departments than had once been the case, and less critical scrutiny of policy developments than had applied in an earlier age. Foster's analysis resonated with the experience of many senior civil servants and some ministers, leading in the mid-2000s to the formation of an all-party group, the Better Government Initiative,[3] which issued several reports designed to improve processes of policymaking and legislation. But critics such as Foster were in turn accused of rosy-spectacled 'golden-ageism' both by those who were sceptical about the historical validity of the 'decline' thesis (such as Vernon Bogdanor[4]) and by defenders of current government processes. The latter thought that an

---

[2] Sir Christopher Foster, *British Government in Crisis* (Oxford: Hart Publishing, 2005). See also Sir Christopher Foster, *Why are We So Badly Governed?* (London: Public Management and Policy Association, 2005).

[3] Comprising mainly retired senior civil servants plus some politicians, academics, and others.

[4] Vernon Bogdanor, 'British Government in Crisis: book review', *PMPA Review* 30 (2005): pp. 12–14; see also George Jones' more positive review of the book in the same issue of *PMPA Review*, pp. 11–12.

expansion of the Parliamentary Counsel's office (the civil servants who draft bills in consultation with departments), together with changes in parliamentary procedures designed to enhance Parliament's ability to scrutinize legislation more effectively, had in fact served to improve the quality of legislation.

Other seasoned observers of the workings of Whitehall focused on loss of institutional memory—the sort of detailed 'knowledge of the files' that one of the great twentieth-century theorists of bureaucracy, Max Weber,[5] had seen as central to what made modern bureaucracies so powerful and effective—as a result of various developments weakening capacities for what they saw as effective decision-making and policy. For example, Christopher Pollitt and Rod Rhodes, two leading analysts of British government since the 1970s, both argued that loss of institutional memory was an unintended effect of three decades of management reform in Whitehall. As Pollitt ironically put it, a sure 'recipe' for suppressing institutional memory and compromising the ability of organizations to learn from experience involved rapid rotation of operational staff, frequent major changes in IT systems with little attention to careful archiving at the point of changeover, frequent organizational restructurings, a tendency to reward management skills above subject-knowledge, and the slavish adoption of every new management fad as it came along—all of which Pollitt saw as characteristic and typical of UK central government operation over several decades.[6] Rod Rhodes, in a study of three Whitehall departments, observed most of the processes in Pollitt's 'recipe', particularly poor record-keeping, a culture of moving young 'fast stream' civil servants rapidly from one posting to another within departments, and high staff turnover, and argued that the consequent damage to institutional memory had deep implications for the way Whitehall departments worked.[7] Sometimes the criticism extended to turnover at ministerial as well as civil service level. For example, the senior civil servant, Sir Richard Mottram, who uttered the famous remark quoted in the epigraph to this chapter, noted in a lecture in 2008 that one of the departments he had headed, the Department for Work and Pensions (DWP), had had six Secretaries of State in as many years, adding tellingly that 'if DWP were a regulated financial institution, this scale of turnover would surely have attracted the regulator's attention'.[8]

---

[5] Max Weber, 'Bureaucracy' (orig. 1911), in *From Max Weber: Essays in Sociology*, edited and trans. by H. H. Gerth and C. W. Mills (London: Routledge and Kegan Paul, 1948), p. 214.

[6] Christopher Pollitt, *Time, Policy, Management: Governing with the Past* (Oxford: Oxford University Press, 2008), pp. 172–3.

[7] Rod Rhodes, *Everyday Life in British Government* (Oxford: Oxford University Press, 2011), pp. 294–5.

[8] Sir Richard Mottram, 'Fifteen Years at the Top in the UK Civil Service—Some Reflections', Speech to the London School of Economics MPA Programme, 6 May 2008, quoted in Anne White and Patrick Dunleavy, *Making and Breaking Whitehall Departments: A Guide to Machinery of Government Changes* (London: Institute for Government and LSE Public Policy Group, 2010), p. 20.

A third strain of concern about the functioning of Whitehall departments is represented by the writing that we referred to in Chapters 1 and 2 about the rise of 'spin' and message control in the bureaucracy. For example, Sir Bernard Ingham, a controversial civil servant who had been Margaret Thatcher's press secretary from 1979 to 1990, argued that operation of the executive government machine came to be transformed, particularly in the 'New Labour' years after 1997, by more centralized and politicized control of 'message' and 'narrative'.[9] And Ingham was by no means a lone voice: one of the central points in Sir Christopher Foster's *British Government in Crisis*, mentioned earlier, was that a growth in emphasis on 'spinning' had damaged trust in government. Indeed, as we noted in Chapter 2, the Blair government's 'spin machine', arguably modelled on US President Bill Clinton's formidable news management apparatus of the 1990s, attracted a great deal of comment, most of it critical. It was commonly claimed that 'presentation' in a changing and arguably more challenging media environment dominated the operation of executive government as never before, with the new lords of spin coming to rule the cabinet as well as the senior civil service. As well as the perceived need to adapt information management to a changing media environment (with more outlets and twenty-four-hour news coverage), the second two decades of the period covered by this book saw the development of more formal systems for disclosure of government information, in the form of an 'open government' regime from the early 1990s which was replaced by formal Freedom of Information (FOI) legislation (passed in 2002 and coming fully into operation in 2005) presenting further challenges for information management. In 2006 Alasdair Roberts argued that in the UK (and other countries), the advent of FOI legislation led in practice to more centralized political control of operation—exactly the opposite of the 'culture of openness' within the bureaucracy that FOI proponents argued would be the result of such legislation.[10]

All of these three sets of concerns represent important claims about far-reaching changes in *process* within executive government, and many of those who have written about those changes based their analysis on personal observation, long experience, and qualitative insights drawn from well-placed interviewees and observers. But none of the writers referred to above offer systematic numbers to back up their claims about changes over time. Of course, qualitative observations are important and many of the changes in social relationships that those writers highlight may not readily

---

[9] Sir Bernard Ingham, *The Wages of Spin* (London: John Murray, 2003).
[10] Alasdair Roberts, 'Dashed Expectations: Governmental Adaptation to Transparency Rules', in *Transparency: The Key to Better Governance?*, edited by Christopher Hood and David Heald (Oxford: Oxford University Press for the British Academy, 2006).

be picked up by any statistical series. Nevertheless, this chapter aims to add to those debates by assessing the three sets of claims with such numbers as are available. Accordingly, we look at documentary evidence that might support claims that over the decades considered by this book, legislative crafting and departmental administration became more disorderly and less meticulous, that presumptions of loss of continuity and deteriorating institutional memory are reflected in evidence of increasing 'churn' in people and structures, and that information and 'spin' came to absorb more central government resources, in people, spending, or both, than before.

Such measurements can be described as *process indicators*, since they are concerned with what went on inside the government machine rather than the inputs going into that machine (what it cost to run) and the nature of its outputs (in the sense of treating citizens fairly and consistently), and thus represent a rather different angle from that taken in the previous four chapters. It also represents a different angle from the main preoccupations of the NPM movement, which was often represented as being more concerned with costs and effective service for 'customers'. As we shall see, the process indicators considered here offer more support for some of the claims mentioned above than for others, even though many of those we interviewed in the course of our investigations strongly subscribed to what might be called a 'heading into chaos' view.

8.2 More Disorderly Policymaking and Less Meticulous Administration?

As mentioned earlier, one line of criticism about changing process in UK central government over the thirty years considered here was the claim that there had been a decline in procedural standards in various ways. Here we look at two possible indicators that might reflect such a decline, namely the incidence of late-stage government amendments to legislation going through Parliament, and the incidence of 'qualifications' of departmental accounts by the public auditor.

Figure 8.1 indicates the number of government amendments (relative to the length of the legislation) made to bills as they passed through the legislative process in two major and politically salient policy domains in which new legislation regularly appeared, namely criminal justice and the National Health Service. The purpose of gathering those numbers—which reflect months of laborious work, much of it from hard-to-track-down-and-interpret, pre-internet-age, paper sources—is to explore whether in those legislative domains there was clear evidence of an increase over time in government amendments (that is, amendments proposed by a minister of the department

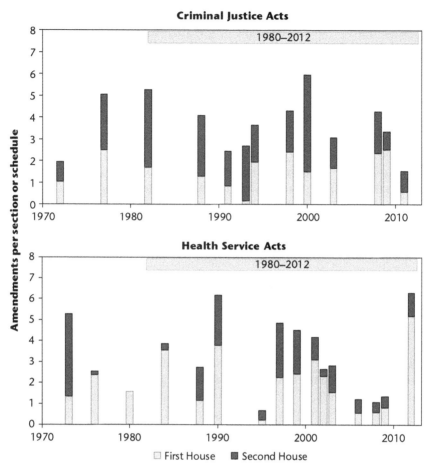

Figure 8.1. Accepted Government Amendments in Two Legislative 'Families' Relative to the Length of the Legislation 1970–2012

Sources and methodology are given in Appendix 4. Graphs in this chapter contain a bar starting at 1980 to facilitate comparison.

sponsoring the bill), particularly at the later stages of the legislative process. If the incidence of such amendments grew over time, it would support Foster's claim, noted earlier, that the quality of policymaking and legislative preparation declined over the period covered by this book. If legislation increasingly tended to arrive in Parliament shoddily prepared and ill thought-through, such that it tended to fall apart in Parliament, necessitating hastily cobbled together, late-stage amendments, does that show up in a count of amendments?[11]

---

[11] The House of Lords *Report on the Working of the House* (HL 9, 1987–88), p. 5, made a similar point over two decades earlier: 'Government legislation has been more heavily amended in the

Figure 8.1 allows us to assess whether that was indeed the case in these two major legislative 'families'. Details of the analysis are given in Appendix 4. A bill starts either in the House of Commons or (less commonly) in the House of Lords, and then passes to the other house, being subject to amendment at various stages in each house. It must be approved by both houses before it receives Royal Assent and becomes an Act of Parliament. Figure 8.1 shows the number of government amendments agreed in the parliamentary stages in each house relative to the length of the legislation (the number of sections and schedules in the Act of Parliament).

Of course there are limits to the validity of such an indicator that cannot be ignored. One of our interviewees thought it reflected a naive 'accountant's view' of legislative production. One or two pointed to technical improvements in the process of legislative drafting that had come about as a result of the adoption of digital technology (which made technical checking easier by the use of search functions, instead of the laborious and potentially error-prone processes of proof-reading paper documents in the pre-digital, letterpress age), more pre-legislative scrutiny both in Parliament and inside the government machine (as a result of formal Impact Assessment processes), and the increased pay and staff numbers in the Parliamentary Counsel's office that dated from changes in the late 1990s. One of our interviewees pointed out that government amendments can reflect concessions made to interest groups with a propensity to 'have a go'[12] and that amendments can be introduced late in the legislative process for reasons that have nothing to do with the quality of a bill's original drafting, for example when anti-terrorism measures are added to bills already in progress (as happened after bombings in London in 2005) to demonstrate activity and thus score political points. Another pointed out that dozens of clauses[13] could be added as a single amendment to a bill, while ten amendments could relate to a single clause. A single word change could lead to swathes of amendments, since each instance of such a word would give rise to an amendment.

All of these points are valid and important. But we might expect such complicating factors to be more or less constant, or at least trendless, over time. And indeed, a leading member of the 'Better Government Initiative' (BGI) told us that the BGI had thought late-stage amendments might be a

---

Lords than in previous Sessions [. . .] which suggests that legislation may have been introduced without adequate consideration'.

[12] Meg Russell, in *The Contemporary House of Lords: Westminster Bicameralism Revived* (Oxford: Oxford University Press, 2013) showed that over half of all agreed 'policy-type' amendments in twelve bills in the House of Lords, although introduced by government ministers, were versions of amendments originally proposed by non-ministerial peers and therefore probably originated with outside interest groups.

[13] The numbered 'sections' in an Act of Parliament are known as 'clauses' in a bill.

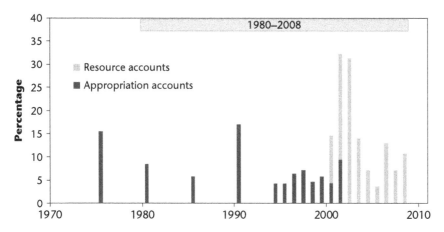

Figure 8.2. Percentage of Departmental Accounts 'Qualified' by the Public Auditor 1975–2008

Sources: Appropriation Accounts sampled at five-yearly intervals until 1990, thereafter National Audit Office *Annual Reports.*

promising proxy for legislative quality and had discussed the issue with the Parliamentary clerks.

Turning to a different aspect of process, Figure 8.2 indicates the percentage of departmental accounts 'qualified' by the National Audit Office (and its pre-1983 equivalent, the Exchequer and Audit Department) in its annual audit of central government accounts from 1975 to 2009. By 'qualified' is meant those accounts about which the Comptroller and Auditor General had some doubts and was therefore unable to give an 'unqualified opinion' that the accounts were true and fair in the sense of accurately representing departments' financial position according to the reporting standards applying at the time.

The figures shown in Figure 8.2 are compiled from two different sources. The numbers from 1975 to 1990 came from 'appropriation accounts', while the numbers from 1994 to 2008 came from the National Audit Office's (NAO) annual reports. During the latter period the accounting system altered, notably with the advent of 'resource accounting'[14] replacing the traditional cash 'appropriation accounts' system which was phased out in 2000 and 2001. The accounting system changed again in 2009–10 with the production of 'whole of government accounts'. In the first two years of the new system of accounts, there were qualifications of those accounts by the NAO, but the reporting system had changed too much to enable meaningful comparison with earlier years, so the analysis shown in Figure 8.2 stops at 2008.

---

[14] Whereas traditional cash accounting was based on recording cash payments, resource accounting aims to measure resources as they are consumed, such that the recorded cost of capital items is spread over their lifetime.

161

Both of these process indicators give a mixed picture, but neither unambiguously supports the 'descent into chaos' view we noted earlier. Figure 8.1 does not indicate that there was a rise in the proportion of late-stage government amendments in the legislative process for the two 'families' of legislation explored, even though several interviewees told us that amendments had become technically easier to insert into legislative documents than had been the case in the old days of 'hot metal' letterpress printing. Legislation did become markedly longer, a point commented on by several of our interviewees (who put it down partly to changing and more long-winded styles of legislative drafting and less densely spaced text on each page, as well as an increasing volume of legislation originating with the European Union). Correspondingly, we found that the total number of amendments in the two families of legislation showed a slight (though not statistically significant) increase.[15]

Other quantifiable changes also took place in legislation over this time. The number of statutory instruments (pieces of delegated legislation) rose steeply during the 1980s and early 1990s.[16] And according to one study legislation also became steadily more indeterminate (that is, expressed in language that in effect leaves it to the courts to complete the legislation),[17] which might help to account for the rising incidence of judicial review we noted in Chapter 6.

But contrary to what might be expected from Sir Christopher Foster's portrait of legislation increasingly ill-prepared within the executive machine and consequently more likely to fall apart at the legislative stage, there was no obvious long-term increase either in the total number of amendments relative to the length of legislation, or in the proportion of late-stage amendments in the legislative process in the statutes analysed here. The pattern shown in Figure 8.1 looks more like trendless fluctuation than long-term change, which broadly chimes with what we were told by interviewees with experience of legislative drafting over the period considered here.

As already noted, such an analysis has its limitations as a test of Foster's thesis. Only two families of legislation are considered here, a count of amendments

---

[15] While the number of Acts of Parliament did not increase, the number of pages of legislation increased from about 2000 per year in 1980 to over 3500 per year in the 2000s. Donald Shell, in *The House of Lords* (Manchester: Manchester University Press, 2007) found that the total number of amendments made by the House of Lords to government bills rose from the 1970s to 2000 and then fell in the early 2000s. Data from the House of Lords Public Bill Office showed that this fall continued (unevenly) during the 2000s and early 2010s. Unfortunately no comparable data on amendments were published by the House of Commons.

[16] House of Commons Library Standard Note, *Acts & Statutory Instruments: Volume of UK Legislation 1950 to 2012*, (SN/SG/2911, 2012).

[17] Matthew Williams, 'Indeterminate Sovereignty and the Rule of Law: A Descriptive Analysis of Changes to Parliament's Use of Language', *British Politics* (forthcoming, 2015).

does not necessarily represent their degree of consequentiality, and it is still possible that weighting the numbers shown in Figure 8.1 according to the salience or importance of the amendments in question—the degree of policy change that they represented—might produce a different picture. But at the least, 'not proven' seems the most appropriate verdict from this analysis.

Much the same 'not proven' conclusion seems to apply to the proportion of departmental accounts qualified by the public auditor, as shown in Figure 8.2. Though the percentage of accounts qualified varied greatly from year to year, Figure 8.2 does not indicate a long-term overall increase in audit qualifications over three decades, as might be expected if there was indeed a long-term departure from a 'Weberian' (rule-following) style of bureaucratic functioning, as many of the critics of NPM developments argued. It is true that Figure 8.2 indicates a notable spike in the proportion of accounts qualified by the auditor after the move from cash accounting to resource accounts in the early 2000s. But it is likely that this can be put down to teething difficulties associated with the switchover rather than heralding a long-term move to more problematic accounting.

8.3 Churn: Institutional Restructuring and Individual Turnover

A second 'process' criticism that we noted at the outset is the view that continuity and institutional memory in the central government machine were damaged by excessive churn, both in the sense of too many institutional makeovers and reorganizations and of increasing staff turnover that robbed the central government machine of long-term experience. Do such numbers as are available back up that view? Section 8.3 analyses two sets of indicators of churn—namely the incidence of measures of restructuring of government organizations including Transfer of Functions Orders (changes in departmental responsibilities made by delegated legislation under a statute originally dating back to 1948) and various measures of turnovers of personnel of various types.

Turning to the first element—'churn' in institutional structures through reorganization—the 'descent into chaos' view might lead us to expect a long-term increase in turnover rates of central government departments and perhaps other central government organizations as well, namely executive agencies and 'quangos' in the sense of 'non-departmental public bodies' (NDPBs).

As far as central government departments are concerned, we noted in Chapter 2 that the overall number of departments was fairly constant at

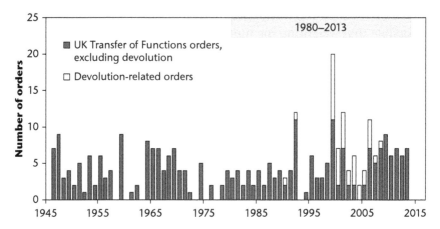

Figure 8.3. Departmental Reorganization: UK Transfer of Functions Orders 1946–2013

Sources: Christopher Pollitt, *Manipulating the Machine: Changing the Pattern of Ministerial Departments 1960–83* (London: Allen and Unwin, 1984), p. 17; Iain McLean (Whitehall database <http://www.nuff.ox.ac.uk/politics/whitehall/Download>); <http://www.legislation.gov.uk>.

between eighteen and twenty-two throughout our three-decade period. That stability went along with considerable rearrangement of departmental port-folios, such that few of the departments that existed in 1980 still had the same names or responsibilities in the early 2010s. But did the rate of 'churn' increase?

Figure 8.3 shows what happened to the incidence of Transfer of Functions Orders over the sixty-odd years for which such orders have operated as the legal means for transferring responsibilities from one central government department to another. That figure shows a considerable year-to-year vari-ation, but it can be seen that the last two decades of the thirty-year period considered by this book witnessed three notable peaks in transfer activity that were higher than any in the preceding fifty years. Some of the Orders from 1999 to 2001 were associated with devolution to Scotland and Wales, but even excluding these, the 1990s and 2000s had a relatively high level of activity.

That is broadly in line with a careful study by Anne White and Patrick Dunleavy who found fifteen departmental reorganizations from 1979 to 1996 and thirty between 1997 and 2009.[18] That represents an increase from an average of about 4 per cent of departments reorganized per year in the earlier period to about 11 per cent per year in the later one (although the reorganizations were by no means evenly spread, being particularly prevalent

---

[18] Anne White and Patrick Dunleavy, *Making and Breaking Government Departments: A Guide to Machinery of Government Changes* (London: Institute for Government and LSE Public Policy Group, 2010), Figure 4, p. 16 and Figure 5, p. 17.

in years following leadership changes and general elections). But it provides at best fairly weak evidence in support of the institutional 'churn' analysis, particularly given that White and Dunleavy found the rate of churn had, if anything, decreased over the longer period from 1950 to 2008. For example, the nineteen departmental reconfigurations carried out during the Blair premiership and the eleven reconfigurations initiated by the Brown premiership did not even come close to the twenty-eight reconfigurations carried out under Harold Wilson's first premiership in the 1960s.

But to probe further into the rate of central government reorganization over time, we need to go beyond changes of portfolios at the level of departments. After all, White and Dunleavy pointed out that the relative scarcity of major reorganizations under the Thatcher and Major premierships coincided with a time of substantial *intra*-departmental reorganization which, as we discussed in Chapter 2, included the formation of the Next Steps agencies, in which departmental delivery functions were carved out into executive agencies. So if we look at what happened to the turnover rate of those agencies, can we find evidence for increasing churn?

Thomas Elston analysed executive agency launches and closures since the introduction of such agencies in 1988 showing that, on average, eight agencies closed and nine were launched each year between 1995 and 2006.[19] The overall closure rate (about 6 per cent per year from 1995 to 2006) rose sharply to reach almost 19 per cent in 2008 and at the same time the number of launches fell, so that by 2010 the overall number of agencies had fallen by some 40 per cent from its 1997 peak. As with the pattern explored earlier for government departments, Elston's analysis gives a measure of support to the 'high churn' hypothesis, in that the agency world exhibited a continuous pattern of launches and closures, and the 'churn' rate somewhat increased after 2006. But again this study gives only fairly weak evidence in support of the 'increasing churn' hypothesis, in that there is no exactly comparable data for the 1980–1995 period, and we cannot rule out the possibility that intra-departmental reorganization ran at a comparable or higher rate in the pre-agency days.

Finally if we turn to NDPBs or 'quangos' as they are commonly called, do we see strong evidence of increasing churn? Our analysis in Chapter 2 showed a steady decrease in the number of executive NDPBs since the 1970s. Building on that analysis, we drew on a database kindly supplied to us by Brian Hogwood, who tracked the fate of NDPBs in each year up to 1994.[20] It

---

[19] Thomas Elston, 'Developments in UK Executive Agencies: Re-examining the "Disaggregation-Reaggregation" Thesis', *Public Policy and Administration* 28, no. 1 (2013): pp. 66–89.
[20] See Brian Hogwood, 'The "Growth" of Quangos: Evidence and Explanations', *Parliamentary Affairs* 48, no. 2 (1995): pp. 207–25.

is notoriously difficult to count 'quangos' as a result of their fluid and chang-ing definitions, but taking snapshots of the executive NDPB population at twelve-year intervals (1982, 1994, and 2006)[21] we attempted to reproduce—in a simplified form—Hogwood's criteria for 'continuous existence' of each NDPB. Of the 350-odd executive NDPBs existing in 1982, about 60 per cent still existed in 1994 and a further hundred had been created. In the second twelve-year period, about half of the 300 bodies existing in 1994 survived as executive NDPBs until 2006 and a further sixty-seven were created.[22] This corresponded to an annual destruction rate of about 4 per cent in the early period and 5 per cent in the later one (ignoring, of course, organizations that were created and destroyed wholly within each twelve-year period consid-ered here). From this analysis we therefore see perhaps a slight increase in instability of NDPBs in the second period compared to the first. But again this can be counted as only weak evidence of increasing 'churn'. Further, many bodies that ceased to be formally counted as NDPBs continued to exist in some other form in the public sector. We cannot firmly say whether the incidence of 'faked deaths' of that kind changed overall over the two periods.

So when we consider all the available evidence regarding reorganization rates for departments, agencies, and NDPBs, we find in each case an indica-tion of slightly increased 'churn' over the past three decades. But the changes observed are hardly of the 'soar-away' variety, and average turnover rates, at between 4 and 11 per cent per year, were generally lower than turnover rates of private sector businesses, which ceased trading at an average annual rate of over 10 per cent from 2001 to 2011.[23] We cannot dismiss the possibility that those observed rises are within the range of measurement error, given the built-in limitations of the available data, but on the consilience principle, the fact that all the three data series considered for organizational 'churn' point in the same direction, gives us slightly more confidence in identifying a weak increase than would apply if those three sources of data pointed in opposite directions.

Turning now to the issue of whether there was a measurable increase in staff turnover in the central government machine that would be consistent with claims of declining institutional memory, tricky issues again arise as to what is the best measure of such movement. Is it movement at the upper or lower

---

[21] 1982 and 1994 data were from Brian Hogwood's database which (for 1994) was similar to the data in *Public Bodies 1994*. 2006 data were from *Public Bodies 2006* and the Scottish and Welsh government websites. Our figures differ somewhat from Hogwood's, because we counted multiple bodies as one and excluded some bodies falling outside our criteria for executive NDPBs. Our analysis is only approximate given the difficulty of deciding whether a body had a continuous existence when it was succeeded in *Public Bodies* by another body with a similar name or remit.

[22] This figure includes the 174 English and Northern Irish executive NDPBs listed in *Public Bodies* 2006, plus thirty-one Scottish and fifteen Welsh bodies.

[23] House of Commons Library Standard Note, *Business Statistics* (SN/EP/6152, 2013), p. 8.

levels of the government machine that matters most? Is it movement within departments, across departments, or in and out of the civil service that matters most? Is it turnover of permanent civil servants or of politicians and their political appointees that matters most? The answers to all of those questions are debatable, and only some of them are available from documentary data.

What we cannot measure from reported documentary data are changes in the 'merry-go-round' of postings within the civil service and inside departments—that is, the average length of time that key civil servants stay in one post before moving on to different responsibilities in the same or another department—even though many of the criticisms of the operation of the executive machine focus on precisely that feature. For example, one of our interviewees who was well placed to observe the process of legislative drafting over two decades commented that many departmental bill teams drafting legislation lacked continuity because many of the members of those bill teams were in post for less than eighteen months, and consequently often tended to be 'learners' rather than experienced players in the matters being handled. Others with roughly the same degree of experience made very similar observations, and one suggested that the 'four-year norm' for senior civil service posts, introduced in 2003, exacerbated this tendency, particularly when too rigidly imposed.[24] But all we managed to obtain in the way of documentary data on this point was a very short run of numbers, kindly provided by the Cabinet Office Senior Civil Service database team, indicating that such turnover had been close to 30 per cent in recent years, as we discuss below.

What we can measure from the (mostly) published numbers for much of the thirty years covered here is turnover of the whole civil service, in terms both of voluntary resignations and of all reasons for leaving, and for shorter periods for the senior grades. We can also measure the length of tenure of ministers in departments (the political merry-go-round criticized by Sir Richard Mottram and others, as noted earlier) and the corresponding tenure of Permanent Secretaries, the civil service heads of government departments.

Taking these items in reverse order, Figures 8.4 show the pattern of tenure of the 'top bananas', namely ministers and Permanent Secretaries. The average lengths of ministerial tenure in each premiership since 1945 shown in Figure 8.4 are drawn from data collated by Samuel Berlinksi and colleagues.[25]

[24] According to the Cabinet Office, the four-year norm for Senior Civil Service postings was designed 'both to avoid too frequent moves . . . but also to change the possible perception of the SCS as a comfortable environment with a guarantee of a job for life.' (House of Commons Public Administration Select Committee, *Skills for Government*, (HC 93-II, 2006–07), p. 68).
[25] Samuel Berlinski, Torun Dewan, and Keith Dowding, *Accounting for Ministers* (Cambridge: Cambridge University Press, 2012), Table 4.2.

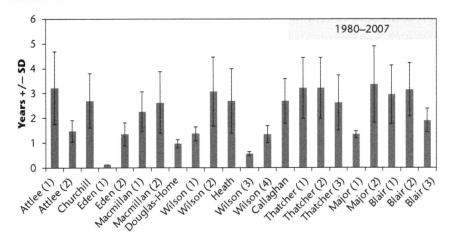

Figure 8.4. Tenure of Ministers by Government since 1945

Source: Data from Samuel Berlinski, Torun Dewan, and Keith Dowding, *Accounting for Ministers* (Cambridge: Cambridge University Press, 2012), Table 4.2.

The data for Permanent Secretaries in Figure 8.5 come from our updating of an analysis by Kevin Theakston and Geoffrey Fry, who calculated the average length of tenure of Permanent Secretaries in each approximately twenty-one-year period from 1900 to 1986.[26] These analyses show that, for these two sets of leaders, there was little sign of the 'merry-go-round' speeding up over the three decades considered here.

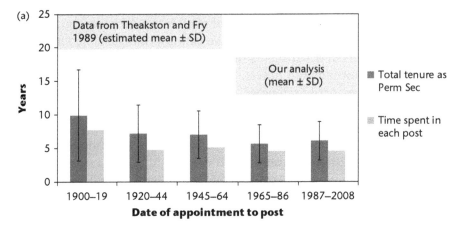

Figure 8.5a. Average Tenure of Permanent Secretaries 1900–2008

[26] Kevin Theakston and Geoffrey Fry, 'Britain's Administrative Elite: Permanent Secretaries 1900–1986', *Public Administration* 67 (1989): pp. 129–47.

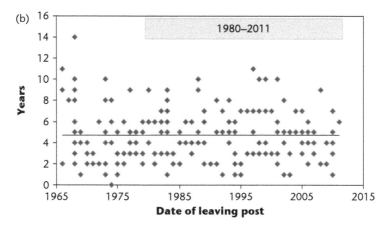

Figure 8.5b. Tenure of Permanent Secretaries in Any One Post (all who left office 1966–2011) with Regression Line

Sources: Kevin Theakston and Geoffrey Fry, 'Britain's Administrative Elite: Permanent Secretaries 1900-1986', *Public Administration* 67 (1989): pp. 129–47; Colin McKie's list of Permanent Secretaries <http://www.gulabin.com/>.

Turning to other civil servants of various degrees of seniority, Figure 8.6 tracks the available data on overall leaving rates and (voluntary) resignation rates from the civil service as a whole and from the upper ranks—both the Senior Civil Service (SCS, formed in 1996 from the old grades 1–5) and grades 6 and 7 (normally considered to be the policy 'workhorses' of the civil service at the upper middle level). Turnover for the civil service as a whole actually fell over the thirty years considered here, but stabilized from the mid-1990s. That fall in turnover was due to a marked decrease in both leaving and resignation rates for female civil servants (the rates for male civil servants hardly changed) and was accompanied by a considerable increase in part-time working for female civil servants.

However, Figure 8.6 shows a different story for the senior grades over the two or two-and-a-half decades for which the numbers are available. The annual incidence of resignation of senior civil servants rose from about 1 per cent in the mid-1990s to about 3 per cent in the 2010s, and the resignation rates of the grades just below the senior level also increased, albeit not quite so much, perhaps because the prospect of promotion to the SCS acted for those grades as an incentive to remain in the service. And overall leaving rates also increased for both sets of senior civil servants in the decade to 2012. Where we knew detailed reasons for departure[27] we saw a considerable increase between 2007 and 2012 in other 'voluntary' cessations such as early retirements and voluntary severance schemes among the senior grades, so clearly 'resignations' alone do not tell the whole story.

---

[27] The Office for National Statistics (ONS) dataset 2007–2012 already referred to.

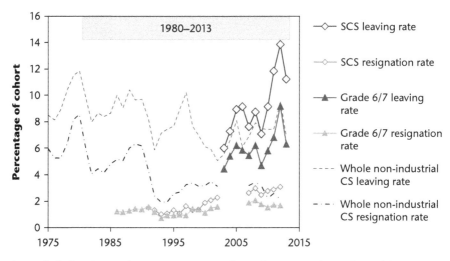

Figure 8.6. Leaving and Resignation Rates from the Non-Industrial Civil Service and from Senior Grades 1975–2012

Sources: Civil Service Statistics and ONS personal communication. *Civil Service Statistics* ceased reporting resignations after 2003. ONS supplied us with numbers and grades of civil servants leaving the service 2007–2012. 'Resignation' was one of the nineteen 'reasons for leaving' recorded by ONS.

A 2013 report from the NAO provided some further information, since it showed not only senior staff leaving the civil service in recent years but also movements between departments and posts, arguably a more meaningful metric for understanding institutional stability.[28] The Cabinet Office, the original source of this data, supplied us with 'total movements out of an SCS Post, 2005 to 2012' which showed that on average over 28 per cent of the SCS moved post in each of those years, with no obvious trend over that period. These numbers cannot be used to make long-term comparisons of the kind shown in Figure 8.6, but a 28 per cent churn rate of senior staff has clear implications for continuity of project management and institutional memory.[29] So it may well not be the Permanent Secretary level that is the most meaningful level at which to analyse churn, since it is the levels below those 'top bananas' that typically depart early for one

---

[28] National Audit Office, *Building Capability in the Senior Civil Service to Meet Today's Challenges* (HC 129, 2013–14).

[29] In 2013, the government attempted to slow this turnover by introducing a 'pivotal role allowance' to encourage key SCS members to remain in post while they managed major projects. See National Audit Office, *Building Capability in the Senior Civil Service to Meet Today's Challenges* (HC 129, 2013–14), p. 9. This approach was criticized by the Review Body on Senior Salaries, commenting '[w]e do not understand why senior managers cannot insist on key individuals remaining in post for longer. The needs of the organisation for continuity ought to override the wishes of the individual to change jobs frequently.' *Thirty-fifth Annual Report on Senior Salaries* (Cm 8569, 2013), para 3.36.

reason or another—a pattern that has also been observed in corporations and local authorities.[30]

Now it is not the purpose of this analysis to identify what might have caused that increase in leaving and resignation rates shown in Figure 8.6, and specifically how far it was caused by disaffection or loss of morale as against other job market factors, such as more lucrative opportunities for people with senior civil service skills and experience during times when employment in the private sector are buoyant (it is certainly noticeable from Figure 8.6 that resignation rates dipped in the recessions of the early 1990s and the late 2000s). That is a separate debate which we do not enter here: rather what interests us is whether and how far there was an increase in early exits from the upper ranks of the civil service that would be consistent with the claims noted earlier about loss of institutional memory and experience.

At the least Figure 8.6 provides quite strong circumstantial evidence that turnover increased markedly for this key group of civil servants from the mid-1990s. And it chimes with other evidence, such as the interview comments noted earlier about declining experience and continuity in bill teams. On a similar theme, one recently retired civil servant we interviewed commented on what he thought was a loss of command of arcane details of public expenditure within the Treasury as a result of a long-term shift of policy leadership from Under-Secretaries with 'a huge understanding of the details' to more work done by younger people, some from outside the civil service, who he described as bright, but with no long-term view or knowledge of previous policy, leading to (in that interviewee's view) much reinventing of the wheel and waste of time.

Accordingly, while the analysis in Section 8.2 did not find clear evidence of increasing disorder in the legislative process as measured by increasing late-stage amendments or of a long-term decline in careful accounting as measured by increasing qualifications of accounts, some of the indicators explored in this section do indeed suggest an increase in 'churn' both of organizational changes (albeit of an uneven kind) and of upper-level civil servants (but not of civil servants as a whole, or of Permanent Secretaries' tenure at the head of individual departments).

Of course, that raises at least three difficult questions of interpretation. One is what is the 'optimum' rate of churn both in organizational structures and of people (it would certainly be hard to argue that zero is the optimum in any organization), and whether an annual resignation rate of less than three in every hundred people is really incompatible with

---

[30] See George Boyne, Oliver James, Peter John, and Nicolai Petrovsky, 'Does Public Service Performance Affect Top Management Turnover?', *Journal of Public Administration Research and Theory* 20 (2010): pp. i1261–i1279.

maintenance of institutional memory in a well-run organization with proper record-keeping.[31] Against that, a number of interviewees told us (consistent with the observations of Christopher Pollitt and Rod Rhodes that we noted at the outset) that filing and record-keeping tended to be poor and that the digital age record-keeping systems were at best second-rate. No one indicated that improved digital filing and record-keeping compensated for higher turnover in maintaining institutional memory, and several suggested the opposite. One recently retired senior civil servant told us that electronic filing had never worked, even in prosperous private sector organizations like law firms, let alone what he described as the 'rubbish systems' in the public service, helping to contribute to serious mistakes caused by lack of experience.[32]

A second key issue of interpretation is whether it is the higher policymaking grades or the lower operational-level grades that are more important for the maintenance of institutional memory, since, as we have seen, turnover fell for the civil service as a whole over the period considered here but rose for the higher grades. Most of the concerns about rising turnover noted above have been directed towards the upper policymaking grades in the bureaucracy as being the main repository of experience and institutional memory. However, an increasing devolution of policymaking roles to delivery agencies in the 1990s and 2000s suggests that this experience started to reside increasingly outside the central Whitehall departments traditionally associated with 'policy' functions.[33]

A third issue is whether the resignation and leaving rates shown in Figure 8.6 are a proxy for what we cannot directly observe, namely the sort of 'merry-go-round' represented by the rate of postings within departments or government as a whole. As already noted, there is no systematic documentary record covering decades of what happened to this element of 'churn', but circumstantial evidence strongly suggests that such churn at least did not decrease. The introduction in 2013 of financial incentives to keep key individuals in post showed that at the end of our period the government still considered churn of this type to be excessive.

---

[31] See Kenneth J. Meier and Alisa Hicklin, 'Employee Turnover and Organizational Performance: Testing a Hypothesis from Classical Public Administration', *Journal of Public Administration Research and Theory* 18, no. 4 (2008): pp. 573–90, for a study showing a U-shaped relationship between turnover and performance.

[32] The Government Office of Science's *Science & Analysis Assurance Review of Her Majesty's Treasury* (London: The Government Office of Science, 2013) made similar points.

[33] See for example Thomas Elston, 'Developments in UK Executive Agencies: Re-examining the "Disaggregation-Reaggregation" Thesis', *Public Policy and Administration* 28, no. 1 (2013): pp. 82–5, and Neil Elder and Edward Page 'Accountability and Control in Next Steps Agencies', in *Transforming British Government*, Vol. I, edited by Rod Rhodes (Basingstoke: Macmillan, 2000), pp. 223–37.

All of those issues are certainly debatable. But the analysis of churn here shows that there is at least a case to answer on this aspect of the 'heading into chaos' hypothesis.

8.4 Changes in Government Information Organization and Resources

A third 'process' issue raised at the beginning of this chapter (and also discussed in Chapters 1 and 2) concerns the much-discussed question of what happened to the role of 'spin' and presentation within the government machine. As we have seen earlier, numerous critics argued that message control assumed greater profile and importance, and many of those critics argued that the change had malign effects on factors such as trust in government, the party-political impartiality of the civil service, and the quality of policy-making more generally.

Again, despite the strong passions that went into debates over 'spin' and the substantial body of writing on that subject, the literature is long on anecdote and short on provision of consistent numbers over time, a characteristic of official reports on the subject as well as more popular literature. Here we aim to explore such numbers as are available for the resources claimed by spin and presentational activity over the thirty years considered here.

Figure 8.7 gives an approximate indication of the number of 'information' or 'communication' staff in the civil service over that period. It puts together three statistical series, namely those who were counted as 'information officers' in *Civil Service Statistics* from 1969 to 1995, those who were listed as information

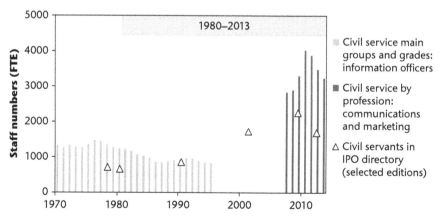

Figure 8.7. Civil Service Staff in Communications Roles 1970–2013
Sources: Civil Service Statistics and IPO Directories.

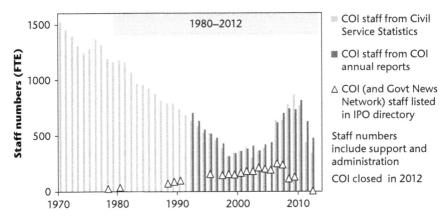

Figure 8.8. Central Office of Information Staff Numbers 1970–2013

Sources: Civil Service Statistics, IPO Directories, and COI *Annual Reports.*

or communication staff in a directory of press officers dating back to the 1970s (titled at various times *Information & Press Officers, IPO Directory,* or *The White Book*), and those who were categorized as 'communications and marketing' personnel in *Civil Service Statistics* from 2007 to 2013. Clearly those series are not fully comparable but the fact that a new category of 'communications and marketing' emerged towards the end of our period, and that the numbers of civil servants listed in the IPO directory more than doubled does suggest some increase in the resources going into communications over this period.

Two other sets of numbers about information and communication civil servants throw some more light on the changes that occurred in this domain. Figure 8.8 shows the staffing of the Central Office of Information (COI), the UK government's central agency for 'presentational' work, which for most of the period considered here comprised the shrunken remains of a massive Second World War Ministry of Information, but was wound up on grounds of cost-cutting at the end of 2011, with most of the staff transferred to the Cabinet Office. To the extent that these numbers represent a consistent series over time, Figure 8.8 indicates two decades of decline in the staffing of this central information office since 1980 (accounted for to some extent by out-sourcing work once done in-house by civil servants), partially offset by a distinct pick-up towards the end of the period, though by no means returning to the levels seen in the early 1980s. So if we looked only at these numbers, it would only be the later 2000s that show marked increases, with an overall decline over more than three decades.

However, other evidence suggests a quite different story. The numbers of communication staff listed in the IPO directory for the Prime Minister's Office, the Treasury, and the Cabinet Office over the thirty years to 2009, reveal a pattern of substantial growth from about 10 to about 40 individuals listed in each case—almost a mirror image of what happened to the COI's numbers. The numbers of communication staff listed by the IPO directory for the Department for Work and Pensions and its predecessors pointed to a similar picture of noticeable expansion, reaching 180 staff by 2006, though in this case the numbers fell back sharply in 2007, in contrast to the reported numbers for the three central policy departments.

Such numbers have to be interpreted with care, because the overall size of the IPO directory (in terms of the number of people listed) approximately tripled over the period considered here, such that the share of the total represented by these departments changed little. But even so the absolute expansion is striking, and when we put this pattern together with those in Figures 8.7 and 8.8, they are consistent with an interpretation that much of the 'action' on government presentation moved from a common service agency (COI) shrinking in staff size as technical tasks were outsourced, to a pattern of 'spinners' clustered in central agencies and around ministers in departments.[34] That was indeed what some of our interviewees told us had happened to the spin operations.

Of course, much of the discussion and criticism of the rise of 'spinners' that we referred to earlier and also in Chapter 2, was concerned not only (indeed not so much) with increased bureaucratic investment in this activity but also with the increased power exerted by so-called 'sultans of spin' within the government machine, over ministers as well as civil servants.[35] The sort of analysis we have conducted here cannot speak directly to that issue, but such documentary evidence as is available does seem to indicate not just increased investment but a different pattern of deployment at the bureaucratic level.

8.5 An Overall Assessment

As in previous chapters, we sum up this analysis in the 'scorecard' represented by Table 8.1 below. This analysis did not confirm many of the claims about changes in process that we set out at the start of this chapter. If less disciplined policymaking within the executive government machine (more casual 'sofa government' replacing earlier more orderly and documented decision processes) could be expected to result in increasing incidence of late-stage government amendments to (increasingly ill thought-out and poorly

[34] See also Christopher Hood, *The Blame Game: Spin, Bureaucracy and Self-Preservation in Government* (Princeton: Princeton University Press, 2011), pp. 116–17, which described growth of media-handling staff in No. 10 Downing Street (and the White House) over fifty years or so.

[35] Nicholas Jones, *Sultans of Spin: The Media and the New Labour Government* (London: Gollancz, 1999).

Table 8.1. Changing Processes inside Executive Government: A Summary Scorecard

Process change	Indicators considered	Observations
More disorderly policymaking and less meticulous administration	Incidence of late-stage amendments to government bills in two legislative families over three decades	No evidence of increasing proportion of late-stage amendments over time
	Number of amendments relative to length of legislation	No evidence of increasing number of amendments per section or page of legislation
	Incidence of departmental accounts qualified by the public auditor	No evidence of increasing qualification of accounts over time
Increasing churn of organizations and individuals impacting institutional memory and continuity	Incidence of reorganization in central departments over three decades, executive agencies (since late 1980s) and non-departmental public bodies (two selected periods)	Some evidence (not very strong) for a slight upturn in 'churn' for all three types of organizations within the time periods considered
	Reported turnover of ministers, Permanent Secretaries (PS), total civil servants, and top civil service grades below PS	No evidence of increased turnover of ministers and PSs; some decrease in turnover of whole civil service, but considerable increase in turnover of top civil service grades below PS
Increasing emphasis on presentation	Numbers of staff identified as 'Information' or 'communication' in civil service	Evidence complicated by data breaks, but it is plausible to infer substantial growth
	Central Office of Information staff	Long-term decline over thirty years before eventual abolition
	Staff listed as media contacts in IPO directories for three central government departments	Evidence of material increase

consulted on) legislation, Figure 8.1 indicated no clear evidence of such an increase. If sloppier administration could be expected to be picked up by rising numbers of departmental accounts qualified by the public auditor, Figure 8.2 showed no convincing evidence of a rising trend there either. If more disorderly processes and loss of continuity and experience could be expected to be reflected in a more rapid 'merry-go-round' of ministers and Permanent Secretaries and of increasing turnover rates in the civil service as a whole, Figures 8.4, 8.5, and part of 8.6 showed either no evidence of change or change in the opposite direction to that expected. If rising emphasis on spin might be expected to be reflected by a big increase in the staffing of the government's central information agency, Figure 8.8 showed, on the contrary, that there was a long-term decline in the size of that agency over the period considered here.

However, some of the other indicators explored here do fit the critics' expectations. Albeit not strongly, Figure 8.3 indicated several spikes in departmental reorganization towards the end of the thirty years considered here, and the analyses of agency spin-outs (and 'spin-ins') and quango changes pointed in the same direction. Figure 8.6 showed that the rate of voluntary resignations and other departures from the SCS (and the grades immediately below) increased notably during the 2000s. Put together, those changes do chime to some extent with claims that the period witnessed an increase in churn that may have reduced continuity and institutional memory and experience. Such turnover may also have contributed to the increasing 'indicator churn' that we discussed in Chapter 3, which itself could be considered an element of 'process quality'.

When it comes to the resources absorbed by 'spin' and presentational activity, Figure 8.8 showed that the staffing of the UK government's central information agency fell to under a third of its 1980 levels by 2000, although it showed a temporary increase in the mid-2000s before its eventual closure. But Figure 8.7 indicated a sharp increase in the numbers of civil servants classified as having information or communication responsibilities, and numbers drawn from the IPO directory showed signs of a quadrupling in people identified as media contacts in key central agencies and departments. Put together, these changes suggest the organization of spin and presentation in central government altered in two ways. It changed shape, in that there was a tendency to run down the direct staffing of the central communications agency, partly by outsourcing, but at the same time communications staff in central departments and around ministers grew markedly. Again, that observed pattern is broadly consistent with the idea that more emphasis went onto high-level presentation within government over this period.

From the summary of the analysis indicated by Table 8.1, the overall pattern therefore seems to point to a verdict of 'partly proven' in relation to the three main types of 'process' concerns identified at the start of this chapter. The two possible indicators of growing administrative 'sloppiness' considered here (late-stage amendments and qualified accounts) point to a 'not proven' verdict. That is perhaps surprising, given that one of the major charges brought by critics of NPM against managerialism concerned the quality of process, though a consideration of indicator churn, as discussed in Chapter 3, might point in a different direction. In the next chapter we turn to an overall assessment of what the evidence presented in the last five chapters tells us about the propositions about change in the government machine that we set out to explore in Chapter 1.

9

Not What it Said on the Tin

Assessing Three Decades of Change

It does exactly what it says on the tin . . .[1]

Chapter 1 began by commenting on the remarkable lack of 'evidence and proof' about the much-discussed aspirations of reformers in many countries to change the way government and public services operate so that they worked better and cost less, particularly by harnessing the transformative power of better management and new information technology (IT). The remainder of this book has aimed to fill the gap for the critical case of the UK by a careful and balanced examination of the available documentary evidence about what happened to running costs and also to the incidence of formal complaints and judicial challenges that reflect perceptions of the consistency or fairness of case-handling in government organizations.

As we have shown, far from falling, running costs rose substantially in absolute terms over thirty years, while complaints soared. That is not exactly 'what it said on the tin' of all those grandiloquent reform makeovers aimed at containing costs and improving administration for citizens. Our analysis in Chapter 4 also shows that what drove running costs up over the three decades was not the wage costs of civil servants (which appear to have stayed relatively constant in constant price terms), but the 'outsourced' elements of running costs, even though outsourcing had tended to figure large in standard recipes for greater efficiency. Indeed, as we saw in Chapter 7, part of what may have lain behind the rise in complaints and judicial challenge may have been a combination of falling civil service numbers and increasing turnover in the policymaking grades, interacting with developments noted by other

---

[1] One of the UK's most famous advertising slogans, used in TV advertisements since 1994 by the UK woodstain and wood-dye manufacturer Ronseal. The slogan has entered the language as a phrase to denote anything that does precisely what it is intended to.

commentators and scholars, such as ambitious IT projects and less determinate legislation.

This chapter aims to review these findings and show why they matter for anyone who wants to assess attempts to reform the working of government and public services over the past thirty years or so. Accordingly, we begin by revisiting the nine possible outcomes of government makeovers that we set out in the first chapter. As we will show, our findings are nuanced, conclusions can hang on how much weight is placed on which indicators, so there is certainly scope for debate as to precisely which of the nine possible outcomes we identified fits best with the findings of the previous chapters. But even so, we can rule out most of the nine, including the most optimistic visions of the true believers in the positive transformative powers of managerialism and IT. After revisiting the 'scoreboard', we turn to discussing the implications of what this study has revealed for our understanding of public management reform. In terms of how we explain or account for public management changes, it suggests that more than a minor tweak of some current received interpretations is needed in the light of these findings, and that our findings throw up new questions for future inquiry. The chapter concludes by considering the implications of this study for public management policy—what if any lessons can be drawn about how to minimize expense and maximize aptitude in government?

9.1 The Nine Items Scorecard Revisited: Did Government Work Better and Cost Less?

In Chapter 1 we asked whose expectations of the outcomes of thirty years of government makeovers best fit what can be observed after the event. Academics are often accused of a tendency to be wise after the event, with 20/20 hindsight of the kind inevitably denied to contemporary decision-makers. But, as we have seen, comparing like with like over time in matters bureaucratic is far from straightforward in this case, because of the challenges involved in putting together consistent data-series in the face of the kind of volatility we described in Chapter 3. The various kinds of (mostly bureau-political) pressures around data continuity that we explored there create a dynamic of data instability that makes it perilous to read too much into small changes. But that is just the reason why we adopted the 'consilience' approach that we described in the first chapter to denote examining more than one source of evidence wherever possible, and seeing whether the different sources add up to a consistent story, rather than putting all the weight on any single source of information. It is also why we have avoided elaborate statistical tests that tend to assume far more of the data (such as normal distributions or consistent measurements) than can be justified in this sort of case.

Nevertheless, as we have shown, given sufficient time and patience, it has been possible to create some reasonably consistent data-series over fairly long periods of time in the past from many of the indicators included in this study. Whether that will continue to be true in the future remains to be seen, and we will come back to that issue later.

On the basis of our analysis over the last five chapters, Table 9.1 summarizes what happened to government cost and perceptions of consistency or fairness in government administration (taking complaints and litigation as the main indicators of such perceptions, as in Chapter 6) over three decades.

So if we go back to the nine possible long-term outcomes of successive UK central government makeovers that we laid out in Chapter 1 (Table 1.1, and redrawn below as Table 9.2) according to their effects on operating costs and performance in terms of perceived consistency or fairness in administration, the observed outcomes of the data summarized in Table 9.1 do not very plausibly fit the hopes and expectations of the reform champions that government makeovers would lead unambiguously to lower cost and better administration. Those who believe that modern management systems linked with the creative development and application of IT can produce an easily observable quantum change in the operation of government, dramatically improving the quality of its output while decisively cutting operating costs at the same time, cannot, at first sight at least, find much general comfort in the results we reported in Chapters 4 to 6.

Table 9.1. Indicators of Running Costs and Fairness/Consistency in Government: A Simple Scorecard for the Period 1980–2013

RUNNING OR ADMINISTRATION COSTS		
	Change in absolute (real-terms) costs	Change in relative costs
Central government administration costs	Cost more	Decreased relative to total public spending[†]
Civil service staff costs	Cost about the same	Decreased relative to total public spending
Tax collection costs	Cost more	Decreased relative to tax yield

PERCEIVED CONSISTENCY OR FAIRNESS		
	Change in citizens' responses	Change in survival rate
Survey data on citizen satisfaction and trust	Opinions mostly worse or unchanged	n/a
Complaints to ombudsmen	Complaints increased	Survival rate decreased
Judicial review	Judicial review applications increased	Survival rate decreased

[†] By 'total public spending', we mean here 'Total Managed Expenditure' (TME)

Of course it is possible (as we were told by several of the practitioners we interviewed) that individual public organizations under outstanding leadership might have bucked the general trend we depict here. We do not deny that at all, though our breakdown of running costs by departmental group in Chapter 4 and the comparison of central departments with executive agencies in Chapter 7, did not clearly establish huge variations among those groups. But it is the big picture, not the history of individual organizations, that we set out to explore in this book. And at that level, those who believe in the power of managerialism and IT changes to produce substantial cost-cutting and a better quality of administration (the top left-hand cell in 1.1 and 9.2), could only argue that such an outcome came about by exercising extreme selectivity in which individual pieces of data to pick and which to ignore from the numerous series explored in this book. For instance, they would have to dismiss the incidence of complaints or litigation as a valid indicator of perceived consistency or fairness in government administration and instead either focus on the minority of survey data-series (as considered in Chapter 6) that point to rising satisfaction or approval, or selectively to pick changes in some broader social outcomes (such as longevity) for which government be held to be partly responsible, while ignoring others (such as obesity). As far as cost is concerned, they would either have to put all the stress on relative rather than absolute running cost levels (at a time when government spending, particularly on transfer payments, increased massively), or by positing sufficiently 'doomwatch' counterfactuals about how much worse everything would have been in the absence of reform. But running cost reduction and better quality administration cannot be 'seen from space', as it were.

However, it is also notable that what we earlier described as the 'mainstream' academic position on New Public Management (NPM) reforms is not very convincingly supported by this analysis either. That position, as we noted in Chapter 1, involves assuming you broadly get what you pay for in government (and perhaps in other areas of life as well). And that implies that cost-cutting is likely to lead to worse performance, particularly in that Weberian-type rule-of-law work involving careful categorization of cases according to rules that we focused on in Chapter 6, or that better performance in such respects can only be achieved by higher cost. But while the analysis here does not support the outcome represented by the top left-hand cell of Table 9.2 (that is, 'worked better, cost less'), nor does it fit with the argument most commonly made about the outcome of those changes by NPM sceptics, as noted in Chapter 1. That is, the claim that NPM measures had a negative effect on the way government worked, due to cost-cutting measures that prioritized efficiency over quality, fairness, and equity, is hard to square with our finding in this book that running costs did not in fact fall at all over the period as a whole, but rather rose substantially in absolute terms—yet the quality of administration as measured in Chapter 6 did not improve.

So the most commonly advanced interpretations of the outcomes of government makeovers in the long-running battle between the true believers in the efficacy of new managerialism (and related remedies for performance problems in government and public services) and the academic and other sceptics ironically seem to be the hardest to reconcile with the overall pattern of the data we presented in the earlier chapters. As we have already noted, it is difficult to argue that the top row of Table 9.2 (that government 'worked better') is clearly supported by our data. To do so would require us to contrive a case that the few indicators showing an improvement in fairness and consistency should outweigh all those that did not, and to argue that rising numbers of complaints and litigation tell us nothing at all about general perceptions of consistency or fairness but only about those (relatively) few citizens—some no doubt 'politically motivated'—who are pursuing a particular grievance in spite of the costs and aggravation involved in doing so. To argue that government clearly 'cost less' seems to be equally difficult, unless we believe that relative costs are more appropriate metrics than absolute costs in an age of steeply rising programme spending, and even then we would have to ignore the periods when relative costs were stable or rising. That also seems to rule out the outcomes in the left-most column, and that is why we have shaded the top row and the left-hand column in Table 9.2 as least supported by the analysis here.

That leaves the four outcomes in the unshaded area of Table 9.2, each of which seems to be capable of being supported to some extent by the data presented in the previous chapters, dependent on how much weight is placed on each indicator and how much validity is attributed to those indicators. As we

Table 9.2. Nine Possible Outcomes Revisited: The Four Most Plausible Outcomes (Unshaded Area)

	Running cost level →		
	1	2	3
	Worked better, cost less *Quantum improvement*	Worked better, cost the same *Doing better with the same*	Worked better, cost more *Doing better with more*
	4	5	6
	Worked the same, cost less *Doing the same with less*	Worked the same, cost the same *No change*	Worked the same, cost more *Doing the same with more*
Performance level in terms of perceived consistency or fairness	7	8	9
	Worked worse, cost less *Doing worse with less*	Worked worse, cost the same *Doing worse with the same*	Worked worse, cost more *Quantum Deterioration*

have seen, the civil service in general seems to have 'cost the same' overall at the end of the period as it had done at the beginning, though per capita payroll costs certainly rose in real terms and overall running costs increased as well, driven chiefly by increased cost of outsourced items such as IT and consultancy. As for indicators representing perceptions of consistent, careful, and fair administration, while public satisfaction survey responses showed no overall trend, complaints and judicial review litigation increased substantially (even though survival rates fell, as we showed in Chapter 6). That means, dependent on how those various elements are weighted, that a case could be made for the fatalist view that all the government makeovers made little difference to cost and performance (cell 5), or even for the radically pessimistic view (as represented by the most out-and-out anti-managerialist critics such as Robert Protherough and John Pick)[2] that managerialist reforms achieved the very opposite of their declared purposes to cut costs and improve performance (cell 9). But the data examined here broadly seems to point to a more middle-of-the-road conclusion that UK central government 'cost a bit more and worked a bit worse' over the thirty years considered here. That conclusion is strikingly at odds both with the heady drumbeat of political and managerial rhetoric surrounding successive makeovers of central government and with the common academic view that NPM and many of the changes that went along with it had major consequences (positive or negative) for government performance.

9.2 What Are the Implications of these Findings for Our Understanding of Government and Public Services?

So what are the implications of such a conclusion for understandings of government and public administration? As for the implications of this analysis for the common view of NPM that we discussed in the first chapter, as a set of public management policies designed to cut running costs and improve the quality of public services, the choice seems to lie between a more conservative approach (in the scientific, not party-political, sense, involving minimal adjustment to mainstream or received views) and a more radical departure from such assumptions.

9.2.1 *Five Minimal-Adjustment Approaches*

There are several possible minimal-adjustment arguments that could be used to reconcile the picture summarized in Table 9.1 with the received view of

---

[2] Robert Protherough and John Pick, *Managing Britannia: Culture and Management in Modern Britain* (Edgeways: Brynmill Press, 2002).

NPM as a movement aimed at cutting costs and improving quality, without totally abandoning that view. One possible argument along these lines is that even if administration and tax collection costs went up, the application of managerialism and new IT may have delivered better value by improving the quality of public services in important ways not explored in Chapter 6, particularly in better social outcomes (such as increased longevity or economic prosperity).

A second is that running costs would have risen even faster and complaints soared yet higher in the absence of new managerialism and IT developments. And a third minimal-adjustment argument, which we referred to in Chapter 4, might be that the orthodox, received interpretation of NPM as a cost-cutting movement is generally correct, but just premature, with the expected running cost savings coming after some bedding-down period, rather than occurring at the outset in the supposedly 'slash-and-burn' era of the Thatcherite 1980s.

Fourth, it could possibly be claimed that the cost-cutting and performance-improving potential of new managerialism and IT developments was genuine but undermined by weak or inept leadership or implementation rather than by any inherent defects in those recipes for improvement. Fifth and finally, perhaps stretching the concept of 'minimal' to the limit or beyond, it might be argued that the results observed in Chapters 4–8 are primarily explicable in terms of major changes in the social context in which government operated over the three decades taken here—such as demographic changes or changes in social behaviour—which somehow had the effect of loading the dice against efforts to cut costs and improve or maintain administrative consistency and fairness, or (to put it another way) forced government to run even to stand still in terms of running costs and administrative quality. Indeed, we came across all of these arguments in one form or another from interviewees and other sources in the course of writing this book.

The first possible minimal-adjustment argument noted in the previous paragraph—that the quality of government's operations went up in ways not included in the analysis of Chapter 6—obviously takes us beyond the scope of that analysis. But to be plausible, such a counter-argument would need to grapple with the tricky problems of causal attribution that beset attempts to link social outcomes to government action, as discussed in Chapter 6. It would have to make difficult choices about which indicators of broader social management to include as measures of government capability or otherwise and which to exclude (for example, changing incidence of obesity, eating disorders, depression, self-harm). It would have to find reasons to dismiss indicators of administrative quality for which government can plausibly be argued to have far more direct responsibility, such as the changing incidence of formal complaints and of judicial challenges that we analysed in Chapter 6, as unimportant or representative only of a tiny minority of malcontents.

The second possible minimal-adjustment argument—that the cost and performance outcomes shown in the previous chapters would all have been much worse without the successive makeovers—rests on a counterfactual which in its nature cannot be proved. But the cost data we discussed in Chapter 4, Figure 4.3, (which indicates that the civil service paybill was falling as a proportion of total government spending long before the era of 'NPM' and the digital age, and that the slope of that decline does not greatly change between the pre-NPM and NPM era) suggests some problems with this interpretation. So does the fact that the slope of the graph of applications for first-stage judicial review in England and Wales did not appreciably alter between the mid-1970s and the mid-1980s, as we showed in Chapter 6, Figure 6.3a.

The third possible minimal-adjustment argument is that the orthodox periodization of NPM developments (as concentrating, at least in the early stages, on cost reductions) was somewhat off the mark but that the underlying dynamic was correctly identified in the conventional accounts, in that the expected cost reductions and/or administrative improvements eventually arrived but more slowly than such accounts assume. The indicators of perceptions of fairness and consistency in administration explored in Chapter 6 do not really fit this delayed-effect interpretation, but the running-cost picture might lend itself to a variant of it. After all, as we showed in Chapter 5, there was a drop in the cost-to-yield ratio for both direct and indirect taxes towards the end of our period, and as far as running costs are concerned, Figure 4.1 in Chapter 4 showed that both for the Conservative governments of the 1980s and 1990s and the Labour governments of the 1990s and 2000s, those costs seem to have been checked more obviously in the later years of each government than in their earlier periods. At first sight, Figure 4.1 suggests not so much a single process of learning and bedding-in but of two long-lasting governments each coming to bear down on running costs in the later years of their tenure.

However, it is not clear that such an interpretation stands up to very close examination. That notable fall in the cost-to-yield ratio of tax collection in the middle of our period between 1993 and 2000 needs to be interpreted against the background of the long economic boom that boosted tax revenue over that period, and it is notable that the cost-to-yield ratio stopped falling in the mid-2000s in spite (perhaps because) of the merger of the two central government tax departments intended to cut tax collection costs. Even then, as our analysis of long-term tax collection costs in Chapter 5 showed (Figure 5.1), the effect was to return cost-to-yield to the levels achieved in the late 1960s, long before the period conventionally associated with NPM and modern IT changes, rather than to some uniquely low level never before achieved.

As far as the running cost data is concerned, it is certainly striking that there was a sizeable (but not sustained) fall in all six cost items in the top three rows of Table 9.1 for much of the 1990s. But the reduction in the ratios of both running costs and paybill costs to Total Managed Expenditure (TME) over the 2000s in part reflects a huge spike in overall public spending and, as we discussed in Chapter 4, in part also reflects a tendency to classify ever-more items as programme rather than administrative expenditure from the mid-2000s—meaning that to some non-trivial extent administrative costs were 'cut' by reclassification as well as, or rather than, by genuine reductions in staff or other actual reductions in spending. So the problem with the 'delayed effect' argument is that it only fits some of the observations presented in Chapters 4–8 for some of the time. As indicated in Table 9.1, summing up our analysis in Chapters 4 and 5, there is no evidence for the period as a whole that the era of new managerialism and modern IT succeeded in cutting absolute levels of wage or running costs to any marked extent despite the massive amount of restructuring, outsourcing, and spending on IT projects over that period, and all the inflated claims that went along with those developments.

The fourth form of minimal-adjustment argument, almost always advanced as a last line of defence when the success of policies or institutional designs comes into question, is to suggest that the basic design, recipe, or strategy was correct but that the outcomes could have been very different if only better leadership or less inept implementation had been in place. The late Joseph Berliner, an expert in Soviet economics and politics, used to distinguish 'jockey' and 'horse' interpretations of the shortcomings and eventual collapse of the administrative-command economy in the former Soviet Union, to distinguish between the claim that the system could have worked better if only more competent leadership had been available and the contradictory claim that the system's inherent defects meant that it would inevitably have collapsed sooner or later even under the best imaginable leadership.[3] Like the second minimal-adjustment argument, the 'jockey' argument rests on a counterfactual that cannot be proved. It is certainly interesting, as already noted, that John Major, stereotypically presented as a 'weak' prime minister compared to the more commanding and decisive images conventionally associated with Margaret Thatcher or Tony Blair,[4] seems from this analysis to

[3] J. Berliner, 'Soviet Initial Conditions: How They Have Affected Russian Transition', paper presented at the International Conference sponsored by Moscow University, Harvard Davis Center, and University of Houston International Economics Program, titled 'Soviet Economy in the 1930s–1970s', Zvenigorod, Russia, 22–24 June 2001, quoted in Paul Gregory, *The Political Economy of Stalinism: Evidence from the Soviet Secret Archives* (Cambridge: Cambridge University Press, 2004), p. 4.

[4] John Major was also prime minister during the debacle of 'Black Wednesday' (16 September 1992) when the UK government was forced to withdraw the pound sterling from the then European Exchange Rate Mechanism (ERM) after spending £27 billion of reserves in an unsuccessful attempt to keep the pound above its agreed lower limit in the ERM.

have presided over what might be a surprisingly effective regime for holding/ driving down running costs in UK central departments, and not just by classifying them away. Indeed, several interviewees with long-term experience in the government machine made the same observation about the efficacy of cost control at that time.

Nevertheless, the fact that the overall period considered in this book spans the reigns of five different prime ministers, six cabinet secretaries, and a much larger array of ministers and top civil servants would suggest that, for this minimal-adjustment account of the outcomes of attempts to make government cost less and work better to be true, the leadership failure in question must have been almost systemic, going across a whole class or generation of political and administrative leaders rather than being confined to any single one.

The fifth possible basis for a minimal-adjustment approach (perhaps it could be considered as a variant of the first two mentioned earlier) is to explain the running cost and perceived administrative quality indicators observed here as a result of changes in government's social context. In particular, changes in the size and composition of the population and its behaviour and attitudes might possibly have served to override what might otherwise have been the decisively cost-reducing and quality-improving effects of successive makeovers of the administrative machine. Such changes in government's human environment might serve to explain why running costs might rise without an increase in perceived administrative consistency and fairness (cell 6 of Table 9.2), or alternatively why administrative quality might fall without a decrease in running costs (cell 8 of Table 9.2). Those outcomes might be more explicable if what happens in society and policy has more impact on the relationship between what government costs and how well it does its job than the details of how the machinery of government is arranged and the deliberate actions of those who manage that machinery. From this viewpoint, there is no compelling reason to expect the relationship between cost and performance to be confined to the four corners of Table 9.2 (as the 'get-what-you-pay-for' attitude we described in Chapter 1 might lead us to expect), and eminently plausible reasons to expect some kinds of change to produce precisely the sort of relationship between cost and quality that is captured by the mid-point cells 6 and 8 of Table 9.2.

For example, precisely those outcomes might be explicable in terms of changing context if politicians or legislatures choose to produce much more complex laws and policies (such as taxes with many more levels, categories, exemptions, and abatements, as we discussed in Chapter 5), and thus consume what might otherwise be the cost-reducing potential of managerial or IT changes in greater policy complexity so that they can fine-tune policy settings to target marginal voters more precisely. Similarly, an outcome that combined higher running costs with no increase in perceived administrative quality might be explicable if developments such as an interaction of changes in demography and political pressures for tougher sentencing for certain kinds of offences, such as sex offences, led to a doubling of the prison population (as has indeed happened in the UK over the past thirty years), or if a massive increase in immigration (as has also happened) presents government with greater challenges in communicating carefully with citizens or service users. Similarly if, to take yet another marked feature of recent decades, there are increasing requirements for compliance with international regulations from the EU and other institutions, those requirements may counteract what might otherwise have been the cost-reducing or quality-enhancing effects of new managerial and IT systems. Such social or policy changes (all of which are readily observable) could indeed be plausibly expected either to increase government's running costs without improving perceived fairness and consistency of administration or to decrease such perceived fairness and consistency if running costs are held constant.

Those sorts of questions go to the heart of attempts to measure government productivity changes over time, and the technical challenges they pose are formidable. But out of the five 'minimal-adjustment' arguments for accounting for the outcomes observed here, this 'changing context' explanation seems to be the most plausible, though as mentioned earlier it could be considered as a variant of the first and second possible arguments (i.e., that our indicators did not capture important aspects of government quality, or that continuation of 'business-as-usual' would have produced much worse outcomes). To explore that possibility carefully would mean investigating government activity in each separate policy domain rather than the government-wide approach that we have adopted in this book, and that may well be the direction that future evaluative research needs to go in, if we are to move further beyond either the hyped expectations of the reform champions or the standard negative assessments of the outcomes of NPM in much of the public administration literature. And as we noted in the first chapter, in spite of the massive funding and effort put into 'NPM research' in recent decades, very little work has been put into the challenging task of tracing out the effects of such contextual changes on government cost and quality, beyond (at best) rather general discussion or prima facie observations.

Nevertheless, even from what we know now, there are some question marks to set against the 'changing context' explanation. One is the observation in Chapters 4 and 8 that running cost increases did not vary greatly among different departmental groups or administrative units, suggesting either that contextual changes had a fairly similar cost-increasing effect on all of them or (even harder to demonstrate) that some might have shown up more obviously as cost or quality successes if their special contextual social pressures were fully taken into account. A second, as mentioned in Chapters 4 and 5, is the fact that the efforts of Patrick Dunleavy and Leandro Carrera to measure productivity changes over time for welfare benefits bureaucracy and taxation, explicitly controlling for some of those contextual factors, indicate flat or even declining productivity in both of those domains over some of the three decades discussed in this book.

9.2.2 Beyond Minimal Adjustment

Now there is much to be said for adopting a minimal-adjustment approach when observed facts seem to be in conflict with commonly asserted interpretations. After all, such an approach avoids over-claiming. It chimes with the 'parsimony principle' in science, the preference for simpler or more economical explanations with fewer moving parts over more elaborate or complex explanations when all else is equal. And it often does not seriously detract from the value of an interpretative theory (unless it is for a horse race, of course) if its predictions kick in rather later than expected. But none of the first four possible minimal-adjustment arguments noted above seems unproblematic, and the fifth—that changing contexts can explain the difference between the outcomes that were hoped for or expected by those who advocated managerial changes or digital transformation and what has been observed in the last five chapters—takes us to the limits of the observable and indeed to the limit of current methodologies for productivity measurement.

So if we do need to go beyond minimal adjustments to received views of the expected outcomes of managerial and other changes in government and public services, what might non-minimal adjustments consist of? One possibility, familiar in several varieties of bureaucratic and interest group theory, might be that management changes and IT developments in government and public services somehow ended up benefitting the 'change-makers' rather than taxpayers or end users of public services, and might even have been intended to have such an effect. A second, also advanced in several variants, is that changing bureaucracy is a political arena in which rhetoric, discourse, image, and 'spin' matters far more than cost and possibly some aspects of performance as well, despite the conventional rhetorical emphasis on 'what works'. A third possibility, also frequently argued in numerous variants in the literature of bureaucracy and public policy, is that entrenched aspects of organizational culture and micro-politics can somehow get in the way of real cost savings or performance enhancement.

That first possible non-minimal-adjustment line of analysis interprets management reforms and information system projects as the sort of public policy or activity that benefits a limited group rather than voters at large, despite claims that such changes will be of general public benefit. There is a family of theories and arguments of this general type, rather than a single one. Over two decades ago Patrick Dunleavy argued that the reshaping of central government reflected what he took to be the preferences and interests of the UK civil service policy elite at that time, who were happy enough to downsize, privatize, outsource, and 'corporatize' the lower-level and 'delivery' parts of government with all their accompanying management challenges, so long as their own power within the inner circle of the policy process was not affected.[5] More recently, Stephen Wilks highlighted the 'colonization' of the UK state by powerful private corporations, both as entrenched for-profit providers of an ever-increasing share of public services and as a key part of the governance of departments and agencies, supplying board members and senior personnel.[6]

In a somewhat similar vein, as we mentioned in Chapter 1, Thomas Ferguson in the 1980s developed an 'investment theory' of politics, arguing that what shaped the policy choices of political parties competing in elections was not the preferences of the median voter (which had become the central proposition in many political-science accounts of party competition by that time, reflecting Duncan Black's mid-twentieth-century discovery of the median voter theorem[7]), but rather the preferences of the organizations and individuals who finance the competing parties' electoral campaigns.[8] And before that, James Q. Wilson had argued that there was a class of policy actions (comprising what he called 'client politics') for which the benefits were concentrated and the maleficiaries diffused, such that a small group of beneficiaries had the motive and opportunity to promote and defend the policy position in question, but the more numerous maleficiaries (those excluded from the benefits) each had low individual stakes and faced greater obstacles in collective action to resist such policies (termed 'rent-seeking' in the loaded vocabulary of public choice analysis).[9]

From all of these perspectives—each of which involves departure from the standard assumption that managerialism and IT developments are intended to cut costs and raise performance—we might expect public management policy to be heavily prone to excessive reorganization and the reshaping of government to suit the interests of the policy elite, funders, or key 'client groups' like consultants and contractors rather than those of the voters and taxpayers at large. After all, some on the left have repeatedly suggested that one of the important political motives for public service reform by right-of-centre governments is to make some public services (notably public schools

[5] Patrick Dunleavy, *Bureaucracy, Democracy and Public Choice* (Hemel Hempstead: Harvester Wheatsheaf, 1991).
[6] Stephen Wilks, *The Political Power of the Business Corporation* (Cheltenham: Edward Elgar, 2013).
[7] Duncan Black, *The Theory of Committees and Elections* (Cambridge: Cambridge University Press, 1958).
[8] Thomas Ferguson, *Golden Rule: The Investment Theory of Party Competition and the Logic of Money-Driven Political Systems* (Chicago: University of Chicago Press, 1994).
[9] James Q. Wilson, *The Politics of Regulation* (New York: Basic Books, 1980), pp. 357–94.

and health care) worse so that middle-class citizens who can afford it choose to exit state-provided services in favour of private alternatives, suggesting that it is cell 7 rather than cell 1 of Table 9.2 that might be the real (if unstated) political objective of such parties and their backers. Such an interpretation is far from unproblematic: after all, there are many government services—such as the issue of passports or driving licences—for which there is no feasible exit option even for the wealthy, and marginal voters still have to be wooed for such parties to succeed electorally. But it reminds us that stated objectives should not always be taken at face value. So if succeeding government makeovers failed to 'do what it said on the tin', the explanation could be either that what was said on the tin did not convey the real purpose of those makeovers or, if it did, that it failed to take account of all the ways that well-placed interests could make use of the makeovers for their own benefit.

A second set of non-minimal-adjustment arguments that might explain the observed pattern as shown in Table 9.2 are those which focus on ideology, discourse, rhetoric, or image than with more concrete benefits or costs to voters at large. As we noted in Chapter 1, Christopher Pollitt portrayed managerialism in public services as an ideology rather than a pragmatic response—that is, an all-encompassing worldview and belief system which provides a perspective on almost any situation and whose adherents will systematically tend to reject any negative information about the effects of its favoured recipes as indicating either that those recipes have not been properly applied or have not been taken far enough (through the process of what the social psychologist Leon Festinger famously termed 'cognitive dissonance').[10]

Those who see public management and administration as an arena for sharply clashing cultures and competing worldviews might draw a similar conclusion. True believers need no 'evidence-based' results to prove the correctness of their ideas.[11] But in contrast to the view of government organization as an arena of deeply conflicting worldviews, others have portrayed managerialism in government as more a matter of rhetoric—persuasive discourse, in the sense of finding the right argumentative key to open a lock—than of fundamental beliefs. And, as we also noted in Chapter 1, particularly for matters that can be portrayed as 'valence' issues for voters (that is, those sorts of issues in which voters choose between candidates or parties on the basis of their perceived competence in pursuit of values most agree on, rather than 'positional issues' like abortion or gay marriage which divide voters), a rhetorical stance that puts effort into conveying an image of shiny 'modernity' and

[10] Leon Fesinger, *A Theory of Cognitive Dissonance* (Stanford, CA: Stanford University Press, 1957).
[11] Christopher Pollitt, *Managerialism and the Public Services*, 2nd edn (Oxford: Blackwell, 1993); Christopher Hood, *The Art of the State: Culture, Rhetoric and Public Management* (Oxford: Clarendon, 1998).

191

purposive energy might be a logical response. If so, that can also explain why government makeovers in the name of cutting costs and improving quality should put more emphasis on 'talking the talk' than 'walking the walk' in the sense of delivering concrete and readily measurable results.

A third set of non-minimal-adjustment arguments might explain the pattern observed in Table 9.2 in terms of deeply entrenched organizational cultures, logics, and mindsets. For example, Patrick Dunleavy and Leandro Carrera,[12] whose work we have referred to earlier in Chapters 4 and 5, have argued that, at least in the British case, inherent biases about concentrating managerial power worked against the sort of cost saving (and better service delivery) that could be drawn from web-based integrative applications of IT. From a rather different perspective one of us has argued that if a logic of blame avoidance rather than credit-claiming dominates organizational design, the architecture of government organization will tend to be dominated by principles that run clean counter to most orthodox recipes for good organization[13]—and that will include a logic of built-in deniability that runs strongly counter to the sort of 'intelligent centre' organizational culture that Dunleavy and his colleagues see as necessary for successful 'digitization' of government.

It is not our purpose here to choose among such non-minimal-adjustment explanations, or even to say what their relative weight might be in some multi-factor explanation. Nor do the three families of alternative ideas sketched out earlier necessarily exhaust the possibilities. But what the analysis of this book does suggest is that there is a case to answer. There is a case to answer because we have shown that NPM and associated digital-age developments over much of UK central government's operations seem to have had little dramatic long-term effect in the area for which the strongest claims were made by both advocates and critics about its likely impacts (i.e., cutting running costs) even in the country often claimed to be the originator of NPM and undoubtedly one of its most enthusiastic cheerleaders. If so, non-minimal explanations such as the ones we have sketched out above need to be taken seriously and tested properly, challenging though it is to tease apart their testable implications.

9.3 Implications for Science and Research: What We Now Know We Don't Know

This study aimed to answer one apparently simple question, namely, did UK government after a generation of makeovers and massive IT developments

---

[12] Patrick Dunleavy and Leandro Carrera, *Growing the Productivity of Government Services* (Cheltenham: Edward Elgar, 2013).
[13] Christopher Hood, *The Blame Game: Spin, Bureaucracy and Self-Preservation in Government* (Princeton: Princeton University Press, 2011).

end up 'working better and costing less'? Like many simple questions, that one turned out to be much trickier to answer than might at first appear, but it shows the importance for students of public management change to include on their agenda close attention to what was actually delivered over a period of decades as well as on the 'talking-a-good-game' purple passages of reform announcements. Further, our answer to that question, as summed up in Table 9.2 earlier, of course raises further questions. Indeed, it is normal in science for answers to one question to create new 'known unknowns' in the form of further questions. And there are at least three such further questions that arise out of what we have found out here.

One is the question, discussed in Section 9.2, of what accounts for the observations summed up in Table 9.2—whether they can be explained by only making minor modifications to the orthodox or standard assumptions about the efficacy of NPM and associated digital-era changes to cut running costs and push up administrative standards in government, or whether some more radical departure from such assumptions is needed. We suggested in Section 9.2 that out of the minimal-adjustment arguments, the 'changing context' variant is the one that seems most plausible. But if a complete departure from minimum adjustment is called for, the question then arises of which of the possible alternatives (some of which we sketched out in Section 9.2) most plausibly fit the outcomes we have observed.

A second question is whether what we have found for the UK represents a general pattern across comparable countries, or whether it is distinctive—a theme that we broached in Chapter 8. This study has been comparative in several ways, since it has been centrally concerned with comparison of UK central government over time, and comparison between different organizations and aggregates in government. But though in Chapter 8 we did refer to such (limited) international public sector productivity comparisons as are available in the literature, this study was not designed as a cross-national inquiry. While we can say that the answers we have found to the question we posed at the outset are significant given that they apply to the critical case of 'NPM's vanguard state', we cannot say very confidently whether the patterns shown here for the UK are typical or exceptional in cross-national perspective. Cross-national comparison on the sorts of measures we have explored here is clearly a logical next step, but as we pointed out in the first chapter, there is no convenient ready-made international dataset for such analysis, and the only feasible way to approach it is by a laborious process of extracting and reconstructing the necessary data country by country.

A third question concerns whether the future will be like the past. That presents a challenge for the future in continuing to try to track long-term cost and productivity trends over time, to assess the cost-reduction and quality-improvement claims associated with current and future administrative makeovers. After all, it seems most unlikely that concerns about how to maximize aptitude and minimize expense in government (Jeremy Bentham's slogan for public management reform, as noted in Chapter 1) will be any less important in the coming decades as they were in the past three—or indeed the past two hundred, since Jeremy Bentham coined that slogan. And there are some obvious limitations in relying on practitioner testimony, 'expert surveys', or population-wide attitude survey data to assess the cost-reduction and quality-improvement claims of NPM or its numerous competitors for the hearts and minds of public managers and those who make public management policy. So, laborious as it is, a careful comparison of reported administrative numbers over time remains important to get to the bottom of what changes in cost and administrative quality over time.

Indeed, this study was partly motivated by a desire to revisit a 'bureaumetric' study of UK central government departments that one of us co-investigated over thirty years ago,[14] to see how far the picture had changed or remained the same since then.[15] And it is tempting to speculate on what another set of researchers might find if they in turn repeated this study in another thirty years, in 2045 or so, to see how—or if—the cost and administrative quality government may be transformed by another generation of technological change and management ideas. But the prospects for such a future generation of research in the 2040s are to say the least uncertain. Even if the UK continues to hold together as a state (an issue settled at least in the short term by the Scottish referendum of 2014), the sort of data breaks we analysed in Chapter 3 are likely to work against consistent comparison over time.

If the observable increase in the data volatility index we developed to measure the stability of performance data-series in Chapter 3 continues or accelerates in the future, the method we used for reconstructing reported administrative data into more-or-less consistent series over time would be rendered more difficult to the point of impossibility. If the future is to be one of ever more high-level data breaks on our volatility index, it seems quite likely that such a mid-century study might have to rely much more on oral testimony, by putting together more fragmentary data, even possibly by the sort of crowdsourcing that TV and radio companies now use to recover lost copies of old programmes. Indeed, even over the three-year course of this research (2010–13), the launch of the website www.gov.uk (ostensibly intended to simplify citizens' interactions with government) meant that many of the online documents such as past editions of departmental annual

---

[14] Christopher Hood and Andrew Dunsire, *Bureaumetrics: The Quantitative Comparison of British Central Government Agencies* (Farnborough: Gower, 1981).

[15] Though it was also motivated by the aim to put the spotlight more clearly on tracking what happened to costs and quality than had been the case for that earlier study.

reports, on which this study relied, disappeared from their original URLs and could thereafter be found only with difficulty if at all. The data collection described in this book would have been far more difficult had we begun the exercise just two years later.

But even if that is what might be expected in the future, there is no reason why the exploration of data breaks that we conducted in Chapter 3 should not still be as applicable in the 2040s as it was in the 2010s. Indeed, if the future really is one of performance data volatility in turbodrive, it will be even more important to take data breaks themselves as the object of analysis and to use those breaks as a 'tin-opener' to discover the bureaucratic politics or other processes that they can reveal.

9.4 A Final Word: Implications for Public Management Policy

If 'minimal-adjustment' arguments to orthodox views and expectations of NPM and IT applied to government can satisfactorily account for our observations in earlier chapters, then the obvious what-to-do policy conclusion to draw is that 'one more heave', more determined application, or better quality leadership can finally deliver those hoped-for running cost savings and improved (or at least not reduced) fairness and consistency in administration. That is the 'must-try-harder' option, and of course it cannot be dismissed. For example, this study has shown that while it may be necessary to cut civil service staff numbers to cut government's running costs, it is not sufficient, and that effective measures to cut such costs have to include a vigorous attack on those elements of running costs other than direct wage costs, notably consultancies, IT costs, and the cost of Private Finance Initiative (PFI) contracts that fund public infrastructure, including many government buildings, from private capital. Similarly, if government makeovers are really animated by single-minded desire to cut running cost and improve administrative quality, it is hard to see how such objectives can be achieved without maintaining more consistency in underlying performance numbers than the increasing churn observed in this study—how can anyone know if government is doing better or worse if the basis of the numbers keeps changing and it takes years of detective work to produce consistent data-series?

However, if some or all of the possible non-minimal-adjustment explanations sketched out in Section 9.3 account for why the pursuit of public management policies do not appear to have made government clearly 'cost less and work better' over the three decades covered by this book, something more than 'must try harder' seems to be called for. And those alternative explanations merit some attention if they can provide pointers to the sort of policy designs or political strategies that might produce different results.

So, if the cause of the outcomes observed in Table 9.2 is indeed a product of some sort of rent-seeking, 'client politics', or elite bureau-shaping processes, then the sort of cases and literature that could inform alternative public management policies must be those that focus on ways to break up such self-serving networks. Indeed, there is a literature in political science about how client politics patterns can be broken up by 'policy entrepreneurs' acting like class action lawyers to change policy settings by pitting the interests of diffused maleficiaries (losers) against the concentrated beneficiaries. For example, James Q. Wilson pointed to the way Senator Ted Kennedy acted as a policy entrepreneur of that type in pushing the 1978 Airline Deregulation Act through the US Congress after a long process of committee hearings and deliberation,[16] and others have pointed out that Kennedy's initiative built on the work and advocacy of a group of economists who believed they had convincing evidence that the then airline regulatory system (in place since the 1930s) served to raise prices rather than to keep them down.[17] That may be a plausible model for an alternative approach to public management reform in the future, but it requires a careful build-up of systematic evidence about the issues considered in this book as well as the availability of suitable policy entrepreneurs.

Alternatively, if public management reform is truly an ideological and visceral issue, the conclusion must be that mobilization for policy change is more important than the sort of assembly of evidence that lay behind changes such as the airline deregulation movement in the 1970s and 1980s. And it is true that evidence about the effects of airline regulation was easier to compile from the careful statistics and records kept over decades by the US Civil Aeronautics Board than applies to the plastic and volatile recording of running costs by UK governments in recent years. But even then, cases from the past involving social and political movements for change in government organization to cut costs or improve performance—such as the short-lived civil service reform under the Wan-li emperor in classical China, the 'Economical Reform' movement in eighteenth-century Britain,[18] or Progressive-era reforms such as the late nineteenth century city-manager movement in the United States—can help to show how such changes come about. In the case of the 'Economical Reform' movement, the creation of HM Stationery Office as a new department

---

[16] James Q. Wilson, *The Politics of Regulation* (New York: Basic Books, 1980).

[17] See for instance, Stephen Breyer, *Regulation and its Reform* (Cambridge, MA: Harvard University Press, 1982).

[18] See, for example, Christopher Hood, 'Reflections on Public Service Reform in a Cold Fiscal Climate', in *Public Services: A New Reform Agenda, edited by* Simon Griffiths, Henry Kippen, and Gerry Stoker (London: Bloomsbury, 2013), pp. 223–4.

of the Treasury in 1786, involving a mixture of parliamentary advocacy (notably by Edmund Burke), wider political mobilization against the cost of public pensions and patents, and some support within the bureaucracy, was a crucial step. That new department enabled the Treasury to challenge the 'patents' (exclusive rights) for the supply of stationery and printing at high prices awarded to favoured suppliers, paving the way for massive cost-cutting through the eventual adoption of a mixture of open tendering and 'meta-phytic' (that is, public–private) competition for those costly items.[19] Given the extent to which running costs seem to have been raised by outsourced items rather than civil service wage costs over the decades examined by this study, the 'Economical Reform' movement and its counterparts such as the Progressive public administration movement in the United States a century later[20] may also provide a relevant historical policy model.

Finally, if organizational or institutional cultures, whether of hierarchical management, blame-avoidance, or something else, are what shape the outcomes of efforts to make government work better or cost less, we need to focus on those exceptional cases in which such cultures change or are overcome, as a result of pressures from outside or inside or both, rather than the general aggregates with which we have been concerned in this book. The islands of competence and high performance (such as the famous Moscow metro system) in the former Soviet state and cases of successful public enterprise in otherwise unpromising settings, provide possible examples here.[21] As already stated, that goes well beyond the ground this book has aimed to cover. But tracing out how well government works and what it costs will and should continue to be a central issue in public management.

---

[19] See Hugh Barty-King, *Her Majesty's Stationery Office: The Story of the First 200 Years, 1786–1986* (London: HMSO, 1986).
[20] See Christopher Hood, *The Art of the State: Culture, Rhetoric and Public Management* (Oxford: Clarendon, 1998), pp. 90–1.
[21] See Scott Douglas, 'Success Nonetheless: Making Public Utilities Work in Small-Scale Democracies Despite Social Capital Difficulties', D.Phil thesis, University of Oxford, 2012.

APPENDIX 1

Interviewees and Focus Group Members

Several individuals held more than one post during their career. The post most relevant to our study is listed here.

Department or organization	Current officials	Former officials
Cabinet Office	3	2
HM Treasury	8	3
No. 10 Policy Unit		1
Ministry of Justice	1	3
Home Office		1
Department for Transport		1
Department for Communities and Local Government	4	
Department for Business, Innovation and Skills (or former Department of Trade and Industry or Office for Government Commerce)	3	3
National Audit Office	5	
House of Lords	1	
Office of the Parliamentary Counsel	2	2
Office for National Statistics	1	
Scottish Civil Service	3	
Local government	2	1
Executive Agency	2	
Law Commission	1	
Parliamentary and Health Service Ombudsman	1	1
Office of Fair Trading	2	
Hansard Society	1	
Better Government Initiative	2	
Non-departmental public bodies		1

Index of Volatility: Classification of Discontinuities for Chapter 3

Discontinuities were classified as 'Large' (weighting 4), 'Medium' (2), and 'Small' (1) as specified in Table 3.1

Table A2.1. Classification of Discontinuities

Date	Weighting	**Administration or running costs** Source: Public Expenditure Statistical Analyses, annual editions
1986	4	First report of running costs (backdated to 1980–81)
1987	2	Property Services Agency (PSA) taken out of costs and some Department of Social Security (DSS) costs restated
1991	2	PSA and Land Registry included
1993	2	Superannuation and casual staff included
1995	2	Civil departmental running costs shown, with MoD operating costs shown separately
1998	2	'Gross' redefined as 'net of inter-departmental receipts'—requiring recalculation of all previous years
1999	2	Administration costs of devolved bodies and MoD omitted completely
2001	4	Net costs could no longer be calculated; gross costs only reported and no receipts reported
2002	2	Resource accounting introduced (made little numerical difference to running costs), and report format changed, with shorter spans of outturn years
2004	1	Only two outturn years reported and no overlap with previous edition
2005	4	Net costs only shown. No receipts shown, so gross costs could not be calculated. Major reclassification of Administration by an unknown amount
2008	2	MoD included in administration budget (known amount)
2011	4	Arms-length bodies included (unknown but very substantial amount, mainly NHS bodies)
2012	4	Large decrease in reported spending of (mainly) DWP and HMRC. This was a combination of reclassifications and actual spending cuts, so no comparison with previous years was possible

(Continued)

Table A2.1. (Continued)

Date	Weighting	Civil service paybill Sources: *Memoranda of the Chief Secretary to the Treasury*, annual editions; *Public Expenditure Statistical Analyses*, annual editions; National Audit Office (NAO) report (HC 818 2010–11); and personal communication from the Cabinet Office
1981	1	'Indirect' remuneration no longer quoted
1986	4	Civil service paybill reporting discontinued (Treasury Memoranda series)
1992	4	Civil service paybill included in PESA, backdated to 1986–87
1993	2	Superannuation and casual staff included
1996	2	MoD armed forces staff costs included
1999	2	Devolved bodies and MoD staff not included
2000	2	MoD civilian staff included
2001	2	MoD staff not included
2005	4	Civil service paybill no longer reported. Gershon reclassifications mean that the PESA administration paybill covers only civil servants within admin budgets (an unknown number of staff)
2008	4	MoD civilian staff included in administration paybill and other substantial changes
2011	4	Staff of arms-length bodies included in the PESA administration paybill (unknown amount). NAO report (HC 818 2010–11) provided the civil service paybill for 2001–2010 based on Cabinet Office estimates and a personal communication from the Cabinet Office provided the 2011–12 and 2012–13 figures
2012	4	Unknown numbers of DWP and HMRC staff reclassified out of administration paybill
2013	4	Further major changes to administration paybill

Date	Weighting	Tax cost-to-yield (c/y) Sources: Inland Revenue (IR), Customs & Excise (C&E), and Her Majesty's Revenue and Customs (HMRC) *Annual Departmental Reports*
1984	1	New format for tables, start of reported income tax c/y
1989	2	C&E report omitted many tables—reinstated the following year
1993	2	C&E ceased reporting c/y (calculation required)
1995	1	IR tables format changed, no functional analysis by tax, Valuation Office Agency staff removed from count (and possibly payroll) but overall c/y unchanged. C&E report format also changed
1999	4	Contributions and Benefits agency merged with IR, National Insurance contributions included in reported c/y (original basis could not be reconstructed)
2000	2	C&E altered how net costs reported, so c/y could only be estimated after this date
2001	2	IR Tax Credit costs included in c/y (c/y reported with and without this change)
2003	1	IR report format changed
2005	4	HMRC formed, no c/y reported this year. Table showing c/y calculations no longer given
2006	2	Overall c/y reported but calculation basis unclear
2007	1	Changed report format
2010	2	Departmental accounts but no annual report produced. C/y figures could be calculated
2011	1	New report format, new tables, but still no table showing c/y calculation basis
2012	2	Overall c/y no longer reported, administration costs completely altered due to reclassifications, c/y estimated from DEL/yield

(Continued)

Table A2.1. (Continued)

Date	Weighting	**Complaints to Parliamentary Ombudsman** *Sources*: Parliamentary Commissioner for Administration *Annual Reports*; Parliamentary and Health Service Ombudsman (PHSO) *Annual Reports*; personal communication from PHSO office
1998	1	Switch from calendar to financial year reporting
2005	4	Number of complaints submitted via MPs no longer reported (only 'total complaints,' a much larger number), distinction between statutory investigations and other interventions removed, departmental breakdown of complaints no longer compatible. (Subsequent numbers of complaints via MPs obtained as personal communication in 2012)
2006	4	No distinction made between Health Ombudsman and and Parliamentary Ombudsman complaints in this year and 2007
2008	4	Health and Parliamentary complaints distinguished. A new metric 'enquiries' appeared alongside 'complaints received'. Departments reappeared in more-or-less consistent form
2011	1	A separate report (*Responsive and Accountable* HC 1551 2010–11) published which gave some more detailed statistical information (but still not the number of complaints received via MPs). A further edition (HC 799 and 800 [statistical supplement]) published in 2012
2013	4	Annual report gave only 'enquiries' and not 'complaints'. *Responsive and Accountable* discontinued. Some information available online, but reporting periods unclear and metrics not comparable with previous years

APPENDIX 3

Dealing with 'Medium' Levels of Data Volatility: The Example of Departmental Running Costs

A3.1 The Problem

The UK Treasury's annual *Public Expenditure Statistical Analysis* (PESA) reports gave outturn figures for running costs for each year of the three decades covered by this book. But simply logging those costs for a run of years to obtain a long time-series would not provide a valid basis for a like-with-like comparison because the classification of what counted as running costs changed so frequently over this period. Indeed the Treasury itself cautioned against forming a time-series by putting together the costs reported for each year. PESA 2010 warned at p. 6: 'Users are strongly advised against simply splicing data together from different editions of PESA as data is unlikely to be directly consistent due to changes in coverage and classification'.

These changes mostly consisted of data breaks at the 'medium' level in our index of volatility (as discussed in Chapter 3 and Appendix 2) because something more than routine recalculations were required to produce a consistent series. But in most years the changes fell short of the highest level in our volatility index because in most editions of PESA the previous years' outturns were reported when recalculated retrospectively on the new basis. So comparing the reports of the same year's outturn in different PESA editions made it possible to gauge the extent of such reclassification changes, which are illustrated in Figure A3.1 for net running costs.

No meaningful picture of cost changes over time could have been obtained without taking such reclassifications into account, because (both for gross and net running costs), those reclassifications frequently resulted in larger changes between one edition of PESA and another than the year-to-year changes reported within each PESA report (differences sometimes running into billions of pounds, and over 20 per cent of the total costs). So the apparent running costs for any one year depended critically on which edition of PESA was consulted.

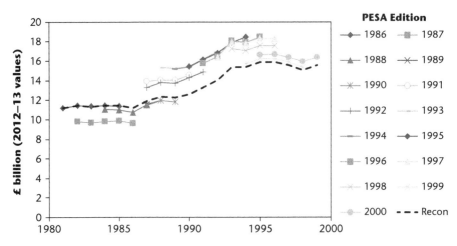

Figure A3.1. Net Running Costs of UK Central Civil Departments 1980–81 to 1998–99 in Real Terms, Showing Successive Reclassifications (£billion, 2012–13 values using GDP deflator).

Dotted line is the reconstruction using the method described in this Appendix

A3.2 A Partial Solution

To overcome this difficulty and make a long-term comparison of running costs possible, we noted that the effect of each reclassification was to increase or decrease all the outturn years by approximately the same amount compared to the previous PESA edition, while the year-to-year changes remained almost the same.

Thus to choose any pair of successive years, say the financial years ending 1984 and 1985, the inflation-adjusted difference in costs between those years reported in PESA 1986, 1987, and 1988 were almost the same, even though the absolute levels varied by over a billion pounds (in 2012–13 values) between PESA editions due to reclassification changes.

We therefore 'stripped out' the effect of the reclassification change by adding the average inflation-adjusted change between 1984 and 1985 (from all PESA editions in which both years were reported) to the costs for 1984, and so on for subsequent years (the dotted line shown in the figure). Provided overlapping outturn years are reported in each PESA edition; a continuous record can be reconstructed by this approach. As this approach uses the difference between subsequent years' costs as reported *in the same edition* of PESA (that is, presumably calculated by the Treasury on the same basis) it would seem to be a valid way of measuring changes in running costs over an extended period.

It should be noted that the absolute costs calculated by this method depend critically on the chosen starting year. We chose fiscal year 1980–81 (the first outturn year reported in PESA 1986) as our baseline, and so whatever was classified as 'running costs' in that year is therefore 'built in' to our results for subsequent years. But this starting figure is not necessarily a 'truer' reflection of absolute running costs than the subsequent reclassified figures, merely a route to like-for-like comparison over time.

Because of this system of overlapping-years reporting, many of the Treasury reclassifications of departmental running costs over the thirty years considered by this book were at the 'medium' level in our index of volatility. But as noted in Chapters 3 and 4, some data breaks scored at the topmost level in our index of volatility, and could not be corrected by this method. In PESA 2005, for instance, administration costs started to be defined in a fundamentally different way, and only net (rather than gross) costs were reported. However, in the previous three PESA editions, only gross costs were reported. So net running costs were not reported in any edition of PESA for the financial year 1999–2000, making it impossible to compare the absolute level of costs after that date with the earlier series.

A further fundamental change took place, starting in PESA 2010. In the most recent editions, the basis for calculating administration costs was inconsistent between different financial years *within the same edition of PESA*, making it impossible to distinguish reclassification changes from actual spending changes by this method.

APPENDIX 4

Analysis of Legislative Amendments: Methodology for Chapter 8

A4.1 Legislation: Selection Criteria

Legislation.gov.uk was searched using appropriate keywords for Criminal Justice and Health Service Acts. Acts were selected with regard to the relevance of the topic of the legislation and the requirement to sample each decade from the 1970s to the 2010s for both families of legislation. Consolidation and amendment acts were excluded, as was legislation that was wholly concerned with the devolved administrations. Acts whose parliamentary process was cut short by a general election were also excluded. The Acts analysed are shown in the table below.

Some definitions: Legislation is referred to as a *bill* as it proceeds through parliament and an *Act of Parliament* when it receives Royal Assent. The numbered *sections* of an Act are known as *clauses* in a bill, while *schedules* are so-called both in Acts and in bills.

A4.2 Sources

Commons committee stage: Minutes of Proceedings of Standing Committees (until the 2005–06 parliamentary session) and Public Bill Committees (from the 2006–07 session) showed the fate of each amendment, and in whose name it was tabled. Amendments tabled without names were assumed to be government amendments, confirmed for a sample of cases by reference to the detailed transcript of the committee debates.

Commons Report stage: Hansard reports of the Commons debates were analysed to determine the fate of each amendment listed in the Marshalled List of amendments for that date.

Lords stages (Committee, Report, and Third Reading): Marshalled Lists of Amendments, hand annotated with the fate of each amendment by the clerks in the House of Lords. These lists were found in the Bill Files in the Parliamentary Archives in the Palace of Westminster. (Bill Files not yet released under the thirty-year rule were reviewed and released under Freedom of Information at our request.)

A4.3 Amendment Analysis

1. Amendments were categorized as 'government' (proposed by a government minister from the sponsoring department, with or without other proposers), or 'non-government' (proposed by an opposition member or a backbencher from the governing party).
2. The fate of each amendment was recorded as agreed (with or without a division [i.e. a vote]), withdrawn, not moved, not called, or negatived with or without a division.

This analysis showed that:

1. Virtually all government amendments were agreed.
2. Backbench or opposition amendments were rarely agreed. Overall, 0.5 per cent of agreed Commons amendments and 8.7 per cent of agreed Lords amendments were 'non-government'. The Lords amendments showed considerable variation, however; in three bills 'non-government' amendments accounted for over a third of all agreed amendments. In the Commons, no bill had more than 3 per cent agreed 'non-government' amendments.
3. Large numbers of amendments were proposed by the opposition and some by backbenchers from the governing party, but the vast majority of those amendments were withdrawn, not moved, not called, or negatived with or without a division.
4. In the House of Commons, the Committee Stage and the Report Stage each accounted for about half of the government amendments agreed by that House (with a wide range, from 8 to 90 per cent). In the House of Lords, the average proportions were Committee: 36 per cent; Report: 45 per cent; and Third Reading: 19 per cent, with a similarly large range.
5. The numbers of government amendments agreed at each stage in the first or the second house (and the sum in each house), whether as absolute numbers or relative to the length of the final legislation, showed no systematic changes over time.
6. No differences in any of these metrics were found between Health and Criminal Justice bills, or between bills first introduced in the Commons or in the Lords.

Table A4.1. Results of Amendment Analysis

Legislation Analysed	Originating house	Length of Final Legislation			Agreed Government Amendments	
		Pages	Sections	Schedules	First house	Second house
Criminal Justice (thirteen bills)						
Criminal Justice Act 1972	Commons	62	66	6	76	65
Criminal Law Act 1977	Lords	128	65	14	198	200
Criminal Justice Act 1982	Commons	168	81	17	168	347
Criminal Justice Act 1988	Lords	160	165	15	233	502
Criminal Justice Act 1991	Commons	126	102	13	98	182
Criminal Justice Act 1993	Lords	102	79	6	14	214
Criminal Justice and Public Order Act 1994	Commons	214	172	11	355	311
Crime and Disorder Act 1998	Lords	177	121	10	318	245
Criminal Justice and Court Services Act 2000	Commons	113	82	8	137	398
Criminal Justice Act 2003	Commons	453	339	38	632	529
Criminal Justice and Immigration Act 2008	Commons	326	154	28	428	350
Policing and Crime Act 2009	Commons	202	117	8	316	103
Police Reform and Social Responsibility Act 2011	Commons	246	158	17	102	168
Health Service (sixteen bills)						
National Health Service Reorganisation Act 1973	Lords	102	58	5	85	248
Health Services Act 1976	Commons	37	24	5	69	5
Health Services Act 1980	Commons	63	26	7	52	0
Health and Social Security Act 1984	Commons	63	29	8	132	11
Health and Medicines Act 1988	Commons	32	28	3	36	49
National Health Service and Community Care Act 1990	Commons	130	67	10	292	186
Health Authorities Act 1995	Commons	53	10	3	3	6
National Health Service (Primary Care) Act 1997	Lords	66	41	3	99	115
Health Act 1999	Lords	112	69	5	179	156
Health and Social Care Act 2001	Commons	91	70	6	236	82
National Health Service Reform and Health Care Professions Act 2002	Commons	101	42	9	118	17
Health and Social Care (Community Health and Standards) Act 2003	Commons	185	203	14	338	277
Health Act 2006	Commons	91	84	9	54	58
Health and Social Care Act 2008	Commons	208	173	15	113	90
Health Act 2009	Lords	71	41	6	38	26
Health and Social Care Act 2012	Commons	457	309	23	1722	367

Selected Bibliography

Afonso, António, Ludger Schucknecht, and Vito Tanzi. 'Public Sector Efficiency: An International Comparison'. *Public Choice* 123, nos. 3–4 (2005): pp. 321–47.

Andrews, Rhys. 'NPM and the Search for Efficiency'. In *The Ashgate Research Companion to New Public Management,* edited by Tom Christensen and Per Laegreid (Farnham, Surrey: Ashgate, 2011), pp. 281–94.

Audit Commission. *Behind Closed Doors: The Revolution in Central Support Services* (London: HMSO, 1994).

Barty-King, Hugh. *Her Majesty's Stationery Office: The Story of the First 200 Years, 1786–1986* (London: HMSO, 1986).

Beck Jørgensen, Torben, and Lotte Andersen. 'An Aftermath of NPM: Regained Relevance of Public Values and Public Service Motivation'. In *The Ashgate Research Companion to New Public Management*, edited by Tom Christensen and Per Laegreid (Farnham, Surrey: Ashgate, 2011), pp. 335–48.

Berlinski, Samuel, Torun Dewan, and Keith Dowding. *Accounting for Ministers* (Cambridge: Cambridge University Press, 2012).

Bevan, Gwyn R., and Christopher Hood. 'What's Measured is What Matters: Targets and Gaming in Healthcare in England'. *Public Administration* 84, no. 3 (2006): pp. 517–38.

Blair, Tony. *The Third Way: New Politics for the New Century* (London: Fabian Society, 1998).

Bogdanor, Vernon. 'British Government in Crisis: book review'. *PMPA Review* 30 (2005): pp. 12–14.

Bondy, Varda, and Maurice Sunkin. *The Dynamics of Judicial Review Litigation: The Resolution of Public Law Challenges Before Final Hearing* (London: The Public Law Project, 2009).

Boyle, Richard. *Measuring Public Sector Productivity: Lessons from International Experience* (Dublin: Institute of Public Administration, 2006).

Butler, David, Andrew Adonis, and Tony Travers. *Failure in British Government: The Politics of the Poll Tax* (Oxford: Oxford University Press, 1994).

Butler, Robin. 'Reinventing British Government'. *Public Administration* 72, no. 2 (1994): pp. 263–70.

Carnwarth, Robert. 'Tribunal Justice—a New Start'. *Public Law* 48, no. 1 (2009): pp. 1–15.

Carrera, Leandro, Patrick Dunleavy, and Simon Bastow. *Understanding Productivity Trends in UK Tax Collection.* LSE Public Policy Group Working Paper July 2009 (London: LSE PPG, 2009).

Carter, Neil. 'Learning to Measure Performance—the Use of Indicators in Organizations'. *Public Administration* 69, no. 1 (1991): pp. 85–101.

Chapman, Richard, and Andrew Dunsire (eds). *Style in Administration* (London: Allen & Unwin, 1971).

Christensen, Tom, and Per Laegreid (eds). *New Public Management: The Transformation of Ideas and Practice* (Aldershot: Ashgate, 2001).

Craig, David, and Richard Brooks. *Plundering the Public Sector: How New Labour are Letting Consultants Run off with £70 Billion of Our Money* (London: Constable, 2006).

Crawford, Rowena, Carl Emmerson, and Gemma Tetlow. *A Survey of Public Spending in the UK* (London: Institute for Fiscal Studies, 2009).

Demetriadi, Stephen. *A Reform for the Civil Service* (London: Cassell, 1921).

Dunleavy, Patrick. *Bureaucracy, Democracy and Public Choice* (Hemel Hempstead: Harvester Wheatsheaf, 1991).

Dunleavy, Patrick, Helen Margetts, Simon Bastow, and Jane Tinkler. *Digital Era Governance: IT Corporations, the State and E-Government* (Oxford: Oxford University Press, 2006).

Dunleavy, Patrick, and Leandro Carrera. *Growing the Productivity of Government Services* (Cheltenham: Edward Elgar, 2013).

Elder, Neil, and Page, Edward. 'Accountability and Control in Next Steps Agencies'. In *Transforming British Government: Volume 1: Changing Institutions*, edited by Rod Rhodes (Basingstoke: Macmillan, 2000).

Elston, Thomas. 'Developments in UK Executive Agencies: Re-examining the "Disaggregation-Reaggregation" Thesis'. *Public Policy and Administration* 28, no.1 (2013): pp. 66–89.

Ferguson, Thomas. *Golden Rule: The Investment Theory of Party Competition and the Logic of Money-Driven Political Systems* (Chicago: University of Chicago Press, 1994).

Foster, Christopher. *British Government in Crisis* (Oxford: Hart Publishing, 2005).

Freeguard, Gavin, and Ian Makgill. *Government Contracting: Public Data, Private Providers* (London: Institute for Government, 2014).

Gershon, Peter. *Releasing Resources to the Front Line: An Independent Review of Public Sector Efficiency* (London: HMSO, 2004).

Gibson, John S. *The Thistle and the Crown: A History of the Scottish Office* (Edinburgh: HMSO, 1985).

Gore, Al. *From Red Tape to Results: Creating a Government That Works Better and Costs Less*, Report of the National Performance Review (Washington: US Government Printing Office, 1993).

Gormley, William T. Jr., and David L. Weimer. *Organizational Report Cards* (Cambridge, MA: Harvard University Press, 1999).

The Government Office of Science. *Science & Analysis Assurance Review of Her Majesty's Treasury* (London: The Government Office of Science, 2013).

Greenaway, John. 'Having the Bun and the Halfpenny: Can Old Public Service Ethics Survive in the New Whitehall?'. *Public Administration* 73, no. 3 (1995): pp. 357–74.

Griffith, John A. G. *Central Departments and Local Authorities* (London: Allen & Unwin, 1966).

Griffith, John A. G. *Parliamentary Scrutiny of Government Bills* (London: Allen & Unwin, 1974)

Heclo, Hugh, and Aaron Wildavsky. *The Private Government of Public Money: Community and Policy Inside British Politics* (London: Macmillan, 1974).

Hogwood, Brian. 'The "Growth" of Quangos: Evidence and Explanations'. *Parliamentary Affairs* 48, no. 2 (1995): pp. 207–25.

Hood, Christopher. 'A Public Management for All Seasons'. *Public Administration* 69, no. 2 (1991): pp. 3–19.

Hood, Christopher. *The Art of the State: Culture, Rhetoric and Public Management* (Oxford: Clarendon, 1998).

Hood, Christopher. 'Gaming in Targetworld'. *Public Administration Review* 66, no. 4 (2006): pp. 515–20.

Hood, Christopher. 'Public Service Management by Numbers: Why Does it Vary? Where Has it Come From? What Are the Gaps and the Puzzles?'. *Public Money and Management* 27, no. 2 (2007): pp. 95–102.

Hood, Christopher. *The Blame Game: Spin, Bureaucracy and Self-Preservation in Government* (Princeton: Princeton University Press, 2011), pp. 9–14 and pp. 116–17.

Hood, Christopher. 'Reflections on Public Service Reform in a Cold Fiscal Climate'. In *Public Services: A New Reform Agenda*, edited by Simon Griffiths, Henry Kippen, and Gerry Stoker (London: Bloomsbury, 2013), pp. 215–29.

Hood, Christopher, and Ruth Dixon, 'The Political Payoff from Performance Target Systems: No-Brainer or No-Gainer?'. *Journal of Public Administration Research and Theory* 20, Suppl. 2 (2010): pp. i281–98.

Hood, Christopher, and Andrew Dunsire. *Bureaumetrics: The Quantitative Comparison of British Central Government Agencies* (Farnborough: Gower, 1981).

Hood, Christopher, David Heald, and Rozana Himaz (eds). *When the Party's Over: The Politics of Fiscal Squeeze in Perspective*, Proceedings of the British Academy 197 (Oxford: Oxford University Press, 2014).

Hood, Christopher, Oliver James, George Jones, Colin Scott, and Tony Travers. *Regulation Inside Government: Waste Watchers, Quality Police and Sleaze-Busters* (Oxford: Oxford University Press, 1999).

Hood, Christopher, and Martin Lodge. *The Politics of Public Service Bargains: Reward, Competency, Loyalty—and Blame* (Oxford: Oxford University Press, 2006).

Hood, Christopher, and Helen Margetts. *The Tools of Government in the Digital Age* (Basingstoke: Palgrave Macmillan, 2007).

Ingham, Bernard. *The Wages of Spin* (London: John Murray, 2003).

Jacobs, Michael. 'Margaret Thatcher's Economic Jackpot: Miracle or Myth?'. *Economic and Political Weekly* 23, no. 3 (1988): p. 1520.

James, Oliver. 'The UK Core Executive's Use of Public Service Agreements as a Tool of Governance'. *Public Administration* 82, no. 2 (1994): pp. 397–419.

James, Oliver. 'Evaluating Executive Agencies in UK Government'. *Public Policy and Management* 16, no. 3 (2001): pp. 24–52.

James, Oliver. *The Executive Agency Revolution in Whitehall: Public Interest versus Bureau-Shaping Perspectives* (Basingstoke: Palgrave Macmillan, 2003).

James, Oliver, and Sandra van Thiel. 'Structural Devolution to Agencies'. In *The Ashgate Research Companion to New Public Management*, edited by Tom Christensen and Per Laegreid (Farnham, Surrey: Ashgate, 2011), pp. 209–22.

Jarvis, Richard. *The UK Experience of Public Administration Reform* (London: Commonwealth Secretariat, 2002).

Jenkins, Kate, Karen Caines, and Andrew Jackson. *Improving Management in Government: The Next Steps* (London: HMSO, 1988).

Jones, George W. *The Future of Local Government: Has it One?* (London: CIPFA, 2008).

Jones, George W., and John Stewart. *The Case for Local Government* (London: Allen & Unwin, 1983).

Jones, Nicholas. *Sultans Of Spin: The Media And The New Labour Government* (London: Gollancz, 1999).

Johnstone, Dorothy. *A Tax Shall be Charged: Some Aspects of the Introduction of the British Value Added Tax* (London: HMSO, 1975).

Keeling, Desmond. *Management in Government* (London: Allen & Unwin, 1972).

King, Anthony, and Ivor Crewe. *Blunders of Our Governments* (London: Oneworld Publications, 2013).

Klijn, Erik-Hans. *It's The Management, Stupid! On the Importance of Management in Complex Policy Issues* (The Hague: Lemma, 2008).

Kuhry, Bob, and Evert Pommer. 'Performance of the Public Sector'. In Public Sector Performance: An International Comparison of Education, Health Care, Law and Order and Public Administration (The Hague: SCP, 2004), pp. 271–92.

Levi-Faur, David. 'The Global Diffusion of Regulatory Capitalism'. *The Annals of the American Academy of Political and Social Science* 598 (2005), pp. 12–32.

Maas, Gerard C., and Frits K. M. Van Nispen. 'The Quest for a Leaner, Not a Meaner Government'. In *Research in Public Administration, Vol. 5*, edited by James L. Perry (Stamford: JAI Press, 1999), pp. 63–86.

Mackenzie, William J. M., and Jack W. Grove. *Central Administration in Britain* (London: Longmans, 1957).

Margetts, Helen Z. *Information Technology in Government: Britain and America* (London: Routledge, 1999).

Martin, Bill. 'The Puzzle behind Britain's Lamentable Statistics'. Financial Times, 23 February 2007.

Martin, Bill. 'Resurrecting the UK Historic Sector National Accounts'. *The Review of Income and Wealth* 55, no. 3 (2009): pp. 737–51.

Moran, Michael. *The British Regulatory State: Hyper-Modernism and Hyper-Innovation* (Oxford: Oxford University Press, 2003).

National Audit Office. *Progress with VFM Savings and Lessons for Cost Reduction Programmes* (HC 291, 2010–11)

National Audit Office. *Managing Staff Costs in Central Government* (HC 818, 2010–11).

National Audit Office. *Building Capability in the Senior Civil Service* (HC 129, 2013–14).

Nye, Joseph S., Philip D. Zelikow, and David C. King. *Why People Don't Trust Government* (Cambridge, MA: Harvard University Press, 1997).

OECD. *Government at a Glance 2011* (OECD: Paris, 2011).

OECD. *Government at a Glance 2013* (OECD: Paris, 2013).

Osborne, David, and Ted Gaebler. *Reinventing Government: How the Entrepreneurial Spirit is Transforming the Public Sector* (Reading, MA: Addison-Wesley, 1992).

Platt, Lucinda, Maurice Sunkin, and Kerman Calvo. 'Judicial Review Litigation as an Incentive to Change in Local Authority Public Services in England and Wales'. *Journal of Public Administration Research and Theory* 20, Suppl. 2 (2010): pp. i243–60.

Pollitt, Christopher. *Manipulating the Machine: Changing the Pattern of Ministerial Departments 1960–83* (London: Allen & Unwin, 1984).

Pollitt, Christopher. *Managerialism and the Public Services: The Anglo-American Experience* (Oxford: Blackwell, 1990).

Pollitt, Christopher. 'Justification by Works or by Faith? Evaluating the New Public Management'. *Evaluation* 1, no. 2 (1995): pp. 133–54.

Pollitt, Christopher. 'Managerialism Revisited'. In *Taking Stock: Assessing Public Service Reforms*, edited by B. Guy Peters and Donald Savoie (Montreal: McGill-Queens University Press, 1998), pp. 45–77.

Pollitt, Christopher. *Time, Policy, Management: Governing with the Past* (Oxford: Oxford University Press, 2008).

Pollitt, Christopher. 'Performance Blight and the Tyranny of Light'. In *Accountable Governance: Problems and Promises*, edited by Melvin J. Dubnick and H. George Frederickson (New York: M.E. Sharpe, 2010), pp. 81–97.

Pollitt, Christopher. 'The Evolving Narratives of Public Management Reform: 40 Years of Reform White Papers in the UK'. *Public Management Review* 15, no. 6 (2013): pp. 899–922.

Pollitt, Christopher, and Geert Bouckaert. *Public Management Reform: A Comparative Analysis—New Public Management, Governance, and the Neo-Weberian State*, 3rd edn (Oxford: Oxford University Press, 2011).

Protherough, Robert, and John Pick. *Managing Britannia: Culture and Management in Modern Britain* (Edgeways: Brynmill Press, 2002).

Rhodes, Rod. *Everyday Life in British Government* (Oxford: Oxford University Press, 2011), pp. 294–5.

Roberts, Alasdair. 'Dashed Expectations: Governmental Adaptation to Transparency Rules'. In *Transparency: The Key to Better Governance?*, edited by Christopher Hood and David Heald (Oxford: Oxford University Press for the British Academy, 2006).

Roberts, Alasdair. *Large Forces: What's Missing in Public Administration* (North Charleston: CreateSpace Independent Publishing Platform, 2013).

Roberts, Alasdair. *The End of Protest: How Free-Market Capitalism Learned to Control Dissent* (Cornell: Cornell University Press, 2013).

Russell, Meg. *The Contemporary House of Lords: Westminster Bicameralism Revived* (Oxford: Oxford University Press, 2013).

Schaffer, Bernard. *The Administrative Factor* (London: Frank Cass, 1973).

Scott, James C. *Seeing Like a State: How Certain Schemes to Improve the Human Condition Have Failed* (New Haven: Yale University Press, 1998).

Seneviratne, Mary. *Ombudsmen: Public Services and Administrative Justice* (London: Butterworths, 2002).

Shell, Donald. *The House of Lords* (Manchester: Manchester University Press, 2007).

Sisson, Charles H. 'The Civil Service After Fulton'. In *British Government in an Era of Reform*, edited by William J. Stankiewicz (London: Collier Macmillan, 1976), p. 252–62.

Soroka, Stuart, Christopher Wlezien, and Iain McLean. 'Public Expenditure in the UK: How Measures Matter'. *Journal of the Royal Statistical Society: Series A (Statistics in Society)* 169, no. 2 (2009): pp. 255–71.

Stewart, John, and Kieron Walsh. 'Change in Management of Public Services'. *Public Administration* 70, no. 4 (1992): pp. 499–518.

Suleiman, Ezra. *Dismantling Democratic States* (Princeton NJ: Princeton University Press, 2003).

Talbot, Colin. *Ministers and Agencies: Control, Performance and Accountability* (London: CIPFA, 1996).

Talbot, Colin. 'Executive Agencies; Have They Improved Management in Government?', *Public Money and Management* 24, no. 2 (2004), pp. 104–12.

Talbot, Colin, and Christopher Pollitt. *Unbundled Government* (London: Routledge, 2003).

Taylor, David and Susan Balloch (eds). *The Politics of Evaluation: Participation and Policy Implementation* (Bristol: Policy Press, 2005).

Theakston, Kevin, and Geoffrey Fry. 'Britain's Administrative Elite: Permanent Secretaries 1900–1986'. *Public Administration* 67 (1989): pp. 129–47.

Treasury Select Committee. *The Merger of Customs & Excise and the Inland Revenue; Ninth Report of Session 2003–04* (HC 556, 2003–04).

Tsoukas, Haridimos. 'The Tyranny of Light: The Temptations and Paradoxes of the Information Society'. *Futures* 29, no. 9 (1997): pp. 827–43.

Weaver, Kent R. 'The Politics of Blame Avoidance'. *Journal of Public Policy* 6, no. 4 (1986): pp. 371–98.

Weaver, Kent R. *Automatic Government: The Politics of Indexation* (Washington, DC: Brookings Institution Press, 1988).

Weber, Max. 'Bureaucracy'. In *From Max Weber: Essays in Sociology*, edited and translated by Hans H. Gerth and C. Wright Mills (London: Routledge and Kegan Paul, 1948), p. 214.

Weber, Max. 'Science as a Vocation'. In *From Max Weber: Essays in Sociology*, edited and translated by Hans H. Gerth and C. Wright Mills (London: Routledge and Kegan Paul, 1948), p. 139.

Whewell, William. *The Philosophy of the Inductive Sciences: Founded upon their History* ([1840, 2nd edn 1847] reprinted by Whitefish, MT: Kissinger, 2007).

White, Anne, and Patrick J. Dunleavy. *Making and Breaking Whitehall Departments: A Guide to Machinery of Government Changes* (London: Institute for Government and LSE Public Policy Group, 2010).

Wilks, Stephen. *The Political Power of the Business Corporation* (Cheltenham: Edward Elgar, 2013).

Williamson, Samuel. 'New values for the UK GDP, are they better?' UK Measuring Worth 2012 <http://www.measuringworth.com/datasets/ukgdp/RewriteUK.php>

Wilson, Richard. 'Trust in Public Life'. *British Academy Review* 12 (2009): pp. 1–4.

Official Sources Bibliography

Dates	Source title	Source number and date
Civil service staff numbers and turnover		
1970 to 2013	*Civil Service Statistics, Annual Editions*	n/a
Civil service paybill costs		
1962–63 to 1971–72	*Estimates (Memorandum by the Financial Secretary to the Treasury)*	HC 142 1961–62; Cmnd 1965 1963; Cmnd 2290 1964; Cmnd 2619 1965; Cmnd 2955 1966; Cmnd 3227 1967; Cmnd 3583 1968; Cmnd 3971 1969; Cmnd 4331 1970; Cmnd 4627 1971; Cmnd 4921 1972
1972–73 to 1985–86	*Supply Estimates (Memorandum by the Chief Secretary to the Treasury)*	Cmnd 5248 1973; Cmnd 5576 1974; Cmnd 6009 1975; Cmnd 6452 1976; Cmnd 6769 1977; Cmnd 7157 1978; Cmnd 7524 1979; Cmnd 7869 1980; Cmnd 8184 1981; Cmnd 8512 1982; Cmnd 8817 1983; Cmnd 9161 1984; Cmnd 9450 1985; Cmnd 9742 1986
Central government 'common services' costs		
1969–70 to 1975–76	*Public Expenditure*	Cmnd 4234 1970; Cmnd 4578 1971; Cmnd 4829 1972; Cmnd 5178 1973; Cmnd 5519 1974; Cmnd 5879 1975; Cmnd 6393 1976
1976–77 to 1984–85	*The Government's Expenditure Plans*	Cmnd 6721-II 1977; Cmnd 7049-II 1978; Cmnd 7439-II 1979; Cmnd 7841 1980; Cmnd 8175 1981; Cmnd 8494 1982; Cmnd 8789 1983; Cmnd 9143 1984; Cmnd 9428 1985
Central government 'running' or 'administration' costs (and civil service paybill 1986–2004)		
1985–85 to 1989–90	*The Government's Expenditure Plans*	Cmnd 9702-II 1986; Cm 56-II 1987; Cm 288-II 1988; Cm 621 1989; Cm 1021 1990
1990–91 to 2012–13	*Public Expenditure Statistical Analyses*	Cm 1520 1991; Cm 1920 1992; Cm 2219 1993; Cm 2519 1994; Cm 2821 1995; Cm 3201 1996; Cm 3601 1997; Cm 3901 1998; Cm 4201 1999; Cm 4601 2000; Cm 5101 2001; Cm 5401 2002; Cm 5901 2003; Cm 6201 2004; Cm 6521 2005; Cm 6811 2006; Cm 7091 2007; HC 489 2007–08; Cm 7630 2009; Cm 7890 2000; Cm 8104 2011; Cm 8376 2012; Cm 8663 2013

(Continued)

(Continued)

Tax collection costs and revenues (direct taxes)

1973–74 to 2002–03	Report of the Commissioners of Her Majesty's Inland Revenue (117th to 146th reports)	Cmnd 5804 1974; Cmnd 6302 1976; Cmnd 6734 1977; Cmnd 7092 1978; Cmnd 7473 1979; Cmnd 7833 1980; Cmnd 8160 1981; Cmnd 8514 1982; Cmnd 8947 1984; Cmnd 9305 1984; Cmnd 9576 1985; Cmnd 9831 1986; Cm 230 1987; Cm 529 1988; Cm 880 1989; Cm 1321 1990; Cm 1767 1991; Cm 2086 1992; Cm 2328 1993; Cm 2665 1994; Cm 3014 1995; Cm 3446 1997; Cm 3771 1998; Cm 4079 1998; Cm 4477 1999; Cm 5029 2000; Cm 5304 2001; Cm 5706 2002; Cm 6050 2003; HC 1062 2004-05

Tax collection costs and revenues (indirect taxes)

1964–65 to 2002–03	Report of the Commissioners of Her Majesty's Customs and Excise (56th to 94th reports)	Cmnd 2842 1965; Cmnd 3153 1966; Cmnd 3490 1967; Cmnd 3873 1969; Cmnd 4256 1970; Cmnd 4555 1971; Cmnd 4826 1971; Cmnd 5163 1972; Cmnd 5482 1973; Cmnd 5789 1974; Cmnd 6307 1975; Cmnd 6694 1976; Cmnd 7050 1977; Cmnd 7455 1978; Cmnd 7807 1979; Cmnd 8099 1980; Cmnd 8521 1981; Cmnd 8826 1982; Cmnd 9087 1983; Cmnd 9391 1984; Cmnd 9655 1985; Cm 5 1986; Cm 234 1987; Cm 453 1988; Cm 780 1989; Cm 1223 1990; Cm 1636 1991; Cm 2054 1992; Cm 2353 1993; Cm 2651 1994; Cm 2980 1995; Cm 3427 1996; Cm 3776 1997; Cm 4067 1998; Cm 4447 1999; Cm 5064 2001; Cm 5309 2002; Cm 5671 2002; HC 52 2003–04

Tax collection costs and revenues (all taxes)

2003–04 to 2012–13	HM Revenue and Customs Autumn Performance Reports, Annual Reports and Accounts	Cm 6691 2005; Cm 6983 2006; HC 1159 2005–06; HC 626 2006–07; Cm 7107 2007; Cm 7251 2007; HC 674 2007–08; Cm 7402 2008; Cm 7509 2008; HC 464 2008–09; Cm 7591 2009; Cm 7774 2009; HC 299 2009–10; HC 981 2010–12; HC 38 2012–13; HC 10 2013–14

Complaints to Parliamentary Ombudsman

1977 to 1997–98	Parliamentary Commissioner for Administration Annual Report	HC 157 1977–78; HC 205 1978–79; HC 402 1979–80; HC 148 1980–81; HC 258 1981–82; HC 257 1982–83; HC 322 1983–84; HC 262 1984–85; HC 275 1985–86; HC 248 1986–87; HC 363 1987–88; HC 301 1988–89; HC 353 1989–90; HC 299 1990–91; HC 347 1991–92; HC 569 1992–93; HC 290 1993–94; HC 307 1994–95; HC 296 1995–96; HC 386 1996–97; HC 845 1997–98
1998–99 to 2003–04	The Parliamentary Ombudsman Annual Report	HC 572 1998–99; HC 593 1999–2000; HC 5 2001–02; HC 897 2001–02; HC 847 2002–03; HC 702 2003–04

Complaints to Parliamentary and Health Service Ombudsman

2004–05 to 2012–13	Parliamentary and Health Service Ombudsman Annual Report	HC 348 2004–05; HC 1363 2005–06; HC 838 2006–07; HC 1040 2007–08; HC 786 2008–09; HC 274 2010–12; HC 1404 2010–12; HC 251 2012–13; HC 361 2013–14
2010–11 to 2011–12	Parliamentary and Health Service Ombudsman 'Responsive and Accountable' Statistical Report	HC 1551 2010–12; HC 799 2012–13; HC 800 2012–13

(Continued)

(Continued)

Complaints to Health Services Ombudsman

1974–75 to 1998–99	*Health Service Commissioner Annual Report*	HC 161 1974; HC 407 1974–75; HC 528 1975–76; HC 322 1976–77; HC 417 1977–78; HC 106 1979–80; HC 650 1979–80; HC 368 1980–81; HC 419 1981–82; HC 3 1983–84; HC 537 1983–84; HC 455 1984–85; HC 481 1985–86; HC 31 1987–88; HC 534 1987–88; HC 457 1988–89; HC 538 1989–90; HC 536 1990–91; HC 82 1992–93; HC 764 1992–93; HC 499 1993–94; HC 544 1994–95; HC 465 1995–96; HC 41 1997–98; HC 811 1997–98; HC 498 1998–99
1999–2000 to 2002–03	*The Health Service Ombudsman for England Annual Report*	HC 542 1999–00; HC 3 2001–02; HC 887 2001–02; HC 760 2002–03; HC 703 2003–04

Judicial review applications and outcomes

1974 to 2005	*Judicial Statistics*	Cmnd 6361 1975; Cmnd 6634 1976; Cmnd 6875 1977; Cmnd 7254 1978; Cmnd 7627 1979; Cmnd 7977 1980; Cmnd 8436 1981; Cmnd 8770 1982; Cmnd 9065 1983; Cmnd 9370 1984; Cmnd 9599 1985; Cmnd 9864 1986; Cm 173 1987; Cm 428 1988; Cm 745 1989; Cm 1154 1990; Cm 1573 1991; Cm 1990 1992; Cm 2268 1993; Cm 2623 1994; Cm 2891 1995; Cm 3290 1996; Cm 3716 1997; Cm 3980 1998; Cm 4371 1999; Cm 4786 2000; Cm 5223 2001; Cm 5551 2002; Cm 5863 2003; Cm 6251 2004; Cm 6565 2005; Cm 6903 2006
2006 to 2011	*Judicial and Court Statistics*	Cm 7273 2007; Cm 7467 2008; Cm 7697 2009 (editions published 2010 to 2012 were unnumbered)
2012 to 2013	*Court Statistics Quarterly (January–March edition)*	n/a

Local government expenditure and revenues

1978–79 to 1986–87	*Local Government Financial Statistics England and Wales*	n/a
1987–88 to 2012–13	*Local Government Financial Statistics England*	No. 1 (1988) to No. 23 (2013)

Index